# A Century of WAYNE COUNTY KENTUCKY
## 1800 - 1900

BY
AUGUSTA PHILLIPS JOHNSON

Southern Historical Press, Inc.
Greenville, South Carolina

This volume was reproduced from
An 1939 edition located in the
Publisher's private Library

All rights reserved. No part of this publication may be reproduced,
stored in a retrieval system, transmitted in any form, posted
on to the web in any form or by any means without
the prior written permission of the publisher.

Please direct all correspondence and orders to:

www.southernhistoricalpress.com
or
**SOUTHERN HISTORICAL PRESS, Inc.**
**PO Box 1267**
**375 West Broad Street**
**Greenville, SC   29601**
**southernhistoricalpress@gmail.com**

Originally published: Louisville, KY. 1939
Copyright 1939 by: Augusta Phillips Johnson
ISBN #0-89308-739-4
All rights Reserved.
*Printed in the United States of America*

JAMES A. PHILLIPS
*1845-1913*

MARTHA ANN
HARDIN PHILLIPS
*1848-1915*

To My

FATHER

and

MOTHER

# FOREWORD

THIS IS NOT A FORMAL HISTORY of Wayne County. It is the accumulation of a mass of data concerning the people who settled here, their background, their lives and accomplishments, and early history. It has been tied together as well as the information available made it possible to do so. It was undertaken under a sort of inward compulsion to discharge an obligation to some of those concerned. I seemed the logical one to do it as much of the material was dug from old manuscripts, newspaper files, letters, Bible records, etc., in my possession.

This work was begun as a history of Joshua Jones, but it became increasingly clear that the whole of early Wayne was closely allied. The ties of kinship or friendship held these families in such a bond that there could be no separate history. And more and more I have been impressed with the splendid character of the men and women who settled Wayne County; and their descendants are worthy of their fine forebears.

I wish to give grateful acknowledgment to all those who aided me by generously allowing use of their family records.

To my father, James A. Phillips, I owe much. It has been a source of deep regret that he did not write a history of this section himself, as he was so well fitted to do. The articles signed "J. A. P." were written for the Wayne County weekly which he edited for a number of years.

It may seem that a disproportionate amount of space has been devoted to some families. The explanation is that they are those who responded to the request for this information.

All material has been left in its original form wherever it was possible to do so.

*December*, 1938.

AUGUSTA PHILLIPS JOHNSON.

# CONTENTS

| CHAPTER | | PAGE |
|---|---|---|
| I. | Coming of White Men—Long Hunters—Revolutionary Soldiers | 1 |
| II. | Creation of County in 1800—Monticello—Joshua Jones—Micah Taul | 15 |
| III. | Wayne County in the War of 1812—Rodes Garth | 43 |
| IV. | Discovery of Oil—Martin Beaty | 63 |
| V. | Early Preachers—Churches—Doctors—Lawyers | 73 |
| VI. | Education—Early Schools—Common School System | 105 |
| VII. | War Between the States—James S. Chrisman—E. L. Van Winkle—Captains Roberts, Saufley, Tuttle, Stephenson | 117 |
| VIII. | Stage-Coach Days in Wayne County | 169 |
| IX. | Oil—Timber—Farm Products—Stock | 187 |
| X. | Biographical, Genealogical Notes—First Marriage Book of Wayne County—Bibliography | 197 |
| | Index | 267 |

# ILLUSTRATIONS

| | FACING PAGE |
|---|---|
| JAMES A. PHILLIPS | v |
| MARTHA ANN HARDIN PHILLIPS | v |
| JAMES INGRAM | 16 |
| GENERAL JOSHUA BUSTER | 17 |
| PENNSYLVANIA HOME OF DANIEL HOOPES AND ISABELLA HOOPES | 17 |
| JAMES JONES AND MARY BUSTER JONES | 17 |
| JAMES STONE CHRISMAN | 32 |
| ANTHONY MCBEATH | 33 |
| WILLIAM MCBEATH | 33 |
| CAPTAIN BOLIN E. ROBERTS | 33 |
| JOHN COSTELLO | 33 |
| MICAJAH PHILLIPS | 96 |
| WATER MILL ON ELK CREEK | 97 |
| RUINS OF MILL BUILT BY JOSHUA JONES | 97 |
| HOME OF MICAJAH PHILLIPS | 97 |
| WILLIAM SIMPSON | 112 |
| JUDGE M. C. SAUFLEY | 113 |
| CHRISTIAN CHURCH IN MONTICELLO | 113 |
| LAST STAGE-COACH USED IN THE UNITED STATES | 113 |
| DR. J. B. FRISBIE, JR. | 144 |
| JOHN L. SALLEE | 145 |
| CAPTAIN JOHN W. TUTTLE AND MOLLIE MILTON TUTTLE | 145 |
| EPHRAIM L. VAN WINKLE | 145 |
| BATTLE OF MILL SPRING, 1862 | 160 |

# A Century of Wayne County
Kentucky, 1800-1900

"They who take no pride in the noble achievements of remote ancestors, will never achieve anything worthy to be remembered by remote descendants."

--- Macaulay

COMING OF WHITE MEN—LONG
HUNTERS—REVOLUTIONARY
SOLDIERS

# CHAPTER I

THE FIRST WHITE MEN, of whom we have any record, to reach the region later known as Wayne County, Kentucky, were the "Long Hunters," who came in the summer of 1770. They made camp near Mill Springs and remained there hunting and trapping for more than two years. It is easy to understand their extended stay, for nature has made this a region of rare beauty. The quiet meadows merging into verdure-clad hills, the clear, running streams on their way to the Cumberland River, make of this a beauty spot not excelled anywhere in the state. And here were fur-bearing animals in abundance.

Among these "Long Hunters" were James and Richard Knox, William Allen, Joseph Drake, Obadiah Terrell, John Rains, Uriah Stone, Henry Smith, Edward Cowan, Christopher Stoph, Humphrey Hogan, Cassius Brooks, Robert Crockett, James Graham, John Montgomery, Abraham Bledsoe, Richard Skaggs, Henry Skaggs, David Lynch, Kasper Mansco, and Russell and Hughes.

They made a camp and a depot for their game and skins near an excellent spring about six miles from the present site of Monticello. They found no trace of human settlement but in dry caves were many places where stones had been set up that covered quantities of human bones. Dr. W. D. Funkhouser and Dr. William Webb, on an archaeological expedition in 1922 for the University of Kentucky, explored the caves of this section and in their book, *Ancient Life in Kentucky*, say:

"Hines Cave, about six miles from Monticello, yielded the most remains of any in Kentucky. The cave is spacious and well drained. The entrance is protected from wind, rain, and snow by high cliffs, yet well lighted for some distance. The bottom is level and dry and this must have been a desirable shelter to the people who occupied it. There were remains from many fires and in the graves were many artifacts, awls, needles, and skinning knives; in the ash beds were bones of many animals. In one grave was found the skeleton of a young woman with a round piece of shining mica of the type that comes from North Carolina. Many skeletons were found and many more artifacts, stone hoes, flint arrowheads, pipes, pottery, and textiles. Animal bones were those of wolf, bear, wildcat, raccoon, fox, deer, buffalo, beaver, rabbit, turkey, quail, turtle shells, and mussel shells. Many other caves in this section indicate they were the homes of the cave dwellers or Indians who lived in caves in prehistoric times."

The hunters separated into groups to meet here again. They built another depot on Caney Fork of Russell's Creek, where Mt. Gilead Church was built later. Some of the hunters returned home. Some built rafts, loaded them with skins and floated down the Cumberland River to the Ohio, thence to the Mississippi and on down to New Orleans. Stoph and Allen were captured by Cherokees. The Indians plundered the camp during their absence, carrying off skins, pots, pans, etc. Bledsoe's profanity is perhaps excusable when, returning, he wrote on a fallen sycamore: "2300 deerskins lost; ruination, by God."

These men were from the settlements on the Holston and Clinch and New River—as hardy a band of pioneers as ever came into the Wilderness. They knew not the word fear. They were skilled in woodcraft and could meet the Indian on his own ground, but they lacked the cruelty of the savages who were even then committing depredations on the Virginia border. In the meantime, growing dissatisfaction with British rule was steadily leading to war. In 1774 Colonel William Preston, commanding the militia in Southwest Virginia, gave orders to Captain Billy Russell, of Russell's Fork, to warn settlers and surveyors in Kentucky of an Indian uprising. Captain Russell selected Daniel Boone and Michael Stoner for this undertaking. They camped about five miles from Monticello, and Stoner liked the country so well that he afterwards returned and made his home there for many years and is buried near Monticello. Lewis Preston Summers, in his *History of Southwest Virginia*, page 226, quotes the following report of a battle between Indians and British and the settlers in Southwest Virginia, as given to Colonel William Preston, Colonel of Militia, by Captain Shelby:

"On the nineteenth of July, 1776, our scouts returned and informed us that they had discovered a great number of the enemy, a force not inferior to ours. We marched out to meet them, not going more than a mile when we were attacked from the rear. Our men sustained the attack with great intrepidity and bravery, immediately forming a line. They endeavored to surround us but were prevented by the uncommon fortitude of our men who took possession of an eminence that prevented their design. Our line of battle extended about a quarter of a mile. We killed many. There were streams of blood every way and it was generally thought there was never so much execution done in so short a time on the frontier. Never did troops fight with greater calmness than ours. Our spies deserve the greatest applause. The troops are in high spirits and eager for another engagement."

It was signed by James Shelby, James Thompson, William Buchanan, John Campbell, William Cocke, and Thomas Madison.

This was known as the Battle of Long Island Flats of the Holston and Clinch. Near here were many settlers who later removed to Kentucky. Joshua Jones was wounded in this battle. The following is a certified copy of an entry on June 16, 1777, in the Journal of the Virginia House of Delegates:

"Resolved as the opinion of the committee (of public claims) that the petition of Joshua Jones, a soldier who received a wound in the battle near Long Island, on Holston River, in his left arm, which rendered it for some time useless, and still remains very weak, is reasonable and that the petitioner ought to be allowed the sum of one pound for his present relief."

Many instances of savage cruelty are related by Summers, but the persistence of the militia on the frontier finally made the border a safer region.

In May, 1779, the Virginia Assembly enacted a law opening Kentucky to general settlement by survey, entry, and residence. In the same year the General Assembly of Virginia passed an act for marking and opening a road over the Cumberland Mountains in the County of Kentucky. Richard Calloway and John Kinkead, of Washington County, Virginia, were appointed to explore the adjacent land on both sides. They effected the opening of the road by December 1, 1781. It was surveyed from Hand's

Meadow, Virginia, through the Clinch settlements, by Cumberland Gap to the Cumberland River, and on to "The Orchard" (Crab Orchard), Kentucky. This was the Wilderness Road over which an unexampled tide of emigration poured for more than ten years.

The privations these pioneers endured and the dangers they encountered make an everlasting tribute to the intrepid spirit of these early settlers.

Many men who had given service in the Revolution came to what in 1800 became Wayne County. Joshua Jones, mentioned before, died in 1816 before the pension laws were enacted. Samuel Newell, that fine old gentleman who was one of the first justices, became reduced to poverty in later years, but pride, it is said, kept him from applying for a pension. He spent his last days in seclusion with his books.

The pension list of the War Department gives the following names of Revolutionary soldiers who emigrated to Wayne County:

Under Act of 1818: Fred Cooper, North Carolina, and Elisha Thomas, Virginia.

Under Act of 1832:

William Acre, North Carolina, born 1753
John Adair, North Carolina, born 1753
Robert Beakley, North Carolina, born 1756
William Bertram, North Carolina, born 1748
Joseph Brown, North Carolina, born 1753
Robert Covington, Virginia, born 1760
Fred Cooper, Pennsylvania, born 1758
William Carpenter, Virginia, born 1759
Reuben Coffey, North Carolina, born 1756
Pat Coyle, Virginia, born 1751
Peter Catron, Virginia, born 1752
Fred Miller, Virginia, born 1750

Died in Kentucky:

John Davis, Virginia, born 1756
George Decker, Virginia, born 1740
Martin Durham, North Carolina, born 1753
Geo. Dabney, North Carolina, born 1758

Rody Daffron, North Carolina, born 1755
Abraham Hurt, Virginia, born 1760
Conrad Henninger, North Carolina, born 1734
William Johnson, Virginia, born 1753
Jas. Jones, Virginia, born 1756
Wm. Keith, Virginia, born 1759
Thomas Merritt, North Carolina, born 1761
Dudley Moreland, Virginia, born 1759
Jas. McGee, Pennsylvania, born 1762
Zachariah Sanders, Virginia, born 1757
Charles Worsham, born 1760 (living in 1840)

James Pierce
Jesse Powers
George Rogers
Isaac Stephens
William Doss
Jas. Woody
Isaac Crabtree
Jas. McHenry
Jas. Turner
John Walters
Charles Warden
Caleb Cooper
Stephen Pratt

This is not a complete list of Revolutionary soldiers who emigrated to Wayne, for some made no application for pension. Here are given a few biographical sketches based on data found in their applications for pensions:

John Adair was born in County Antrim, Ireland, in 1754, and came to Baltimore with his father in 1762. They moved to Pennsylvania in a short time, thence to Sullivan County, North Carolina, where he enlisted as a private in the militia under Colonel William Campbell, with Captain Brooks. He served on the Holston, fought with the Cherokees, and when the war was over emigrated to Kentucky.

Conrad Henninger was born in Northampton County, Pennsylvania, in 1752, of German parents, moved to Maryland when ten years old, thence to North Carolina, where he served in the militia with Captain Billingsly under Colonel Lock. He settled in the upper part of Wayne where he became prosperous.

Joseph Chrisman served with George Rogers Clark in his campaign of the Northwest and was with him at the capture of Vincennes. He took an active part in the early life of the county. He left a line of distinguished descendants.

John Sanders, born in Lunenburg County, Virginia, in 1754, served in the militia with Captain Robert Cary, under Colonel Tucker and General Lawson. He was guard at Albemarle Barracks. He married in Wayne County, Kentucky, Sarah Jones Buster, daughter of Joshua Jones and widow of Charles Buster, in 1804.

Reuben and Lewis Russell Coffey were Revolutionary soldiers. Reuben came to Wayne County in 1800 where he settled in Elk Spring Valley. He received a pension for his services. His application states that he was born in Albemarle County, Virginia, September 16, 1759. He moved to Amherst County where, in 1777, he volunteered for "as long as my country needs my service," with Captain Moses Guess, under Major Joseph Winston, Colonel Benjamin Cleveland. He also served with Colonel Isaac Shelby. He was at the Battle of King's Mountain. After the war, he went to Wilkes County, North Carolina, and thence to Wayne County, Kentucky.

Reuben, Lewis Russell, and James Coffey were sons of the Rev. James Coffey and Elizabeth Cleveland, sister of Colonel Benjamin Cleveland, who was with Shelby at King's Mountain.

James Coffey, who had obtained land in Wayne County, returned to North Carolina, exchanging his Wayne County land for Lewis' North Carolina tract. Lewis Russell Coffey married Biddy Moore in North Carolina. Their children were: Elizabeth married Richard Cullom (former Senator Cullom was their son); Rachael married Jefferson Jones; Mary married Joshua Oatts; James married Sally Strange; Henderson married Minerva Alexander; Cullom married Rachael Isaacs; Jesse married Eliza Griffin; Shelby married Emerine Meadows; Cleveland married Sophronia Oatts; Franklin married Mary Ann Worsham; and Coleman married (1) Polly Havens, (2) Jane Miller, (3) Sarah Havens, (4) Amanda Hudson Stone.

Lewis Russell Coffey founded the family of that name in Wayne, a numerous and highly respected family. He is buried just east of Monticello in the Elk Spring Valley Cemetery, where a shaft erected by the family is in a fair state of preservation. His is one of the Revolutionary soldiers' graves that is easy to locate, thanks to the foresight of his descendants.

Jesse Powers was born in Prince William County, Virginia, in 1759. His family removed to Charlotte County, where he enlisted in 1777, with Captain Thomas Williams, under General Gates. He also served with Captain Goode in the Fourth Regiment of the Continental Army. He was with General Stephenson at Camden. After the Revolution he removed to Halifax County and soon came into Wayne County, where he was given a grant of land for his services. This was sold later to the grandfather of Judge Joseph Bertram. He was buried near Gap Creek, near two other Revolutionary soldiers, whose names are not now known. The graves are not marked.

Powersburg was named for Jesse Powers, and his descendants still live in that section. His son Charles was father of Daniel Powers, who was father of M. W. Powers. M. W. Powers married a Miss Burnett and removed to Lincoln, where he remained a few years. He returned to Parmleysville where he has been postmaster during the past twenty-five years. He is clerk of old Bethel Church, founded by Raccoon John Smith in 1810.

William Tarleton Taylor of Loudoun County, Virginia, served with General Morgan. He was at the siege of Yorktown. He had a large family of which his Bible gives a complete record.

Major George Bruton, born at Spartansburg, South Carolina, came to Madison County, Kentucky, and there a pension was granted him. He came to Wayne in 1802 where he resided until his death.

Joseph West was born in Sussex County, Delaware, December 1, 1762. He removed to Montgomery County, Virginia, in 1779, where he served as an Indian spy with Captain Thomas Wright. Later he enlisted under Captain George Paris. Afterwards he moved to Madison County, Kentucky, and thence to Wayne County.

Frederick Cooper gave signal service during the Revolution. He was born in York County, Pennsylvania, in 1759, and entered service in 1777. He drove a provision wagon to Valley Forge, coming in contact with George Washington. In 1780, he moved to Rowan County, North Carolina, where records of the county show he enlisted as corporal in Captain Enoch's Company under Colonel Lock. Later, under General Gates, he was captured by the British but managed to escape in a few days. He served under General Morgan at Cowpens and at Eutaw Springs. After the close of the war, he married Dorothy Brown and removed to Wayne in 1799.

William Acre was born in Frederick County, Maryland, in 1752. He moved to Guilford, North Carolina, where he entered the Revolutionary service with Captain Dugan in the militia under Colonel Martin. He later moved to Wayne County and settled on Otter Creek, where he was still living in 1840.

John Francis emigrated to Wayne from Virginia. He received a Revolutionary pension for his services. His family Bible records were filed with his application on which was noted: "Father of John Francis was Henry of Wythe County, Virginia. John killed the Tory who shot his father in battle."

John Denny was born in Amherst County, Virginia, August 8, 1766. He gave valiant service during the Revolution with Captain Cabell in the Virginia Militia throughout 1780 and 1781. He settled in Wayne and lived to a ripe old age, receiving a pension for his services.

Charles Worsham's application, dated June 24, 1833, for Revolutionary pension reads as follows:

"Personally appeared in court, Charles Worsham, a resident of Wayne County, Kentucky, age 77 July 22nd, states that he volunteered in the summer of 1777, the particular month not recollected, shortly after the commencement of the War, when he was 23 years of age; that he volunteered during the War as a private, under Captain Mays, Powhatan County, Va., his christian name not now recollected, and served in the 2nd regiment under Col. Randolph. We rendezvoued at Powhatan Court House and were marched down James River under the command of Col. Hubbard and were at a small skirmish or battle at Hood's on James River. We marched in various directions and were occasionally commanded by Col. Dimot and Gen. Steuben, near Petersburg, Virginia. About this time a Light Horse Company was wanted and by the consent of my Captain Mays, I volunteered with sixty others who could supply themselves with good horses under a Captain Littleberry Mosby in order to pursue the British with more speed and success, and under Captain Mosby we marched to Williamsburg, then to Petersburg Battle and then to Chesterfield Court House where we joined a large force. Tarlton was in pursuit of us, but he stopped at Four Mile Mill, destroying all the flour and the mill, having previously destroyed the arms and flour at Chesterfield Court House. I, the said Charles Worsham, with a detachment, was ordered to go back and watch the movements of Tarlton, under a Sergeant. We went back as far as Four Mile Mill and Court House and found that Tarlton had gone back towards Petersburg. We then returned and reported to the army. I was at the battle of Guilford, N. C., under Captain Mosby and under Gen. Lawson and we fought under General Green at said battle, at which said battle David Jones, Ned Balew, David Tyree, were shot down in my section and taken off. On the same evening, we gave way and marched to the iron works, thence we marched to Deep River, got there just after the British crossed over. Here one Tory was hung, for taking up arms against his country three times. The Small Pox broke out in North Carolina Troops, and by General Green's orders we had a furlough or permit to go home to Virginia. Some short time later, I was called upon by my first Captain Mays, at Powhatan County Court House, to meet him and to go to the siege of York. I marched with him and was at the siege of York. While there I was sent in a small detachment to Amelia County after cattle for the use of the French army and we bought 200 head, I being well acquainted there. Sometime after the siege and surrender of Col. Wallace, I, with the balance of my company received a discharge again from Captain Mays, my first Captain.

"I, the said Charles Worsham have no documentary proof. I know of no person whose testimony I can procure who can testify to my service in the State, but am known by Lewis Coffey, Roger Oatts, and William Simpson, of Wayne County, my neighbors. I was born in Chesterfield County, Virginia, where I lived for some years. I then moved to Powhatan County, Virginia, and lived there during the war. Afterwards I moved to Prince Edward Co., Va., then to Henry County, where I lived three years, then to Spartansburg, S. C., lived there one year, then to Dandridge on the French Road, State of Tennessee, one year, then to Garrard

County, Kentucky, one year; thence to Monticello, Wayne Co., Ky., where I now live and have lived for 25 years."

Declaration of his widow, Polly Worsham, age 75, who appeared November 27, 1843, states she was married to him June, 1787, and that her husband died March 11, 1841. She was Polly Ellington, and they had seven children; one was Cannon Worsham, age 46 in 1845, another was Letitia Grey, age 57.

James C. McGee: "was born in 1762, in Cumberland County, Pennsylvania, and when four years of age moved with his parents (whose names were not stated), to Bedford County, Pennsylvania. While residing in Bedford County, Pa., he volunteered and served as first sergeant in Capt. Samuel Moore's Pennsylvania Company, as Indian spy, as follows: from May, 1777, six months: from May, 1778, six months, and from April, 1779, was in several small skirmishes with the Indians and was severely wounded in the thigh by a bullet. Shortly after the termination of the last named service he volunteered in Westmoreland County (date not given), and served six months as first sergeant in Captain Locheroy's or Lougherty's Pennsylvania company of Indian spies and was discharged in the Fall of 1781. All the above service was rendered at forts and on the frontiers, protecting the inhabitants from the attacks of the Indians. After the Revolutionary War he moved to the territory of North Carolina (which was later East Tennessee) and lived there for some years; thence to Lee County, Virginia, where he lived a while; thence to Anderson and Campbell Counties (Tennessee), where he resided many years. He was commissioned Captain in Anderson County, Tennessee, by John Sevier, Governor of Tennessee, and later commissioned Major in Campbell County, Tenn., by Gov. Sevier. In February, 1833, he moved from Campbell County, Tennessee, to Wayne County, Kentucky. He was allowed a pension on his application executed Nov. 25, 1833, while a resident of Wayne County." He died Aug. 1, 1839.

Thomas Merritt: "was born in 1761, in Warren County, North Carolina. He entered the service in February, 1780, and served three months as Private in Capt. Thomas Chrisman's company, Col. Jas. Allen's North Carolina regiment. He again entered the service early in 1781 and served three months as a Private in Capt.

Geo. Nazie's company under Lieutenant-Colonel Guilford Dudley and was discharged May 13, 1781. He enlisted July 1, 1781, served as private in Capt. Benjamin Bailey's North Carolina company under Major Blount; was in the battle of Eutaw Springs and was discharged May 1, 1782; length of service in all, 15 months. After the Revolutionary war the soldier moved to Kentucky, where he had lived 33 years, when he was allowed a pension upon his application executed Aug. 27, 1832, at which time he was living in Wayne County."

CREATION OF COUNTY IN 1800—
MONTICELLO—JOSHUA JONES
—MICAH TAUL

JAMES INGRAM

*Born in England in 1761; came to Virginia when a child and later came to Wayne County*

Pennsylvania home of Daniel Hoopes, the boy immigrant (1683), and Isabella Hoopes, grandmother of Hannah Todhunter

GENERAL JOSHUA BUSTER
*Officer in the War of 1812*

JAMES JONES AND MARY BUSTER JONES
*Married in Virginia in 1798 and came to Wayne County in 1799*

## CHAPTER II

On December thirteenth of the year 1800 the State Legislature of Kentucky passed an act creating a new county, said county to be named Wayne in honor of General Anthony Wayne, the Revolutionary hero. The act specifies the following bounds:

"All that part of Pulaski and Cumberland included within following bounds: Beginning at mouth of Indian Creek on Cumberland River and running by James Sanduskie's cabin to the road that leads from Captain Thomas Johnston's to Major Alexander McFarland's on Indian Creek; thence to top of Poplar Mountain; thence with same until it intersects State line; thence east with said line so far that a north line will strike Rock Creek on main South Fork of Cumberland River; thence down the same to the beginning shall be one district and called and known by the name of Wayne."

The territory of Wayne had been, variously, a part of Lincoln County when Kentucky was divided into only three counties; then a part of Green when that county was carved from Lincoln; then a part of Cumberland, and was finally, in 1800, created from parts of Cumberland and Pulaski.

In 1803, a small part of Adair County, "from mouth of Wolf Creek to Cumberland River," was added to Wayne "for convenience of citizens." In 1817, an act was passed "to alter division line between Wayne and Pulaski," throwing a small part of Wayne into Pulaski and a small part of Pulaski into Wayne. In 1836 Clinton County was created from parts of Wayne and Cumberland, and in 1912 a part of Wayne was taken to form McCreary County, leaving Wayne with its present area of 478 square miles.

Between the close of the Revolution and 1792, when Kentucky was admitted to statehood, Virginia had made a number of military grants of land in this section, and Kentucky continued the practice. All grants up to 1797 were military. A grant by Virginia to General George Rogers Clark in 1784 included several thousand acres in the northern part of what later became Wayne County, and the first deed recorded in the county was made by General Clark to Jacob Vanhoozer. Major Alexander McFarland was also located in the upper part of the county as well as Captain Thomas Johnston. After 1797 the unappropriated lands were opened by grants under "headrights" by which any man twenty-one years of age could acquire from 100 to 200 acres of land by making survey and entry and living upon it one year.

These surveys were made by surveyors with varying degrees of ability, giving cause for many land suits later to settle boundary lines and establish title. There was much inaccuracy and overlapping. Confusion was inevitable under these conditions, but in the main, differences were adjusted amicably enough in Wayne, due to the intelligence and fair-mindedness of the settlers and the superior ability of the man who was appointed first surveyor of the county, Joshua Jones.

Joshua Jones had been a surveyor for thirty-five years in Virginia. He had been engaged in surveying as early as 1763 and made the first surveys in southwest Virginia on the Holston and Clinch rivers, where he settled after his marriage in 1767. Appointed to survey "the publick lands" by the governor of the new state, he sold his ironworks in Augusta County, Virginia, in 1794 and came to Kentucky.

He surveyed and entered two tracts on Elk Spring Creek in the then county of Cumberland and began at once the operation of an ironworks. On the same day in which the county was created, there was passed an act granting "to Joshua Jones certain lands." The preamble states:

"Whereas it is represented to the present assembly that Joshua Jones has a bloomery in great forwardness in the county of Cumberland and it is deemed expedient to grant unto said Joshua Jones a certain quantity of unappropriated lands contiguous to the said bloomery for the better carrying the same into complete effect: Therefore be it enacted by the General Assembly that one thousand acres of land be granted to Joshua Jones in the said county of Cumberland, to be laid off in not more than five surveys anywhere within the compass of six miles of the said bloomery: Provided however, that the said Jones shall not be at liberty to include in his surveys any salt lick or spring, or any person now actually settled thereon.

"With two hundred acres to be laid off around the same by lines running to the cardinal points, including said improvement in the center.

"Sec. 2. And be it further enacted that the said Joshua Jones shall pay into the public treasury of this state thirty dollars per hundred acres for all the land he may have secured to him under this act on or before the 1st. day of December, 1805: Provided however, that no grant shall issue for the same until the money hereby required to be paid for the same, together with the interest at the rate of six per cent annum thereon from the passage of this act, shall be paid into the public treasury as aforesaid; and provided also that the said Joshua Jones shall have the term of twelve months from and after the passage of this act to pay into the public treasury as aforesaid; and provided also that the said Joshua Jones shall have the term of twelve months from and after the passage of this act to locate and survey the said lands: and upon his, the said Joshua Jones, fully complying with the requisitions of this act, the land hereby granted, with all and singular its appurtenances, shall be the complete bona fide property of said Joshua Jones and his heirs forever, any law, custom, or usage to the contrary notwithstanding. Provided always that if the said Joshua Jones, his heirs, or assigns, shall not on or before the first day of December, 1805, produce to the register of the land office a certificate from the county court of Cumberland, attested by their clerk, that bar-iron hath been made at his said works, that then the lands herein granted shall revert to the Commonwealth, anything in this act to the contrary notwithstanding. This act shall commence and be in force from and after the passage thereof."

December 2, 1801, an act for benefit of Joshua Jones provided that he "be allowed two years longer to locate the land granted to him last session and that he be permitted to locate eight surveys."

December 18, 1804, an act giving Joshua Jones "five years longer to pay the state price for his lands in five installments."

There had come into this region, under the early Kentucky grants, the following: Jonathan and James Ingram in 1796, Cornelius Phillips in 1798, Isaac West in 1799, James Simpson in 1799, Nicholas Lloyd in 1799, Henry Garner in 1799. By 1800, there were the first justices mentioned below; the three who composed the court of quarter sessions; the first tavern keeper, Roger Oatts; the first merchant, Joseph Beard; another merchant, McNutt, "the Irishman"; Lieutenant William Jones; James Jones; Bartholomew Hayden; John Buster; Lewis Coffey.

From 1800 to 1810, each year brought a large number of families. Grants under the "Headrights" provision were made to the following: William Adams, Joseph Alexander, Daniel Andrews, James and John Alcorn, Samuel Ayers, James Brumett, James Bates, William Brown, William Carter, John Caldwell, Peter Catron, Frederic Cooper, James and Lewis Coffey, James Conn, Charles and Samuel Denny, Charles Dibrell, Thomas and Leonard Dodson, David Ewing, Walter Emerson, Elisha Franklin, Elizabeth Fuston, William Green, Edward Gibson, John Gibbs, Henry Guffey, Richard Harris, Christopher Huffaker, Thomas Calhoun, Elias Kelley, Thomas Kennedy, Nicholas Koger, John Long, William Low, John Loveall, James McHenry, Nicholas Lloyd, John Martin, John Miller, John McCollom, Nathan Parker, John Peveyhouse, Moses Phills, John Reed, Samuel Rector, James Rice, Amos Wright, John Roberts, Abraham Sharp, John Sanders, Robert Strain, John Stephenson, Mathew and William Smith, Reuben, John, and James Simpson, William Sutton, Isaac and Richard Summers, Elisha Thomas, Solomon Turpin, James Tuttle, Henry Tuggle, Francis Vicory, William Walker, John Wade, Solomon West, John Wakefield, Thomas Merritt, John Parmley. Some of these had received grants for Revolutionary service, and this was additional land taken up in this way.

There were doubtless others, as records can never be assumed to be complete. In the decade following many more came while many passed on to the rich valleys of middle Tennessee. This was the great Indian route to the South. Cornelius Phillips' brother Richard went on to Tennessee as did some of the Cullom, Shores, Jones, Ewing, Berry, Miller, and McGee families as well as others.

In 1801 a tract of public land was set aside for the town site and on February 13, 1802, "William Beard and Joseph Beard with Hugh McDermott and Henry Beason (bound by distance) make title to thirteen acres of land adjoining the public ground on which the court has established the town."

In 1805 the Cherokee Indians ceded to the United States a tract embracing part of Tennessee and including a strip along the eastern border of Wayne. These were known as the Tellico lands. The name of the town Jellico was so corrupted from Tellico.

W. R. Jillson in his *Kentucky Land Grants* says: "The small and unique group of grants from 1803 to 1853 were given upon warrants from the Register of the Land Office. These grants in Wayne lie mainly on the Little South Fork, a few on Rock Creek, Otter Creek, and Wolf Creek, and two in Elk Spring Valley.

These include:

| | |
|---|---|
| Berry Adkins | James Cooper |
| Moses Anderson | Nick Kanatzan |
| John Adair | Julius Keeton |
| Joseph Abbott | Miles Keeton |
| Edward Baker | Allen Keeton |
| Thomas Branscomb | Moses Kirkpatrick |
| John Branscomb | James Kinder |
| William Bell | Robert Livingston |
| David Bell | Thomas Merritt |
| James Bell | Fred Miller |
| Jacob Bertram | George Miller |
| Elisha Blevins | Joel Long |
| Jonathan Blevins | Joseph Minzes |
| Henry Beason | John Parmley |
| James Beasley | Robert Parmley |
| Samuel Brents | Samuel Young |
| John Bookout | Washington Young |
| Isaac Burnett | John Coger |
| Reuben Burnett | James Coffey |
| Cornelius Cooper | John Davis |
| Isaac Cooper | Azariah Denney |

| | |
|---|---|
| Henry Denney | Francis Emerson |
| Ann Deering | Lewis Faust |
| Osburn Davenport | Fleming Gregory |
| William Dobbs | Mordicai Gregory |
| Edward Doran | Andrew Higginbotton |
| David Duncan | James Jones" |
| James Evans | |

The act creating the county provided that the first meeting of the county court should be held at the home of Henry Garner, and accordingly, on the 16th day of March, 1801, the first county court assembled there. The first justices were Charles Dibrell, Martin Sims, Edward Cullom, James Montgomery, Raleigh Clark, James Jones, James Evans, and Samuel Hinds. The three men who composed the court of quarter sessions were Samuel Newell, Hugh McDermott, and Isaac Chrisman.

Steps were taken at once to provide a courthouse, and a log structure was erected in the center of the square that was laid out by Joshua Jones. Micah Taul was appointed first clerk of both courts. He was then less than sixteen years of age.

At the April term of the county court held at Henry Garner's it was ordered that a courthouse be located on William Beard's land "provided he build a house of hewn logs 30 by 20 feet, two stories high, two floors, two doors, in workmanlike manner."

It was also ordered that "Joshua Jones, gent., survey 13 acres of William Beard's land for the town, lay off the publick square and determine the location of the court house." This courthouse was located in the center of the public square. There were four families living in the town at this time. They were those of William Beard, Joseph Beard, Roger Oatts, and Henry Garner. In 1810 there were twenty-seven people living on the "thirteen acres" that constituted the town. Micah Taul's *Memoirs* tell how the name of Monticello came to be chosen.

The first trustees appointed for the town were Anthony Gholson, George Singleton, Roger Oatts, John Hammond, and Isaac Crabtree. The first constable was Joseph Wheeler.

It was some time, apparently, before a jail was needed and then "Roger Oatts, tavern keeper," was designated as first jailer. He used a log house adjacent to his tavern for a jail. The jail was the last house at the top of the hill above the town spring, near the tavern.

Tavern prices were fixed by court order at "1 and 6 for dinner and 1 for breakfast or supper," using the phraseology to indicate English money, that was one shilling for breakfast or supper, and one shilling and sixpence for dinner.

John Francis, Gent., was the first high sheriff of the county, which office he held until 1813, when Abel Shrewsbury was appointed by the court. Solomon Brents was the first attorney who qualified in Wayne County. Francis Emerson, a qualified attorney, appeared before the court as early as 1807. On the occasion of this April term of court, Joshua McDowell was fined "10s for profanely swearing twice."

The first tax list made in Wayne, in 1801, gives the following statement:

"Tax list of Wayne—District of Pulaski, south of the Cumberland River (the part of Wayne taken from Pulaski):

Total amount of taxable property:

- 162 acres of 1st rate land
- 10,351 acres of 2nd rate land
- 200 acres of 3rd rate land
- 113 white males above 21 years of age
- 14 white males above 16 and under 21
- 28 blacks above 16—62 total blacks
- 276 horses, mules, etc.

Part taken from Cumberland County, William Jones, Commissioner:

- 209 acres 1st rate land
- 12,590 acres 2nd rate land
- 19,055 acres 3rd rate land
- 231 white males above 21 years of age
- 43 white males above 16 and under 21 years of age
- 31 blacks above 16 years of age—total blacks 206
- 473 horses and mules

Commissioners: Edward N. Cullom
Samuel Cowan
William Jones"

The minutes of the courts for the few years after the county was formed are much concerned with the opening and improvement of roads, and these early roads were first, mainly, the means of reaching mills that were located on the water courses. The first mill mentioned is VanWinkle's Mill, on Elk Creek. It was two miles south of Monticello, built by the VanWinkles on land later owned by Micajah Phillips.

Jones' Mill, later known as Marshall's Mill, was built by Joshua Jones. Denney's Mill, near Gregory, was an early mill, as was Eads' Mill in the western section of the county. The mill at Mill Springs was owned and operated at a very early date by the Metcalfe and Tuttle families.

Ferrill's Mill was probably the first in that part of the state. The mill was necessary to the existence of the pioneer as his grain had to be taken to the mill and ground before his family could be supplied with bread.

Young's Mill, on Little South Fork, later owned by John Sandusky, was built at a very early date. It was a marker on the boundary of Public School District Number 29 in 1838 when it was referred to as "Young's Old Mill" by the surveyor. It is thus recorded in the Minute Book of the Commissioners.

Of this period Micah Taul's *Memoirs* give us a graphic account. They were published in 1887 by J. A. Phillips in the *Monticello Signal* and later in various other papers. They cover the years from 1800 to 1850, largely in Wayne County. We get a vivid picture of the life of that early day in his descriptions of "Court Day" when candidates met often for debate. He tells an amusing story of Colonel Lyon, who was candidate for Congress in 1803.

"Colonel Lyon arrived at Monticello on Saturday evening, before the May court in 1803, and put up at the tavern of Roger Oatts, the only one in the town. I called upon him on Sunday morning and invited him to dine with me. My young wife prepared the best dinner she could upon such short notice. Strawberries then grew spontaneously in the barrens about Monticello and were getting ripe. She went herself and gathered perhaps a quart, which constituted the chief article of dessert at dinner. We had at the table with us Col. Lyon and Mr. and Mrs. Haden (my wife's sister) and her little daughter, two or three years old. Col. Lyon dined heartily and when his plate was changed he was furnished with a saucer and spoon and asked if he would take some cream and strawberries. He answered in the affirmative and said he would help himself—the strawberries had been put in a deep plate on the table near him. He seized the plate, placed it before him and *ate up all the strawberries* to the amusement of myself and Mr. Haden and to the infinite distress of the child, who screamed out lustily when she saw the last of the fruit disappear, to the great annoyance of her mother but without disturbing the equanimity of our ill-mannered guest.

"Haden and myself told this next day to the plain, honest people of the county who were delighted. They swore by their Maker that 'Matthew Lyon was their man' and they were as good as their word and his majority in the county was large. He was elected to Congress in opposition to Mr. Walker."

In 1804-5 the Judicial system of Kentucky was changed. The District and Quarter Sessions Courts were abolished and Circuit Courts established, with a judge and two assistants in each county.

In 1807 the Academy or Seminary lands were ordered to be set aside by the State Legislature, the revenue from these to be used for building and carrying on academies of higher learning. The court therefore ordered these lands to be surveyed by Joshua Jones. James Jones, Roger Oatts, and Cornelius Phillips were named justices in 1809, and a road was ordered improved to Rogers Grove Meeting House.

The Legislature that convened in December, 1809, included Edward Cullom in the Senate and Isaac West in the House from Wayne County. It occurred to these gentlemen that the town of Monticello was in a unique position—it had never been formally incorporated. While the Legislature of 1800 that created the county had ordered a town to be laid out, that was all that had been done. Consequently we find on January 18, 1810, "an act for the better regulating of the town of Monticello in the County of Wayne":

"Whereas it is represented to the present General Assembly that there has been no special law passed heretofore for the regulation of the town of Monticello in the County of Wayne and that it is necessary that some special law be passed for that purpose: Be it enacted that the free male inhabitants of the town aforesaid meet at the Court House on the second Saturday of March, 1810, and elect five trustees."

And there follow four pages of specific instructions as to the management of the municipality.

Court notes of 1831 show that John Dick was appointed Sheriff by the governor. William Hardin, attorney, was Justice of the Peace as was Archibald Woods, who served in this capacity for many years. James Jones was Justice of the Peace.

Leo Haden, "a young man of honesty, probity, and good sense produced license from two circuit judges and took the several oaths as attorney of the court."

Sherrod Williams was appointed attorney for the county court. He was born in Pulaski County and moved to Wayne where he married a sister of Lucy and Frank Stone. He was a brilliant but erratic lawyer. He represented Wayne in the Legislature several terms. He later removed to Mississippi. His son, Tom Williams, was also a brilliant lawyer.

In 1813 Abel Shrewsbery was appointed jailer to succeed Roger Oatts, and in 1815 Stone and Berry were licensed to run "an ordinary." On petition of Joshua Jones in 1816, his son James Jones was appointed deputy surveyor of the county and in 1817 Joshua Jones resigned and said James Jones was commissioned surveyor. In 1819 Joshua Oatts and Cannon Worsham were licensed to keep a tavern. By 1810 the county had a population of 5,430 and there were 37 people living in the town. The population of the county increased by about 2,500 in the next ten years as there were 7,951 in 1820. By 1830 there were 8,685.

A cause celebre in Kentucky was the case of *Moore's Heirs against the State*. This trial ran through the courts for several years until it was finally disposed of by Justice George H. Robertson in favor of the plaintiffs. The case had all the elements of a first-class mystery story.

"On a summer afternoon in 1835, a boy of eighteen took his last whipping from his mother. Parental chastisement was more common then than now. William Perry Moore's father, John S. Moore, had died and his mother had married Isaac Shepherd.

The boy may have found it easier to submit to his mother's whipping than to a step-father's discipline, or he may have been slow to assert his budding manhood against the maternal hand. The Moores and Shepherds were people of standing in the community and this discipline was not the unthinking brawling of coarse people. At any rate, vowing his mother should never see or hear from him again, he left home secretly in the night, riding away on his step-father's horse. He returned the horse by the mail carrier from a point where he found other conveyance. This fact testifies to a certain uprightness of character and points to the injustice of the punishment at which he rebelled.

"When he rode away that was the last of him so far as his mother or his family and his home town of Monticello ever knew. His mother's efforts to find him were futile. Here is a description taken from the court records: about 5 feet 9 1-2 inches, weight 160 to 170 pounds, shoulders broad and rather stooped, hair light brown, eyes bluish gray, skin fair, small scar on edge of left jaw, dimple in chin.

"The scar is important because it, with other evidence, served to identify both a soldier of the Texan Army of Independence who had been killed and buried, as well as in later years a peaceful citizen who had married and reared two daughters in Columbus, Georgia. It served to eliminate a third and maybe a fourth. All claimed to have been William P. Moore, son of John S. Moore, of Monticello.

"In 1841, the mother heard of a William Perry Moore in Columbus, Georgia. She asked some men driving stock to this point to find out if it was her son. They reported on their return that this man was not her son. The mother wrote to him anyway, but when an answer came in the wife's handwriting, Mrs. Shepherd felt sure it was not her son. William P. Moore went from Columbus to Baltimore and died there. Soon his widow and daughters appeared in Monticello to claim the estate held by his mother, but she would have nothing to do with them, although the girls were named Mary Evaline and Sarah Adelaide, the names of William Perry Moore's two sisters.

"In 1854, the daughters filed suit at Baltimore to recover the estate. There had appeared the Texas soldier, William Perry

Moore, making a case difficult to decide. Judge George Robertson, of the Court of Appeals, after eleven years of litigation rendered a decision in favor of the plaintiffs."—*Courier-Journal*.

Of this first half century of life in Wayne an article by James A. Phillips, based on Micah Taul's *Memoirs*, already referred to, gives a striking picture.

## MICAH TAUL

We trust that it will not be deemed a species of maudlin sentimentalism or weakness, which gives pleasure to the mind, as in imagination it beholds in "fancy's misty light" the spectral forms of the revered dead, who, one hundred years ago were living, active factors in forging deeds which make the annals of the first chapter of our country's history. Oftentimes these airy shapes pass before our mental vision; we can see the venerable form of the old surveyor, Joshua Jones, Jacob Staff in hand, on his way to survey a plot where the sound of "stick-stuck" was never heard before, nor the compass brought into requisition to establish artificial lines of dominion where once savage beasts and the more savage Indian exercised an undisputed title.

We can behold the seven first justices: Charles Dibrell, Martin Sims, Edward Cullom, James Montgomery, Raleigh Clark, James Jones, and James Evans, assembling at the house of Henry Garner for the purpose of holding the first county court. And those three dignified old gentlemen are Samuel Newell, Hugh McDermott, and Isaac Chrisman. These men compose the court of "quarter sessions." They are trying to find a rude temple of justice in which to hold court.

That man is Roger Oatts and those other two are Joseph and William Beard. They are the only citizens who live in the town: the first mentioned, Roger Oatts, keeps a hotel; Joseph Beard is a merchant, Ben Gholson is his clerk; McNutt, the Irishman, is another merchant who came from Winchester, Virginia. It is county court day: then as now, the good citizens have assembled—a clerk is to be elected—the town is to be named. Some are gathered at the town spring, others are drinking, fighting, and pillaging "for fun." A squad of militia, commanded by Lieutenant Bill Jones, is drifting near the spot where the old jail stood. We can see in the crowd, Joseph Chrisman, William Cullom, Anthony Gholson, Isaac West, Bartholomew Hayden, John Buster, Louis Coffey, Squire Baker, Thomas Eades, Solomon Dunagan, Leonard Dodson. These first settlers came mainly from West Virginia, North Carolina, and Tennessee.

But look! They have all vanished like the gigantic shapes and shadows of the beleaguered city. The actors on this stage have disappeared, having in life illustrated the full gamut of human virtues. They fell asleep on the lap of Mother Earth, there to rest until the resurrection morning.

These are the men with whom Micah Taul came in contact, more than one hundred years ago, after the organization of the county. They were nature's own product, tall, stalwart sons of the mountains and the forests, brothers of the pine and massy oaks, beside which they grew. They had led an outdoor life, where strong lungs inhaled the pure air of heaven, had from childhood been familiar with nature in all her majesty, and unconsciously absorbed her rugged strength, apart from the influences of vice and luxury, which contaminate; having neither fear, hypocrisy, nor avarice they learned the lessons of courage and self-confidence by grappling with the hardships and privations incident to primitive conditions. Thus equipped with but little book knowledge but with much "mother wit" our ancestors had emigrated farther west, to find new homes and to plant Anglo-Saxon civilization, where erstwhile rude savages dwelled.

On the 16th day of March, 1801, the first session of the county court was held at the house of Henry Garner. Before this court appeared Micah Taul, Hugh McDermott, Samuel McKee (long afterward a distinguished member of Congress and father of Colonel McKee who was killed at the battle of Buena Vista), and quite a number of other candidates. Taul was chosen clerk of the court and soon thereafter he was appointed clerk of the court of "quarter sessions." He was two months less than sixteen years of age when he was entrusted with the records of both courts.

Since we now have installed our clerk in both offices, them "to hold during good behaviour," permit us to go back for a time and find out something about his antecedents.

Micah Taul was born in Montgomery County, Maryland, about twelve miles north of the city of Washington, on the 14th day of May, 1785; his father's name was Arthur Thomas Taul; his mother's maiden name was Mary Anne Johnson. He was the youngest of six sons born unto them. In the year 1787 the family moved to Kentucky, and settled in Fayette County. Micah was two years old, but old enough to remember that in coming down the Ohio in a boat he fell into the river and was rescued by his father, and that two of their Negroes were drowned by the overturning of a canoe. His parents were Baptists.

He was taken, upon one occasion, to hear the pastor, Rev. John Price; after the sermon quite a number of persons were baptized, and the next day, said he: "I joined some little girls at play. Whether I voluntarily offered, or the little girls out of mere wantonness got me preaching, I do not remember; so it happened, however, I preached them a sermon and baptized them one and all. I did not hear the last of it for years; I must have been very young, probably not more than 5 years old."

His education was limited, as at that day little opportunity was offered, even in Fayette County, for education. "At the county school" said he, "nothing but reading, writing, and cyphering was taught in those days. The Bible, testament, and Dillsworth's spelling book were the only school books. I was fond of going to school, fond of learning, and I can say it without vanity that I went ahead of all the boys. Although I was industrious, I did not want to be a farmer—wanted to be something else—though I hardly knew what."

At thirteen years of age Micah entered the office of Captain David Bullock, then clerk of the Clark County Court—he had been a captain in the Revolutionary War and was a most excellent clerk "one of the best and altogether the laziest man I ever saw." In a few months after writing in Captain Bullock's office he was considered by everybody as good a clerk as the "old man." In less than a year Bullock hardly ever had an occasion to come to the office.

The truth is Micah Taul never knew what it was to be a boy as he said himself, he ranked with men when he was sixteen years of age. At eleven years of age the decision was made that he was not to be a farmer, then it was that William Leary, a Scotch merchant, of Lexington, refused to employ him, not on account of his abilities, but his diminutive size; and at thirteen, when the average "outlaw" as Judge Owsley used to call them, was "linking it over the lily white lea" robbing bird's nests and watermelon patches, this staid young fellow was acting the part of a man in the clerk's office at Winchester.

So we need not be astonished that one so young took charge of the offices at Wayne County with so much self-confidence. At the age of fifteen he was offered the clerkship of Floyd County upon its organization, which he refused. After his appointment to the offices here he kept the office at his residence half a mile from the courthouse and did all the writing himself until the fall of 1807, when Daniel Mays, a very handsome and sprightly boy from Fayette County, entered the office and remained less than a year. Mays subsequently became a distinguished lawyer and Circuit Judge. Anthony Dibrell, who was afterward Treasurer of the State of Tennessee, wrote in the office for a time during the years 1803-4. Dibrell was an excellent and agreeable boy and made a valuable and useful man. John Chrisman, known more familiarly as "Jack" Chrisman, wrote in the office after this, and upon the resignation of Taul he became the chief clerk.

To an antiquarian it produces a delightful sensation to observe the free and flowing handwriting of our first clerk traced in regular lines with a goose quill upon the unruled pages of the first deed book. The very first deed recorded therein is a historical document itself and of peculiar interest; a deed from the celebrated George Rogers Clark to Jacob Vanhoozer, of 100 acres of land at Price's Meadows now "Meadow Creek," consideration paid 105 pounds.

Had we never come across the *Memoirs* so kindly loaned us by Judge M. C. Saufley we should have been able to deduce with some degree of certainty, from internal evidences connected with his handwriting, one characteristic of the man. The free and uncramped chirography unmistakably indicates a frank, unselfish disposition. How easily we can trace the influences of Micah Taul's style to some of those who came after, perceptibly in Jack Chrisman, some of the elder Phillips's, and William Simpson. Wayne County has much cause to be proud of the day this young scrivener took charge of her public records.

Having some regard to unity, we dealt with Micah Taul as a clerk—the Custos Rotulorum of the courts then existing—and concluded this feature of the history of a man, who has more sides than one. So far as this part of the country is concerned he was simply a name, a shadowy figure, becoming more dim as newborn generations came upon the scene. The fancy picture painted in youth has been almost totally wrecked, and instead of the venerable form of "Old Colonel Taul" bent with age, moving amid the Druid oaks which surrounded the two-story log house a half-mile from the courthouse on the place where the late Micajah Phillips long resided, we behold quite a young man, full of life, vigor, and ambition at the age of twenty-nine retiring from the offices to which he had been chosen to assume the graver responsibilities of legislator in the Congress of the United States.

In recalling these early impressions of the subject of our sketch, we find that imagination is a fraud and that tradition is unable to tell more than half a truth. Under recent lights it develops on us that Micah Taul was a positive force, an entity, acting, felt along many lines, that he was a military leader, a lawyer and a good one, a statesman; and while by accident we have rescued from oblivion some of the characteristics of the man, yet it is to be bewailed that neither art nor tradition have left a trace of the human face divine—the voice, the eyes' magnetic beam, these have perished, lost in the fleeting memory of contemporaries. The old house, too, long used as a barn, like "Palmyra Central in the desert" has disappeared. Many times we have gazed at the well-hewed logs and the wooden pegs in the roof and dreamed of its occupants. Here it was that Dorothy Gholson reigned the queen of this chalet and blessed Micah Taul with her radiant smiles, and here it was that Thomas Paine Taul (the brilliant young lawyer who was associated with John Rowan and W. T. Barry in the prosecution of I. B. Desha) was born, as

JAMES STONE CHRISMAN
*Confederate Congressman from Kentucky, 1861-1865*

ANTHONY McBEATH
*He entered the Confederate Army*

WILLIAM McBEATH
*The brother who joined the Union Army*

CAPTAIN BOLIN E. ROBERTS
*Morgan's Cavalry, C. S. A.*

JOHN COSTELLO
*Young Union soldier who wanted only "to meet his Rebel friends in peace"*

also his brother Algernon Sidney Taul—and Louisiana, who became Mrs. Buford—but we are getting along rather too fast.

In the fall of the year 1801 Anthony Gholson moved from Botetourt County, Virginia, to Wayne County and settled five miles northeast of Monticello. The next spring his son John and his youngest daughter Dorothy passed Isaac West's house where Micah Taul was boarding. It was a damp, cool evening and Dorothy was "wrapped up in a large blue cloth cloak, her face veiled and an umbrella over her." Micah Taul had never seen her before, but he remarked to his brother Jonathan that "that young lady" was to be his wife. A few days afterwards he saw her at the marriage of Abel Shrewsbury to Tebitha Van Hoagan, fell in love with her and in six days thereafter led her to the hymeneal altar. He was only seventeen and Dorothy younger. Said he "of course we were a very young couple, too young. I am in favor of early marriages, but it is possible to marry at too early an age. I thought seriously on the subject at the time, young as I was, but I ranked amongst men, was the clerk of two courts, had a license to practice law which I had obtained in the preceding month of March from Samuel McDowell and John Allen, two of the judges of the District Court of Kentucky."

Isaac Chrisman, Joseph Chrisman, and Bartholomew Hayden, each married daughters of Anthony Gholson, hence we learn that "Jack" Chrisman, who succeeded Taul in the office of clerk was his nephew by marriage. In 1827 Mrs. Taul died at Winchester, Tennessee. Her husband thus speaks of her: "I feel myself wholly incapable of doing justice to the memory of this admirable woman, the wife of my youth—in person she was small and very delicate, her weight at no time in life ever exceeded 100 pounds. She was however generally very healthy. In mind she was a giantess. Her early education like my own was limited, but she was fond of reading, and I made it a rule when at home to read everything I did read, in her hearing—as a daughter, wife, mother, mistress, friend, sister, and neighbor, she was blameless; as a housekeeper she had no equal, order and neatness everywhere prevailed. To cap the climax of her character she was a devout christian. A member of the Baptist church, she was baptized in the Cumberland River by the Rev. Thos.

Chilton about the year 1810. Her sister, Nancy Gholson, attended her for several months in her last illness."

Thos. Payne Taul, the oldest son, became quite a distinguished attorney. Beside the celebrated Desha case he prosecuted James W. McClung at Huntsville, Alabama, when no one else would dare to do it. After this he unfortunately became engaged in a difficulty in which he shot a man by the name of Dwyer at Winchester, Tennessee. He was killed himself by his brother-in-law, Rufus K. Anderson, in 1828 in the same town.

Micah Taul was now left with an only daughter, Algernon Sidney having died before. "I have passed" says he "through many painful and tragical scenes the remembrance of which is poignant almost beyond endurance." He was married the second time but we cannot ascertain from the *Memoirs* who his second wife was, or how many children blessed this union. Nor are we able to give a further account of himself as the *Memoirs* come to a sudden stop about the year 1850. Written in Talladega County, state of Alabama, we conclude that he died about this time in that county.

"How the subject theme may gang" in endeavoring to compress such a variety of incidents in a short sketch along so many different lines taxes the art of the writer. We shall retrace our steps and pick up a thread or two dropped from our woof. But few, if hardly any, persons know that the name of dear old Monticello with its wonderful history, much of which gathers around the old courthouse that once stood in the center of its plaza—"public square"—around the old jail and the never changing "town Spring," was suggested by Micah Taul. The vanity of the Joneses, a strong-minded and bumptious family of people, wanted the town called "Jonesboro" in their honor. There being some controversy about a suitable name, Taul was appealed to for a name. He mentioned Monticello, the name of Jefferson's villa, which was adopted by the court. Said Taul, "the family threw the blame on me and were sore about it for a while but ultimately became friendly."

In this connection we give another incident of a clash with a member of the Jones family. This was with William Jones, the oldest son of Joshua Jones. We quote from the *Memoirs*: "I was elected Military Captain in opposition to Wm. Jones—a new company had been formed by dividing an old one. Jones had been Lieutenant in the old company and expected to be elected Captain of the new one without any opposition. When the election came on to his great surprise I was put up as a candidate in opposition to him and was elected by a large majority. Jones was so much disappointed that he became quite enraged. Swore I should not command the company and that he would whip me on the spot. He considered himself a very stout man and advanced upon me in a menacing attitude. His rage unmanned him and as luck would have it I whipped him, according to the fighting phrase of the day. After a hard fight, fist and skull, biting, gouging &c, I came off victorious. It was a long time before Mr. Jones got over his defeat. He was unfriendly to me for several years, but ultimately became a warm friend. He was a member of a numerous and respectable family, who did not sympathize with him in his hostility to me although, before this occurrence, a portion of the family became displeased with me on account of the naming of the town at the seat of justice."

The William Jones mentioned above was the father of "Tanner," Jimmie Jones, a highly respected citizen, who died at Steubenville several years ago.

We have heretofore considered Micah Taul as a clerk and also somewhat as to his domestic relations. It now behooves us to speak of him in the more active or strenuous scenes of life in which he participated while a citizen of Wayne County.

There was fight in the blood of the Tauls. Most any kind of fight, whether provoked by pride or patriotism. When the bugle called to arms Micah was always ready. There being some apprehension that the government of the United States would have trouble in taking possession of the Louisiana Territory upon the ratification of the treaty of purchase, President Jefferson was authorized by Congress to call into service a number of volunteers. Kentucky's quota was 5,000. Taul raised a company (1804) but they were never called for. We have heretofore alluded to the company which he led out in 1812-13. The competitors for the command of this company were Taul, Lewis Coffey, John Dick, and James Jones. Taul was chosen to command the company.

This company returned to Wayne County in the spring of 1813. Again about the month of June in the same year General

Harrison made a requisition on Governor Shelby for 5,000 mounted volunteers. Says Taul: "The call was responded to as might have been expected from the chivalrous character of the Kentuckians and of their noble old chief (Shelby). I raised a large company in Wayne County without any difficulty. Stephens was elected First Lieutenant, Bartholomew Hayden, Second Lieutenant, Andrew Evans, Ensign. In August we were called upon to rendezvous at Cincinnati. I immediately issued an order for my company to assemble on the day appointed at Monticello, well-mounted and prepared in all respects to take up the line of march. I don't think there was an indifferent horse in the company. I am very sure there was not an indifferent man. I well remember, when we marched through the city of Lexington several of my acquaintances said to me, 'yours is the best looking and the best mounted company that ever marched into this place'— they were in a truth, a noble looking set of fellows, stout, able-bodied, well-dressed, and in fine health." The detachment having marched to Urbana, Ohio, was organized. "I was appointed to the command of the 7th Regiment which was considered at the time by myself and friends as a very high compliment. I was then only 28 years of age and was the youngest Colonel in commission in the State."

This regiment was composed of six companies commanded respectively by Captains Wilson, James Gholson, Sam C. Tate, Thomas Miller, and Craig. The Battle of the Thames was fought on the 5th of October, 1813, but Colonel Taul was in such bad health he could not participate in the engagement. After the defeat of the British the troops were discharged at Maysville and those who volunteered from Wayne came home as best they could.

In the year 1811 Judge Montgomery, of Lincoln County, was a candidate for Congress in the district of which Wayne made a portion. It was understood that the congressional district was formed for the benefit of Montgomery and Tunstall Quarles as his residuary legatee. Quarles boasted that no man in the district could beat Montgomery. This was said in the presence of Colonel Samuel Newell, who remarked that "Micah Taul, of Wayne, could beat him." Whereupon Quarles remarked that, "Montgomery could beat Taul in his own county." Said Micah, "my pride was offended and my ambition somewhat excited and I determined to be a candidate." In this first race for Congress Judge Montgomery beat Taul only 62 votes in the district. In Wayne, Montgomery received only 18 votes out of 1,200. In the year 1814 Montgomery and Taul were candidates again for Congress, the latter was elected by 1,262 votes.

In the course of the summer after returning from Washington, Micah Taul became dissatisfied with his residence in Wayne County, and determined to make a change. In the fall he removed to Winchester, Kentucky. Said he, "the worst selection I could have made, in the state or elsewhere." In summing up the mistakes he had made, he mentioned three: 1st, voting for the "Compensation Bill"; 2nd, moving from Wayne County; 3rd, selecting Winchester as a place of residence. While living in Wayne he made money at the practice of law, but spent it or rather as he frankly confessed "lost it at the card table." "It was then fashionable," said he, "among the profession to play cards for money. The card table was set out every night or every day. There were gentlemen attending court who studied Hoyle more than they did Blackstone and generally won all the money made by others. If I had never played cards I might have been a very wealthy man long, long ago. It is a ruinous vice."

After removing to Winchester he made money fast and might have retained his practice which was good but he indulged in the fashionable habits of the day and neglected his business. For two or three years he was the most popular attorney at the Paris bar, being associated with such men as John Rowan, Beverly Clark, and Thos. F. Marshall. In speaking of Rowan he said that he was "a man of decided talents and commanding eloquence, but I always thought he had as much character as he deserved."

In the spring of 1819 or '20 Colonel Taul was back in Wayne we suppose for the last time. Upon his arrival he found the people excited beyond measure on account of the arrest of three men, who were charged with committing a rape on a woman of the county. The influential citizens prevailed upon him not to undertake their defense. He, however, conferred with the defendants and came to the conclusion they were not guilty of the charge. Said he, "many of my good Wayne County friends were sorely vexed with me for defending them. I never saw a community so inflamed." The men were considered desperate and strong guards were employed by the sheriff to guard the woman. She was marched between double files with the sheriff at the head to the grand jury room that an indictment might be found. "Judge Montgomery," said Taul, "was a very impulsive man; he was not only the personal enemy of the men charged, but he was my personal enemy. I had beaten him for Congress in 1814 and he seemed determined never to forgive me for it."

Amid much opera bouffe demonstration the trial came on. As soon as Taul began his speech, the judge left the bench and did not resume his seat until he concluded his argument. Says Taul, "I never managed a case better, never made a better speech. I convinced the jury that all three of the men were innocent. I dwelt with severity upon the conduct of the judge in having the witness guarded to and from the court house. I told them that the conduct of the judge was a libel upon the county, that his object was to add to the too great excitement for the purpose of producing the conviction of the persons charged. Possibly, gentlemen, said I, his Honor may consider you all savages as you voted against him for Congress in 1812-14." At each of these elections Montgomery had only received eighteen votes in the county. Years afterwards Judge Montgomery told Colonel Taul that the reason why he did not remain on the bench was that he saw the "devil was in him." He said that he was satisfied that Taul intended to arraign him for his conduct before the jury and he could not stand it. "I should," said he, "have ordered you to jail, the consequence of which would have been the acquittal of the prisoners by acclamation. The people of Wayne County would not have seen you carried to jail by my order. No sheriff could have laid hands on you there in safety. Instead of you being taken to jail, I should in all likelihood have been mobbed and thus the whole matter would have ended."

One of these men moved to Texas and another, Charles Cox, the youngest son of a highly respectable man, who had been a member of the Virginia and Kentucky legislature was hung in

Arkansas for murder. He was the father of Rebecca Cox who now lives in Monticello. They had got themselves into this great difficulty by dissipation. They had been the preceding day at a "deer hunt" and "fish fry," where they had indulged freely in drinking, stopped at a doggery, where they became involved with the woman in the case.

We cannot forego giving in this connection an anecdote, which took place during the canvass for Congress in 1812 between Colonel Taul and Judge Montgomery. It occurred in Lincoln County, the home of Montgomery. The judge was disposed to treat Taul with disrespect, did not accord him the usual courtesies that should exist between candidates, in fact would not recognize him or speak to him. The candidates, Montgomery, Taul, and Captain Henry James, of Pulaski, met at Stanford. Montgomery made his speech without any arrangement with the others. Said Taul, "I was young—of an ardent temperament, gay, buoyant, and happy, laughed at his impudence and presumption. He undertook to injure my private character by raking up a lawsuit I had with a man in Clark County, growing out of a transaction between us before I was sixteen years of age, in which he attempted to swindle me out of one hundred dollars."

Two different messengers were sent to Clark County for the purpose of obtaining copies of the records—one was a cousin of Montgomery's, the other a peddler, both lame. The transcript was read and several certificates to prove falsehoods. After he was through, Taul addressed the people and recognized in the crowd "the noble and majestic form of Isaac Shelby then a candidate for Governor." "I was confident," said he, "I had the advantage of my opponent upon this occasion. I was in the county and town of Montgomery's residence and instead of treating me, a young man who had never injured him, with courtesy and respect, he made a wanton attack upon my character, surrounded with personal and political friends. Having been arraigned at the bar of Old Lincoln as a criminal everybody seemed willing to hear me.

"I told them I was a candidate—that my name was Micah Taul—that I was the same Micah Taul named in the transcript;

that I was a young man, having no relatives, and but few acquaintances in the county. I proceeded and said I was not so silly as to flatter myself that I would escape the arrows of calumny and detraction. No candidate that I knew of had been so fortunate in the country, no not even the venerable hero of King's Mountain (Shelby) then present, who had consented to become a candidate for the office of Governor on the sole condition that war was declared against England. He had not escaped; foul charges had been made against him, but he cared as little for them as the stag did for the gadfly that lit upon his horn; and young and humble and friendless as I might be supposed to be I could say to my accusers—my opponents—that their attacks upon me had created in me not one moment's uneasiness; on the contrary I ought to be thankful to them for affording me a good excuse for proving to the people who I was and what I was—to prove to them, in fact, that I had a character of which I had the right to be proud, and of which I was proud, but in relation to which, under ordinary circumstances, it would be indelicate for me to speak [here the speaker read various letters, certificates, etc., to prove his character from boyhood]. I then remarked that I had never thought about the charge against me and of the instruments used in collecting evidence and propagating it—the one being a lame peddler and the other a hopping deputy clerk—without having my risibility excited; it always brought to my recollection Homer's description of the Prince of Slanders:

> " 'Thersites clamored only in the throng,
> Loquacious, loud, and turbulent of tongue,
> Awed by no shame, by no respect controlled,
> In scandal busy, in reproaches bold,
> His figure such as might his soul proclaim,
> One eye was blinky and one leg was lame.'

"My friends shouted and roared at the top of their voices, the crowd was taken by surprise and laughed heartily. Montgomery and friends were completely crestfallen. One of the lame men spoke up (they were both lame) and said his eyes were not blinky, to which I replied that Thersites was a much handsomer man than he. The cheering was resumed and lasted for some time." Montgomery had fled and Micah concluded by saying that "the battle was over and won."

We have given the above circumstance connected with Taul's first race for Congress to show his calmness and equanimity under a brutal assault upon his character; his skill in the employment of the *ad captandum* art that catches the crowd; and above all his literary culture and readiness in its application when needed. Had he remained in Wayne County he would have been returned to Congress in a few years. The little disturbance to his popularity would have been transient. We doubt if there was any one in the congressional district who was his peer in all that goes to make the ideal Congressman.

That Micah was not a teetotaler, we have the direct testimony of John Stephenson, who informed us several years ago that he had seen him "full" many times on his way home from town. Says Taul, "It was no objection to a man in those days that he drank. I will not assert that it would have been an insuperable objection to a candidate to drink for I do not remember that there were any such characters then, but this I can say with perfect truth, a temperance man would not have been likely to succeed at the regular election."—*Monticello Signal*.

# WAYNE IN THE WAR OF 1812—
RODES GARTH

## CHAPTER III

IN THE WAR OF 1812 Wayne County took a part far out of proportion to her population. These men were almost all Revolutionary soldiers, or their sons, from Southwest Virginia and the northwestern part of North Carolina, and when the call came they responded eagerly. The first volunteers from Wayne left August 24, 1812, under Captain Taul. At the same time David McNair led a company from Cumberland County, and William Cross one from this section of Kentucky. These were all among the Kentucky Volunteers called in August for six months' service.

Micah Taul in his *Memoirs* says (of his company): "At the call for volunteers, Captain James Jones volunteered as a private as did Captain Lewis Coffey and Micah Taul. Rodes Garth was Judge Advocate. He was a member of the Monticello bar and was afterwards frequently elected to the Legislature. Micah Taul was elected Captain and led his men to St. Marys, Ohio, where they spent the winter. They were discharged March, 1813, at Cincinnati. They reached Monticello the third Sunday in March."

In June, 1813, General Harrison made a requisition on Governor Shelby for 5,000 mounted volunteers. Governor Shelby took command in person. Captain Taul raised a company in Wayne of which the roster will be given below. On reaching headquarters, Taul was promoted to colonel, and Miller was made captain to succeed him. They advanced to Lake Erie where Taul became ill and was sent to Detroit. The battle of the Thames was fought October, 1813, and the Americans were almost exclusively Kentuckians, says Taul. Of his mounted volunteers he says, "It was the finest company in the state. They aroused admiration as they went through Lexington." He speaks of them at length in his *Memoirs*, an extract from which has been given in Chapter II.

The roster of Captain William Cross's Company of volunteers of August, 1812: Captain Cross; Lieutenant James Cowan; Ensign Henry Gabbert; Sergeants, Thomas Logan, Samuel Cowan, John Owens; Corporals, William Montgomery, John Carter, Andrew Cowan; Drummer, William Ford; Fifer, Thomas Franklin; Privates, Josiah Beckett, Alfred Ballew, George Bromley, William Bright, Isaiah Burcham, Abel Blankenship, John Carpenter, William Cooksey, Thomas Cowan, James Calhoun, John Cooksey, Benjamin Clark, Thomas M. Flowers, David Gabbert, John Gross, Zebedee Hawley, Asa Harper, James Harper, James Kennedy, William Ledford, Abraham Lester, Samuel Linn, Thomas Mills, James Martin, David Murray, Lott R. Mathews, Zerah Martin, Isaac Miller, James Mackey, Lewis Right, William Savage, Alexander Smith, Richard Scott, Andrew Smalley, Jacob Speck, James Wood, John Witham, Zephaniah Worsley, Jesse Wells, John Young, Jr.

The names of the men composing Captain Taul's Company from Wayne were: Captain, Micah Taul; Lieutenant, Joseph H. Woolfolk; Ensign, John Bartleson; First Sergeant, James Givens; Fourth Sergeant, John Shannon; First Corporal, John Dodson; Third Corporal, Thomas C. Pemberton; Fourth Corporal, Noah Wilhite; Drummer, William Cowan; Fifer, Stephen Hines; Privates, Joshua Baxter, Welsher Buckhannon, William Barnes, William Blair, John Buster, Esquire Baker, James Cotton, Tillman Cullom, Edward N. Cullom, Lewis Coffey, Alexander Davis, Solomon Dunagan, John Dick, Thomas Decker, Daniel East, North East, Walter Emerson, Samuel England, John Easter, David East, Jesse Flinn, Samuel Ford, John Foster, John Garovir, James LeGrand, Mordecai Gregory, Rodes Garth, Anderson Garland, John Hicks, Parkman Howard, William Hall, Samuel Ingraham, Augustus Johnson, Benjamin Jones, James Jones, William Jones, James Langston, Cyrus Logan, Jonathan Moore, William Miller, John Montgomery, John M. Newell, Daniel Peveyhouse, Joab Rowe, George Rudd, James Ridgeway, John Ray, John Roberts, William Summers, Richard Savage, John Shrewsbury, Jacob Souther, James Tuttle, Henry Tuttle, Moses Tucker, John Tuller, Thomas Terrell, David Vestol, Isaac Van Winkle, Micajah Van Winkle, Adam Vickery, Valentine Worley, Isaac West, Ballenger Wade, John Wright, James Young.

Rodes Garth kept a journal of the daily occurrences in Captain Taul's Company, beginning with their departure August 24, 1812. This journal was loaned, by one of Garth's descendants, to Judge James A. Phillips, editor of the Wayne County *Outlook,* and was published in this paper in 1898. A copy is subjoined.

It will be remembered that there were seven companies that went out in 1812, under the command of Colonel Barbee, to fight the British. We have heretofore given the names of two of these companies, commanded respectively by Captains Micah Taul and William Cross. Below we give the names of the company commanded by Captain David D. McNair, of Cumberland City. The four other companies of the regiment were commanded by Captains James Barbee, of Mercer, Peter Jordan, also of Mercer, Garret Peterson, of Washington, and John Shelby, of Adair. The names of those composing the company are:

Captain David McNair from Cumberland City, Geo. Allen, Lieutenant, Nimrod Maxwell, Ensign, Wm. Cole, Wm. Morgan, Lemuel Stockdon, Elijah Christman, Nathan Martin, David Spicer, George Martin, Henry Winters, Jas. Price, Wm. Wisdom, Francis Wisdom, Isah Cuzzart, Richard Blackwood, Gardner Green, Richmond Green, John Harvey, Henry Lacy, Jacob Shutts, Abednago Bays, Wm. Chamberland, Jo Weaver, John Wisdom, Josiah Akin, Wm. Smith, Anthony Pennington, Arthur Carrigan, Gilbert Rollin, Michael Crews, John Shutts, Labsum Thurman, Isaac Harris, Wm. Degraffenreed, Wm. Brook, James Brown, John Smith, Sr., Asa Elliot, Wm. A. Walthal, John Mary, Chas. Hibbitts, John Obanion, Joseph Larton, John Onton, Wm. Macksey, Josiah Cheatham, Ezekiel Dop, Elijah Michel, Robert Lawton, John Holland, Isher Stockton, John Smith, Sr., Isaac Rayfield, Wm. Carter, Wm. A. Lucke, Andrew Long, Nathan Cary, James Wisdom.

## "FORWARD MARCH"

(We copy from the *Journal*)

Captain Taul and company of volunteers generally started from Monticello under the command of General Henry Harrison on the 24th day of August, 1812, the expedition of six months against the Indians and British and marched as far as Cumberland River and camped.

August 25, Isaac West returns home and the company continues their march to Maple Swamp at a seat of North East, Esqr. and camped during the night.

August 26, they marched through Stanford, arrived at Danville in the evening, joined Captain Barbee's Company, marched together five miles beyond Danville and were hospitably treated by the citizens of the town and county without cost, and a large number of people were collected.

August 27, the companies returned through Danville and camped at Fisher's pond, about a mile off in the direction to Newport, our expedition being changed by General Hull's surrender of Detroit.

August 28, the company continue their march and camped near Nicholasville.

August 29, continued our march and camped on the road from Nicholasville to Frankfort. The citizens on the road very kindly affording necessaries to the company.

August 30, ordered to change our course, we continued our march and camped on the road in a direction to Georgetown; Captain Taul very sick.

August 31, Captain Taul mends a little; continue our march and in the evening arrived at Georgetown, in the bosom of a polished and generous people. Captain Taul much mended.

September 1, 1812. We left Georgetown about 1 o'clock and continued our march to Little Eagle and camped. Jas. Jones discharged for bodily infirmity.

September 2, continued our march and camped in the evening on Dry Ridge, which is forty miles long and on it is some good land.

September 3, continued our march and in the evening camped at Brumbacks and James Dunigan discharged.

September 4, continued our march and in the evening camped at the foot of Dry Ridge on Banklick creek.

September 5, continued our march on this day and two or three past met many cowards and women and children, leaving the Ohio and its frontier, some going to Virginia and Kentucky for safety; in the evening camped at Newport on the bank of the Ohio river at which place we overtook Colonel Poage's Regiment of Dragoons from Kentucky.

September 6, continued at Newport from the 5th to the 13th, performing military evolutions and Colonel Poage's and Simeral's regiments crossed the Ohio river, saluted with a discharge of cannon as they cross. The balance of our regiment arrive.

September 13, Portman Howard and George Neal were left sick. We crossed the Ohio river, saluted with a discharge of cannon, marched through Cincinnati and camped ten miles on our road to Dayton, it being a cold wet day.

September 14 and 15, continued our march, passed Lebanon, a fine town, and country very flourishing, and the people generally more patriotic than about Cincinnati.

September 16, continued our march and arrived at Dayton on the great Miami river about 11 o'clock a. m. the adjacent country rich and this a flourishing town about 57 miles North of Cincinnati just below the confluence of Still Water and Mad rivers in the great Miami. Poage's, Jennings', and Barbee's Regiments, 400 mounted men and a company of light horse ready to march. About 11 o'clock a certain athletic young man huzzaed for Hull and cursed the Kentuckians, and said they would not dare show their faces in his presence. They ducked him and made him run the gauntlet about a mile with many severe bruises. On the West of Dayton is a large settlement of Dunkards who depend upon their heels, and mercy of the savages rather than to resist them.

September 17. We started to Piqua, the most of us waded the river and camped 5 miles on the road in a field and on the same evening five beehives were pressed by some of our Regiment.

September 18. Continued our march in the morning through the ruins of a Hurricane, the timber prostrated upon the ground about a quarter of a mile long. It is said it happened in the twinkling of an eye, with a great noise. We passed through level country until we came near the Miami river and found rich land on and near it. We passed Staunton, crossed the Miami and we were at Troy, a small country town and camped in a field near the banks of the great Miami river, met a great number of Ohio Militia returning from Fort Wayne and understood General Harrison had started a few days before from Fort Wayne for the town of the Potawatomies with 1,500 men.

September 19. Continued our march, arrived at Piqua about 10 o'clock with Jennings' and Poage's regiments and several hundred mounted riflemen. Colonel Jennings' regiment starts to St. Marys. Piqua an elegant county seat. Three men deserted us and were brought back and kept on guard until next day.

September 20. Sunday. Poage's regiment and the mounted men start to St. Marys. By the order of the colonel a wooden horse was prepared and our Regiment formed in a hollow square and the three deserters arraigned, and by their great entreaty and fair promises to the colonel they were pardoned. In the evening one Indian came into camp, and an express from Harrison that he had burned and destroyed five Indian towns, 120 acres of corn and upward of 70 head of cattle and no Indians seen. Dry and cold.

September 21. Monday. Still camped at Piqua waiting further orders, nothing of importance transpires. Three Indian squaws came in a detachment under Captain Barber from our Regiment consisting of 40 men of Rodes Garth and others, order to be ready to start the next day to escort upwards of 200 head of cattle to St. Marys.

September 22. Tuesday. Rodes Garth, John Garner, and John Shrewsbury, and the rest start to guard the beeves from Piqua to St. Marys, upwards of 30 miles through a wilderness, pass through a tolerably level country of second-rate land, meet about 60 wagons and 200 Ohio men returning home from Fort Wayne, camped the same evening at Fort Lawremy on a river of the same name running in the great Miami, here we had very bad water to use.

September 23. Wednesday. Started from Fort Lawremy with the cattle, met about 45 wagons, a number of Kentucky and

Ohio troops returning from Fort Wayne, passing through second-rate, level soil to St. Marys which place arrived about [?] o'clock, with all the beeves safe, and camped that night here, here found Captain James Logan, an Indian and nine or ten others who were friendly to us, and overtook Colonel Jennings' and Colonel Poage's Regiments, who are employed in cutting a road from St. Marys to Defiance about 60 miles through a howling wilderness.

September 24. Thursday. Captain Barbee and his detachment ordered to guard the public stores at St. Marys. General Harrison goes to Piqua to Barbee's regiment and Colonel Finley, of Ohio with 150 of Ohio volunteers marched against the Tiowa Indians.

September 25. Our detachment still stationed and guarding the public stores; a porcupine taken and brought into camp and one killed; Colonel Poage's Regiment employed in improving the fort at St. Marys, and Colonel Jennings' regiment marched and still employed in cutting the road to Defiance and ordered to build a blockhouse about halfway to Defiance.

September 26. Saturday. Our detachment still employed in guarding the public stores; Rodes Garth, John Garner, and John Shrewsbury take a small tour in the prairie to the west of St. Marys and behold in prospect farther than the eye can see, 20 miles or more. Not a tree or shrub about the prairie. Three miles broad in the general, a grand prospect for those who never saw the like. Here is grass thickly set from five to six feet high, tall majestic trees ranging on either side, and sometimes penetrating the glades or prairie a few hundred yards. Here the western sun sinks below the grass in the western horizon and gradually disappears into night; the site of St. Marys an elegant place and country for farmers, the land level and rich, the prairie affording hay and grass for the horses of the army, sufficient for a million horses.

September 27. Sunday. Still employed at the public stores at St. Marys; Colonel Barbee's regiment arrive from Piqua and Colonel Findley's detachment return from the Tiowa Town of Indians of the Northeast, after burning it and 70 acres of corn; no Indians seen, having fled a few days before; one man of the detachment killed by going beyond the lines of the sentry unknown to the sentinel, who shot him; a deserter from Captain McNary's Company brought back and pardoned by the Colonel.

September 28. Monday. Colonel Barbee's Regiment remain waiting for farther orders; General Harrison returns sometime in the night; a guard under Richard Johnson bring six Miami chiefs from Ft. Wayne to St. Marys to treat with General Harrison, who were taken near Ft. Wayne to St. Marys to treat with Harrison, and taken to Ft. Wayne as spied by Colonel Simeral's regiment. They are large tall sprightly men, the principal chief called Rising Sun; they are well dressed, painted with red and black paint, ornamented with silver, a large war club, a battle ax and bows and arrows brought with them. They are said to be great archers, about 250 warriors, living upon the head waters of the Wabash and adjoining the Potawatomies.

September 29. Tuesday. The six Indians brought into camp before General Harrison and for the want of an efficient interpreter detained, hospitably treated; Colonel Simeral's troop of light horse and all the mounted men return from Ft. Wayne and camp at St. Marys. A great number of friends gladly meet and salute each other.

September 30. Wednesday. This day Captain Barbee and detachment are relieved from guarding the public stores and join the Regiment. This a fine clear day and Colonel Barbee's Regiment marched one mile in the great prairie and mustered, and performed many military evolutions with great skill; whilst we were mustering an express arrived from General Winchester near Ft. Defiance that the advanced troops under him were likely to be attacked by 2,000 or 3,000 British and Indians, and that he had five spies killed and scalped by them, laying in ambush, Colonel Barbee's and Poage's Regiments and the light horse and riflemen present, quick as possible got ready to march to Defiance and by an hour before sundown marched and the same evening camped on the road about six miles from St. Marys all baggage and tents being left, each man taking provisions enough to supply him three days and stagnated branch water tasted very well. The road level and rich, low land.

October 1. Thursday. The sentinels are heard before day, fired two guns and an alarm raised and in less than five minutes the whole army was in battle array, the alarm being over each man took a broil or snack and by the time it was clearly light the army marched. About 8 o'clock it commenced hard raining and continued the whole day. We marched upwards of 24 miles through the mud and rain, our ammunition being much damaged by the rain, and another express met us and informed General Harrison, that the Indians and British had retreated down the river towards the rapids from Ft. Defiance. General Harrison and all the light horse and mounted men, push forward for Defiance, and our two Regiments at night camped on the Oglaves at a block house commenced by Colonel Jennings' Regiment. Before our arrival Colonel Jennings' Regiment were hourly expecting an attack from the Indians and had made considerable breast work around their camp. It continued to rain hard all night. We made fires on the cold wet ground and lodged without tents or whiskey, the Oglave here about 40 yards wide and a great quantity of first rate land.

October 2. Friday. Colonel Jennings engaged in finishing the block house and Colonel Barbee's and Poage's Regiments ordered to cut the road to Defiance about 30 miles, our Regiment finish drying their clothes, clean their guns, and dry their ammunition, several of the Shawnee Indians follow General Harrison. Our Regiment on half rations and no whiskey.

October 3. Saturday. This day Colonel Barbee's Regiment started to clean the road and guard the cattle to Defiance and proceeded about two or three miles, and an express met us from General Harrison directing our Regiment to return to St. Marys, to guard the place and to wait further orders, the Regiment with not half rations in the evening started to St. Marys and camped the same evening about seven miles on the bank of the Oglaves. The most of us had to regale ourselves with hackberries, grapes, haws, hazelnuts, and crabapples the day being wet and dry by turns.

October 4. Sunday. We marched early in the morning and arrived at St. Marys very hungry at about 3 o'clock, about 23 miles. A dry piece of bread was a great rarety to us. At St. Marys we found 500 Ohio mounted men waiting to join General Harrison and we are informed that the Indians are again around Ft. Wayne, had killed two of our men and a boy had killed one of them.

October 5. Monday. This day cold and rainy by turn and a very frosty night and 76 of the Ohio mounted men start to Defiance to guard the wagons and John Gloover starts to see General Harrison.

October 6. Tuesday. This a clear day General Harrison with the 76 Ohio men and the mounted men under Colonel R. M. Johnson from Kentucky return from Ft. Defiance, the Kentucky mounted men about to return home, being discharged by General Harrison.

We are informed that the troops in advance had suffered much for provisions and clothing had become impatient and were addressed by General Harrison and by his promises were better satisfied. Here met a number of old acquaintances and about to start home indulged the social glass, Captain Joseph Boyd and Harrison Mundy of the first troops from Kentucky, attended at Captain Taul's markee after night with some of our Regiment and drank a few bumpers. Captain Mundy was one of about 17 spies of the advanced army who were attacked by 60 Indians. He charged upon them and drove them and as he says, bragged them out of the victory. Captain I. Boyd was among the foremost with Major R. M. Johnson in burning one of the greatest Indian towns, and he said in one of our glasses, he would not desire more than three men and three good tooting horns and he would toot all the Indians through the country and make them run before him. Nearly half the mounted men lately assembled from the Ohio State disorderly, and dishonorably leave their camp and return home.

October 7. Wednesday. The troops under Colonel R. M. Johnson from Kentucky start back home. General Harrison formed the remaining mounted men of Ohio in a close column about four hundred men under the immediate command of Colonel Trimble, and to be under the command of General Tupper when he should join them about 12 o'clock. They were addressed by General Harrison in substance as follows:

"Fellow soldiers and citizens, by my orders and request you have assembled at this place for an expedition as yet to you unknown. With you I have a common pride for the State of Ohio for I was a citizen of it in a territorial state and was your first representative in Congress. I knew there must be some influential, disaffected men from Ohio, otherwise such a number of troops would not have thus disorderly left their camp and deserted the best interests of their country. The valor of the citizens of Kentucky is great. I have under my command now from that state about 5,000 men, and 2,400 mounted men are on the waters of the Wabash. I know your valor is equally as great but greater it cannot be.

"My views since I requested you to assemble at this place have changed. I was then a Brigadier General, and it was then my intention, with about 2,500 mounted men by a speedy march to surprise and retake Detroit. Since then I have been appointed a Major General of all the Northwestern army and I feel it my duty to command and be with them. We would be in a deplorable situation were we all to march now and our provisions and communication be cut off. I have therefore planned a small but important expedition for you to execute under General Tupper, of our own state, and which will be made known to you in due time. The expedition is one to which you are completely adequate. I have provided spies and guides to take you a route unexpected to the Indians, and their towns most contiguous to Ft. Wayne by which you may surprise the Indians before they hear and fly your approach. The Kentuckians have turned, not regarding horses or pay, if they should be well paid by Congress, if not they are satisfied, for property to them is nothing when put in competition with their dearest rights and liberties when invaded by the Indians and British. And if liberty and personal security are incentives to valor in the Kentuckians, much more should it be to the people of Ohio. For should the views of Government and this army be defeated, let me ask you who would be the first and greatest sufferers, you or the Kentuckians? You certainly would. I know then for your own security and safety, the pride and patriotism of your state among the Union, you will not shrink from your duty and the best interest of your country because feed is not provided for your horses and you may not have the greatest certainty of pay. If the little corn of this place was delivered to you your horses might have two or three feeds a piece, but the wagons bearing provisions to the advanced and advancing army must stop and the great object of retaking Detroit and Malden this season must fail. As to pay, you are better situated than the Kentuckians, for I am informed that by the laws of your state provisions are made for payment of expense of troops called out by your Governor. You then have a double lien for compensation to the Kentuckians. But you as free agents have come here to defend your own rights and not that of kings and nobles as in England and other despotic countries, and now unless you are willing to march I do not want you to go. Although during this campaign I am your General in a little time my power will cease, I shall mingle with you but without any more power than any one of you, and in some future campaign your children may be chief commander and my own common soldiers. If but 20 men turn out Colonel Trimble must take them and march but had rather you all would go on the expedition."

Colonel Trimble then addressed them thus:

"Shoulder arms! All you who are for marching on the expedition will face to the right and march to the right and all you for returning face to the left and march to the left." The patriotic band with but few exceptions marched to the right, fixed their guns and huzzaed for joy and general approbation— an interesting scene.

Colonel Barbee's regiment still employed in guarding beeves and the public stores and improving their encampment. General Harrison leaves St. Marys to meet the Pennsylvania and Virginia troops, about 2,500 in number, bearing of cannon and etc., which compose the right wing. The Ohio troops under General Tupper, the center and the Kentucky troops under Generals Winchester and Paine to compose the left wings.

October 8. Thursday. The most of the Kentucky mounted men for 30 days return home very much fatigued and horses very poor. News reaches camp that one of the detachment to Ft. Wayne was shot by an Indian and slightly wounded. Each of them fired. Also that a man was wounded near Ft. Jennings and one killed and scalped on the opposite shore, near Ft. Defiance. This day John Bartleson, Ensign Berry Hinds, Welsher Buchanan, Joseph McMillan, and Daniel Peveyhouse, make a small scout of eight or ten miles to the Northwest of St. Marys for Indians but saw none and found the country by turns rich, swampy, and level.

October 9. Friday. Colonel Simeral's regiment of light horse arrive at St. Marys much fatigued and hungry.

October 10. Saturday. Colonel Barbee's regiment still stationed at St. Marys and Colonel Simeral's Regiment of Light Dragoons. Two men died and were buried with the honors of war. We are informed that considerable baggage of the army of the Wabash was taken by the Indians and several of the guards killed.

October 11. Sunday. This a cold wet day and a certain Mr. Offerd of the light horse came into camp and stated that on the evening before he was hunting his horse two or three miles from camp without arms that two Indians came up to him and compelled him to go to their camp. They tied his hands with a handkerchief. That they had several horses and in a hard rain he slipped his hands loose and made his escape from their pursuit. Major McDowell with about 60 troops of light horse pursue them, find their camp fire and sign of horses, but they left it in such a manner that they could not be pursued. Colonel Simeral and Regiment start to Piqua and the settlement to recruit themselves and horses. John Dick, James Tuttle, and Thomas C. Pemberton of our company very sick. Wagons and 200 bullocks start to Ft. Defiance escorted with about 108 men under Captains Burnett and Jordan. Colonel Barbee broke his cane over one of Captain Sherley's men because he refused to march, which rendered him considerably unpopular with the soldiers and many of the officers. Adjutant John Powell hurt his knee and leg against a stump in a fray with one of the men. The Rules of War in this instance by them trampled upon and disregarded.

October 12. Monday. This a clear day a cold night and frost and the most of the Regiment closely employed in stockading of about four acres around and adjoining the fort. Hickabod Stogdon starts on an express to Ft. Wayne a very dangerous route. John Johnson, the Indian agent, informs us that the Indians brought in here to treat for the Miami tribe were spies and that they had solicited the Delawares three times to take up arms against the Union and that they meditated an attack in the latter end of October. The sick of our company recovering.

October 13. Tuesday. This a clear day the sick recovering and our regiment employed in stockading. About twenty of the Shawnee men and squaws came into camp riding with corn, potatoes, moccasins, broaches and etc., for sale. The squaws ride astraddle on their horses; expert traders clothed with moccasins, leggins, of blue and red cloth and petty coats of the same kind with the border near their ancles, a calico shirt and a clean white blanket with a handkerchief around their head their hair long and platted affect to be very ignorant of our language. They are considered by us to be very treacherous and deceitful some of them in features resembling a little some of our acquaintances in Kentucky. About 8 o'clock at night Alexander Davis a sentinel fired a gun at noise approaching him, our Regiment instantly formed in a few minutes the alarm ceased and we were ordered to our tents.

An hour before day Robert Lawrence starts on express to Ft. Wayne proceeded about two miles saw two Indians on the road one whistled in his charger, which was again returned further up the road he said and that it was prudent to return.

October 14. Wednesday. The company mostly recovered, this a clear morning and warm sunshine, animating all to labor and industry. Being closely engaged in stockading and doing much work, a party having started early in the morning to scour the adjacent country and saw no Indians. About 20 of the Ohio troops desert from Colonel Trimble, forgetting their patriotic tender of services and say on tomorrow one Major and about 100 would be in our camp. The danger, fatigue, and fear of losing their horses induced them to return. It appears that one reason of the general combination of the Indians against us was produced from a belief that a large number of their Ohio neighbors were cowards, their bravery but a parade, that they had nothing to fear from them, when only the name of a Kentuckian cast a damp over their spirits and they generally retreat before them. Many pheasants, black squirrels, and pigeons killed in small scouts near camp.

October 15. Thursday. This a clear warm day and Major Edward with nearly 100 men return disgracefully from their voluntary expedition, without doing anything but drawing and rating the United States provisions and leaving Colonel Trimble near Ft. Wayne.

Joseph H. Wolfolk, lieutenant, with Welsher Buchanan, Daniel Peveyhouse, John Havens, and Sam Ingram took a scout for Indians eight or nine miles to the Northwest of St. Marys, but saw no fresh sign, found one United States horse in their route. The Regiment nearly well and still engaged in stockading.

October 16. Friday. This a clear warm day and Captain Taul, Mordecai Gregory, Lewis Coffey, W. Emerson, N. East, N. Newell and 60 men from our Regiment start to guard the wagons and packhorses from this place to Ft. Jennings. And Rodes Garth starts to Dayton to receive 1,700 gallons of whiskey for the army. The stockading finished and a six-pounder twice fired.

## FROM MICAH TAUL'S MEMOIRS

The Wayne soldiers spent the winter at St. Marys, Ohio, an uneventful period, and returned to Wayne, arriving the third Sunday in March. They were met at the Cumberland River which was the line between Pulaski and Wayne (Burnside) by a large number of people on the Wayne shore, among them Anthony Gholson, then near 80. At the homes, on the way from there to Monticello, people had gathered to welcome them. Ensign Bartleson, a very worthly young man and excellent officer, was riding with me as were two or three more of the company who remained with us. The next day was county court day and I had the pleasure of taking by the hand the fathers and brothers of the young men who had been in my care for the preceding six months.

Shortly after, the patriotic citizens of Wayne gave us a barbecue. It was on a large scale and I delivered an address to them in which I endeavored to do justice to the worthy men who had served under me.

In the second campaign—Sergeant Thomas Miller was a bold, energetic man. He made a fine officer, later removed to Missouri and died early.

Company returned in October and were discharged at Maysville, Kentucky.

---

The soldiers who went with Colonel Taul have been immortalized in his *Memoirs* and Rodes Garth's journal and a tardy recognition is here given to those who fought with Captain Adam Vickery under Colonel Slaughter at New Orleans.

Smith's *History of the Battle of New Orleans* says:

"No troops engaged on the American side did more fatal execution upon the enemy's rank and file than did these Kentucky troops. Every man of the regiment was in rifle range and all did deadly work."

Captain Adam Vickery's Company, Slaughter's Regiment, Kentucky Detached Militia commanded by Lieutenant Colonel Gabriel Slaughter included:

Lieutenant John Garner
Ensign John Barrow
Sergeant Hiram Gregory
Sergeant Thomas Brown
Sergeant Moses Barnes
Sergeant Alexander Brown
Sergeant Harmon Elrod
Corporal William Hurt
Corporal George Dodson
Corporal Thomas Ryan
Corporal Lapsley Hall

Privates:

James Ard
Andrew Alexander

Peter Acre
Owen Burnham
John Bell
John Ballard
James Burnett
James Baker
Stephen Baker
William Barnes
Willis Bowman
Enos Barnes
Lewis Brown
Barnabas Brown
Cornelius Bertram
John Craig
John Casson

William Coughron
Enos Cook
David Cox
Caleb Cooper
John Duffey
James Dean
William Davis
Charles Dabney
Adam Elrod
John Foster
Jesse Gray
Samuel Gholson
Stephen Gibson
Abraham Gooding
Thomas Gibson
John Hains
William Hill
Henry Hall
John Kennedy
William Kogar
John Lee
John Luster (Lester)
James Lenn
Henry Lambert
Robert Livingston
George Miller
Solomon McGowan

Ulysses Mills
David Moore
David Mays
Jesse Neal
Alexander Row
John Ray
John Southwood
John Shaw
John Shelton
John Savage
James Shelton
William Smith
Peter Stephens
Henry Smith
Thomas Stephens
George Smith
William Sallee
John Tiller
John Thornton
John Wade
James Woods
Joshua Welsher
Joseph West
Elisha Wade
Daniel Wray
Barnabas Wallace
John Willis

At least one company of the Fifty-third Regiment, Kentucky Militia, was organized in Wayne in 1805-1806. The tax list of those years and thereafter until 1825, shows the names of the officers. These were Joshua Buster, William Jones, Adam Vickery, Lewis Coffey, captains, with various officers of lower rank noted in the 1812 muster rolls. Micah Taul tells of succeeding William Jones as captain at the outbreak of the war.

By that time, in Wayne, as in the rest of the state, the militia had been gradually disbanded. When the War of 1812 came on, the Wayne division was a fairly well-knit, though informal, organization that responded to General Harrison's call for volunteers in the Western Campaign and to Governor Shelby's call the next year. They also took part in the Southern Campaign, culminating in the Battle of New Orleans.

Samuel Ingram, son of James Ingram, was born in Virginia about 1793. When nineteen years old, he enlisted at Monticello, Wayne County, Kentucky, and served from August 23, 1812, until March 23, 1813, as a private in Captain Micah Taul's Company of Kentucky Militia. He married November 14, 1813, in Wayne County, Kentucky, Elizabeth Parmley. He died February 22, 1881, at his home which was about five miles east of Monticello, Kentucky.

Elizabeth Parmley Ingram born about 1794, died about 1894. She was allowed a pension on her application executed June 18, 1881, at which time she was eighty-seven years of age and was living in Wayne County about six miles southwest of Monticello with her daughter.

The records of the War Department show that James Jones served in the War of 1812 as a private in Captain Micah Taul's Company of Infantry, Seventh (Barbee's) Regiment, Kentucky Militia. He is shown to have entered the service August 23, 1812, to serve six months, and to have been discharged for bodily infirmity, date of discharge not shown.

# DISCOVERY OF OIL—MARTIN BEATY

## CHAPTER IV

SINCE THERE HAS BEEN MUCH CONTROVERSY from time to time about the first oil well, it seems advisable at this point to reproduce an article written some years ago by Captain John W. Tuttle of Monticello and published in the *Signal*. This article, written by an expert claim and title attorney, was the result of exhaustive research, and the name of Captain Tuttle is a guarantee of honesty. Therefore, it would seem that the claim of Wayne to the distinction of having the first oil strike made in her borders is substantiated.

### THE BEATY SALT WELL
#### By J. W. Tuttle

The close of the War of 1812 found all the industries of the new Republic so prostrated and paralyzed that the simplest necessaries of life were only to be obtained upon payment of fabulous prices.

The item of salt alone, which was more indispensable than any other manufactured product, was especially scarce and high. With the return of peace came a revival of its manufacture, however, under the stimulus of the fabulous prices prevailing—$25.00 per barrel for salt. Every salt spring and well was being worked to its utmost capacity to supply the demand. Not only this, but new sources were as eagerly sought as was ever the fountain of youth.

The Legislature of the Commonwealth of Kentucky had to come to the relief of the public, and passed acts to encourage the manufacture of salt, January 31, 1811; February 2, 1813; December 22, 1814; and January 3, 1817. Thus it came to pass that, during the summer of 1817, John Francis and Richard Slavey, both of Wayne County, Kentucky, and Stephen T. Conn, a salt worker of Abingdon, Virginia, jointly began boring and blowing and making experiments and trials for salt water on the Big South Fork of the Cumberland River, opposite the mouth of Bear Creek in Wayne County, Kentucky, claiming to own by entry 1,000 acres of land which included the place where they were boring, lying part in Whitley and part in Wayne County, Kentucky, founding their title upon Acts of the Legislature of Kentucky, passed to encourage the manufacture of salt.

Said Francis and Slavey, owners of said entry, after successfully manufacturing 1,000 bushels of salt from brine obtained thereon, were to pay into the State Treasury, $10 per 100 acres for title in fee to said land.

After a fair supply of brine was encountered in the well, Martin Beaty, of Abingdon, Virginia, September 19, 1817, bought of John Francis, his undivided one-third interest in said land and business, upon the advice of expert Stephen T. Conn.

Shortly afterwards, and perhaps on the same day, Stephen T. Conn who already owned a one-third interest, purchased the right and interest of Richard Slavey, an undivided one-third interest in said land and business.

On or about the same date, Martin Beaty and Lilburn L. Henderson, both of Abingdon, Virginia, purchased the said undivided interest bought by the said Conn from the said Slavey, from the said Conn.

Conn, Henderson, and Beaty, September 19, 1817, entered into a contract of co-partnership, by the terms of which the 1,000-acre tract of land and business was to be considered as joint stock and held in common, each one-third, and that all the expenses incurred in preparing to manufacture salt and in manufacturing were to be borne jointly by the three; and said Beaty and Henderson were to bear the expense of procuring the legal title; also they were to pay balance of purchase money due to Francis and Conn, Beaty to pay Francis and Henderson to pay Conn.

The business was therefore conducted in the name of Conn, Henderson, and Beaty, as a co-partnership. Conn assumed control as active agent of the firm. Merchandise to the amount of $2,000.00 and "metal for boiling," to the amount of $1,000.00, was shipped to the works soon thereafter, and the town location was styled Saltville.

An increased flow of brine, by deeper drilling, hurried Conn to Abingdon for the purpose of notifying his partners in interest, in November, 1817. Salt was manufactured up to 1840, when the works shut down permanently.

In December, 1817, Martin Beaty of Abingdon, Virginia, purchased of John Francis, who had entered and surveyed December 24, 1817 (Surveyor's Book No. 1, Page 370, Wayne County, Kentucky, records), 1,000 acres of land lying and being on the South Fork of Cumberland River, three miles above the mouth of Bear Creek, adjoining the South Fork, the 1,000-acre survey, known as the Beaty Salt Well Tract, upon which there was also a prospect of obtaining salt water, for which Beaty executed to him the notes of the firm.

It being not deemed important to take 1,000 acres under said warrant, only 727 acres were surveyed and afterwards (December 28, 1821) patented, founding their title under Act of the Legislature of Kentucky, passed February 2, 1813, to encourage the manufacturing of salt, Martin Beaty, John H. Fulton, and Lilburn L. Henderson, patentees. This tract became known later as the "Beaty Oil Well Tract."

This 727-acre tract of land was demised, leased, and let to Marcus Huling and —— Zimmerman, both of Pennsylvania, but later from Lee County, Virginia, near Cumberland Gap, Tennessee, after fashion of "wild catters" of all ages, for the purpose of operating thereon for salt water, upon a royalty, or rather "rental" as then called.

The majesty of the law was invoked to settle a dispute as to the title of this tract, but pending litigation the well was drilled by lessee.

At a depth of 536 feet, a veritable "gusher" of petroleum "burst into view" described by an eye witness as follows:

"A stream of oil and carburetted hydrogen was entered which ascended the orifice, pervaded the atmosphere, ran down the bank and spread over the river—but subsequently caught fire and was only checked by throwing sand in the well and plugging the hole."

Petroleum being then of little or no value, the work was abandoned.

Here is another account of the well from the pen of William Bibb, at one time, a half century ago, Governor of Ohio:

"In the valley of the South Fork in early times, were worked Beaty's Salt Wells. Boring one well a little deeper, oil was struck which overflowed at such a rate as to ruin the little salt works. The value of the oil being then unknown, the well was stopped up to prevent the 'nuisance.'"

The following is from the *Cincinnati Gazette*, December 9, 1865:

"The product of the Beaty Oil Well is estimated at 100 barrels per day, but the well is plugged because the oil cannot profitably be removed until navigation of the Big South Fork is opened."

During the summer of 1819, Martin Beaty won the suit to quiet the title to said 727-acre tract, and finally ousted Huling and Zimmerman. The tract thereafter merged into the assets of the firm of Conn, Henderson, and Beaty.

Nothing daunted, Huling and Zimmerman, with the sublime faith in the wisdom of the Creator, which believes that nothing was made in vain, after being satisfied that the product of the salt water well was either "tar or grease and worth money," soon perfected plans for marketing a sample of the product (now locally known as "Devil's Tar") by the South Fork and Cumberland River route.

A number of stout barrels were manufactured, and two of them filled with the "tar," were lashed to a perve—a sort of "dugout"—and started down the river on a medium high tide in charge of two experienced fishermen, Pierson Watson and John Spradling.

While passing through the "narrows" in Devil's Jump the perve dashed to pieces on the rocks—the barrels burst, and the "crew of the vessel" made a narrow escape with their lives by climbing the huge rocks in midstream from whence they were afterwards rescued.

Nothing daunted, Huling and Zimmerman made another attempt to ship the product of the well.

Watson and Spradling were again placed in charge of a perve, newly and specially made for the trip. Two barrels of tar were lashed to the perve, one on each side, as before, with instructions to land near the head of Devil's Jump and take one barrel at a time through the Narrows. When in sight of Devil's Jump, the vessel became unmanageable in the swift current and dashed to pieces on the rocks, the same as before. Watson, being a poor swimmer, narrowly escaped drowning. Shipment by river was thereafter abandoned.

Messrs. Huling and Zimmerman were positive in their opinions that the "Devil's Tar" had an intrinsic value—latent they admitted, of course—but they reasoned that as God had made it (as they believed) it was good for something, and they wanted to know what that something was.

Barrels of the tar were thereafter carted to the neighboring towns and villages and sold to merchants who in turn disposed of it to manufacturers of British Oil, Seneca Oil, Mustang Liniment, etc.

The drilling had been done with pole and augur, 5-inch hole, and at a depth of 536 feet oil was struck.

To Marcus Huling, of Pennsylvania, and to Andrew Zimmerman, a Pennsylvania Dutchman, belongs the honor of being the principals in the drama, "The First Oil Strike." This well, drilled in 1819, an oil "gusher" 77 years ago, was not only the first oil well drilled in the United States, but the first in the world.

---

Near the site of the old salt well are the ruins of an old mill. The mill stone is about all that remains. There has been some effort to interest various organizations in re-opening and improving the old road and placing a memorial to Martin Beaty on the spot. W. A. Kinne, of the Stearns Lumber Company, is much interested in this project.

## THE NEAL WELL

Fulton, Beaty, Ingram, all of Abingdon, Virginia; Irvine and Zimmerman, originally from Pennsylvania, and later from Cumberland Gap, Tennessee, in order to get an increased supply of salt water for the Salt Works at Saltville, in 1820 employed a contractor, John Neal, from Cumberland Gap, Tennessee, to put down a well on the east side of the South Fork near the mouth of Bear Creek, the consideration being in part payment, a Negro boy named "Surk," a slave.

Isaac Powell and Mike Castello were the "blowers for the large hole for the crib" and afterwards worked as drillers. James and Tommy Ryan, then sixteen years old, were employed as assistants. The Negro boy "Surk" also worked on the well, which transferred him to Neal—a singular example of the irony of fate.

Mr. Thomas Ryan, now deceased, was a hale and hearty old man only a few years ago, living on Marsh Creek, Whitley County, Kentucky.

He remembered that when they drilled five feet in one day they thought they were doing extremely well and "knocked off" and went "a-fishing."

Mrs. Ryan's memory tallies with that of Mrs. Cynthia Baker of Oneida, Tennessee, who well remembers the Neal well and the Negro "Surk" and how Johnnie Neal brought her a little salt one time as a present.

"The Neal Well" was finished in the latter part of 1820, and produced a fair supply of salt water, but the brine was so badly "tainted" with "Devil's Tar" it had to be abandoned.

The Conn well bored in 1822 by and for Stephen T. Conn of Abingdon, Virginia, for salt further down the South Fork, near where the road from Monticello to Williamsburg crosses the river, below the mouth of Rock Creek, in Wayne County, proved to be an "oil well" and subsequently abandoned on account of the superabundance of oil.

Huling and Slaughter, also Huling and Napper, in 1823 and 1824, bored for salt water in Casey County, Kentucky.

Thomas Ryan and Davenport Brothers also bored for salt water in 1824 in Casey County, Kentucky, on the Little Fork. Drilling being very hard—one foot per day on an average—work was abandoned.

Later on other wells were drilled near Liberty, Casey County, Kentucky.

*Kentucky Land Grants* compiled by Willard Rouse Jillson gives this item:

"Martin Beaty—Big South Fork—1817—100 Acres."

Martin Beaty first came to Wayne County in 1817 and bought land on the South Fork. He operated salt works, boring wells on his land. In 1824 he was elected to the State Senate. In 1832 he was Presidential elector on the Whig ticket of Clay and Sergeant. Again in 1839 he was elector on the Harrison and Granger ticket. He was elected to Congress in 1833 as a Whig and was elected State Representative in 1848.

He was chairman of the first Board of Common School Commissioners in Wayne from 1837 to 1847.

He died at the home of his daughter in Owsley County in 1856.

Beattyville in Lee County was named for his family who were from Abingdon, Virginia.

# EARLY PREACHERS—CHURCHES—LAWYERS—DOCTORS

## CHAPTER V

THERE IS MUCH EVIDENCE that the early settlers of Wayne, as well as the surrounding counties, were people with a deep-laid religious nature. The war for independence had been fought and won, the frontier had been conquered and they were free to give full play to this religious impulse. There were signs of a great religious awakening that reached to the outposts of civilization.

The construction of log houses of worship quickly followed the erection of homes. These earliest settlers were chiefly Baptists from southwest Virginia and North Carolina, largely from the settlements on the Holston and Clinch where there was an active group of Baptist churches, the Holston Association.

Old Concord Church on Big Sinking is thought to be the oldest church in Wayne County.

George Rogers, affectionately known in later life as "Father Rogers," came into this section in 1798. He gathered a congregation and built a church and held services in different sections of the county.' Father Rogers was born February 6, 1764, and was a Revolutionary soldier from Fauquier County, Virginia.

"NOTE—Father Rogers was a Revolutionary soldier under General Morgan at Cowpens. He was at the siege of Yorktown and in many other battles. He was a Christian who bore his sufferings with great fortitude.

      (Signed) "William Simpson
         "Clk. Wayne County."

He died November 18, 1858.

The Rev. Elliott Jones solemnized the first marriage recorded in the county, that of Thomas Stewart and Hannah Allen, May 27, 1801, and most of the marriages for the next few years.

Two marriages in 1801 were solemnized by the Rev. Mr. Hill.

In 1801, Anthony Gholson gave land for a Baptist church and burying ground at Steubenville. This log structure was razed in the eighties and a frame house built. Anthony Gholson was buried here.

In 1804, John Smith came from Stockton's Valley to the Little South Fork, married and built the Mt. Pisgah Church. He was not an ordained minister and Richard Barrier, a young preacher, was called to the church. There was a very early church at Parmleysville. Early congregations began by meeting at the homes of the settlers, but it was soon evident that they felt there should be a house, if only of logs, set apart and sanctified to the worship of God. The first church in Monticello was built on the hill across the creek, where later Joshua Buster built his home and where, in the old Buster graveyard, some of the earliest settlers were buried. This was the scene of many religious meetings up to 1830.

Many ministers' names figure in the early annals of the county. Isaac Denton from Clinton County, a godly man, mentor of John Smith, came to Wayne to preach. He officiated at the wedding of John Smith and Anna Townsend in 1804.

John Adair was authorized by the court in 1807 "to solemnize matrimony."

Dibrell's Meeting House on the Cumberland River was built before 1810, and the court in 1809 ordered "the road to Rogers Grove Meeting House be improved, overseer appointed to carry this order into effect." Lockett's Chapel was another early church in this section while Bethesda dates back almost to the beginning of the county. Old Salem Church and Alexander's Chapel in the northern part of the county have modern frame buildings superseding the early log structures that showed their early origin.

About 1800, William Lockett, for whom Lockett's Chapel was named, moved into that neighborhood. The original building was erected on land donated by him. His daughter married Rev. Lewis Parker of Pulaski County, and their daughter married Rev. Thomas G. Harrison.

William Lockett and his wife were deeply religious. Their religion was of that quality that enabled them to meet a most unusual and trying situation with the serenity that marks the true Christian character.

The following narration, by one of their descendants, tells graphically the story of their dilemma and how they met it:

"My great-grandmother Lockett's maiden name was De Forrest. She lived in Virginia and married there, probably in the 1780's, a man whose name I am unable to recall certainly, but I think it was Pepper. He was also a resident of that state and they continued to live there after their marriage. Some three or four years later, when their baby girl was about two years old, he had occasion to go to Europe, leaving his wife and child at their home. For some reason, I do not know whether on account of shipwreck, capture or what, he did not return to America for some twelve or fourteen years, maybe longer. His wife concluded after some seven or eight years that he was dead, as she heard nothing at all from him or of him during this interval, and she married my great-grandfather, William Lockett, and they came to Kentucky, bought a farm and settled out in the Lockett's Chapel neighborhood.

"After some years, when she and her second husband had two or three children, the first husband returned to their home town in Virginia. Informed of his wife's marriage, after he landed, and that she and Lockett had come to Kentucky, he followed at once and came to the neighborhood where they lived. Instead of going to see them when he got there, he decided that the better course would be, if they were living happily, simply to slip away and leave them to continue to think that he was dead. Uncle Mike Castillo told me that his father told him that he, that is, this first husband, stayed at his house two or three days, and that he took him, Mr. Castillo, into his confidence and told him his story. He said that he investigated sufficiently to satisfy himself that Lockett and his wife were happy and comfortable and that he had decided to go away without letting them know that he had been there or, for that matter, that he was still alive. But he said that he wanted to see his child. Mr. Castillo told him that he would arrange for him to do that. He accordingly arranged for her to come for water to the big spring near the house (in those early days many residences were located with reference to a spring, then the most convenient source of water) and her father came riding by casually, while she was there and stopped to get a drink. He talked to her for some time, but without disclosing his identity, but he told Mr. Castillo that the hardest fight of his life was to keep from telling her who he was and taking her in his arms. He went away then, and I know nothing of his subsequent history. Uncle Mike told me that his father said he gave an entirely satisfactory explanation of his detention in Europe and of his inability to communicate with his wife, and that he impressed him and the other two or three neighbors who met him as a man of integrity and intelligence.

"He requested that nothing should ever be said to his wife or any other member of the family of his visit, as he preferred that they should continue to think of him as probably dead. But somebody, for some reason, told Mr. Lockett about it after awhile, and he, feeling that it was the only honorable course, told his wife, explaining to her that while it would ruin his life to give her up, she must settle the matter as she thought best. She was a very religious woman (I have heard one of my mother's older sisters tell of her taking her with her to the grove of trees near the house where she went every day for secret prayer), and she told Mr. Lockett that she wanted to study and pray over the matter for a few days and would then tell him her decision. She came to him three or four days later and told him that she had reached a decision—that she had loved her first husband, but had, with good reason, believed him dead and mourned for him and been true to his memory, and that she had concluded that under all the circumstances her proper place was with her present husband and children. That is, she decided that it was her duty to stay with her second husband, and this she did. Lewis Parker, a young Methodist preacher from New York, married in 1824, Matilda Lockett, one of the children of this second marriage. My information is that in order to establish her marriage status and legitimatize the children of the second marriage, proper steps were taken to do so by court proceedings or legislative action.

"No information is available as to the subsequent history of the first husband. The daughter remained with her mother and step-father. In young womanhood she married and moved to one of the western states, where, there is a tradition in the family that one of her sons became governor."

The Wayne Circuit was organized in 1803 by Jacob Young. This included Wayne, Clinton, Cumberland, Pulaski, and Russell counties. Lewis Parker was the preacher of that circuit in 1824.

About the year 1830 Colonel Walter Emerson moved from Tennessee and settled in Wayne County, Kentucky, near the Pulaski County line. Indeed, a part of his farm lay in Pulaski County and a part in Wayne. After he had established his home, it was used as a preaching place by the Methodists for a number of years. In 1852, William Alexander was appointed to the Wayne Circuit and secured a deed from Colonel Emerson to a lot lying in Pulaski County on which a modest frame building 28 by 32 was erected. It was about this time that Isaac W. Emerson, a member of the Louisville Conference, married Miss Sally Parker, daughter of Rev. Lewis Parker of Pulaski County. It was also about this time that Colonel Emerson's youngest daughter, Miss Myrtle, married the Rev. R. C. Alexander who, for many years, was a useful and highly esteemed member of the Louisville Conference.

When the little church referred to above was dedicated and named Alexander's Chapel, it was the only Methodist church within a radius of 10 miles, but there are now four charges, Monticello, West Monticello, Mill Springs, and Wayne Circuit, embraced within the territory which was then served by the original Wayne Circuit. In this territory there are now fourteen Methodist churches. There was an organized Methodist church in the home of Colonel Emerson at least fifteen years before the Alexander's Chapel church building was erected. Lovell's Chapel church, which is located up South Fork of Cumberland River across from Burnside, is an offspring of Alexander's Chapel. It was erected about 1905.

The old church at Alexander's Chapel was torn down in 1912 and a new brick church erected at a cost of about $4,000 and this has served the community as a place of worship since that date.

The records are incomplete but they show that the following have served as pastors of this historic church since it was erected: William Alexander, James L. Edrington, B. A. Cundiff, Thomas G. Harrison, W. T. Davenport, P. A. Edwards, John S. Keen, Robert W. Stone, James G. Freeman, George H. Means, W. C. Brandon, J. V. Guthrie, Jesse L. Murrell, G. W. Shugart, D. F. Walton, Pat H. Davis, Frank E. Lewis, James E. Wooldridge, and T. L. Hulse, presiding elder of that territory from 1907 to 1911.

About the same time a Methodist church was erected at Meadow Creek on land given by Archibald Woods. It was the first of four churches, in that section of the county, which comprised the Mill Springs Circuit. Archibald Woods had invited the Methodists to use his home as a place of worship. This was done until the Meadow Creek Church was erected about 1830.

Thomas J. Chilton was a minister in this section in this early period. He is mentioned as having baptized Isaac T. Reneau.

In 1808, John Smith was ordained a minister in the Baptist church. William Burke from Green County was probably the first Methodist preacher to visit Wayne. James Lair was long a minister of this faith in Wayne. Francis P. Stone was a clergyman at Monticello in 1830.

A few Scotch Presbyterians came into this section and became affiliated with the Baptists and worshiped with them. The first Presbyterian meeting ever held in Wayne was by Thomas Cleland in 1809. David Rice, a prominent Presbyterian preacher, also visited Wayne at an early date and James McGready took part in the great revival in this region.

In this period, the first and second decades of the nineteenth century, there began a great religious controversy and the storm center was the Cumberland and Green River section. Out of this grew the Christian Church and its history closely parallels the history of "Raccoon" John Smith. He was deeply troubled by doctrinal teachings and was in grave doubt when there fell into his hands "The Christian Baptist" written by Alexander Campbell who, disturbed by the number of divisions in the Protestant Church, wanted to restore its original unity. He had only one creed—"only to believe as the early Christians at Antioch."

Smith went to Central Kentucky where a great meeting was in progress. He heard Alexander Campbell. He felt inspired himself to speak. The congregation were disposed to make light of the mountaineer in homespun. "Who is he?" they asked.

He arose and in dramatic fashion said: "I am John Smith from the Little South Fork in Wayne where saltpeter caves abound and raccoons have their homes."

Then he proceeded to electrify the vast assemblage. He won the name Raccoon John Smith that he kept throughout life. He was called to Central Kentucky churches to preach.

A prominent citizen of Monticello wrote asking him to come to Monticello. He returned to Wayne and "for eight days and nights taught the people from house to house." He was urged again to return and in 1831 he advised the group of his followers to meet every Lord's Day. They followed his advice and thus was organized the first congregation of the Christian Church in Wayne County, in October, 1831.

The first building was a log house on the hill where the old Buster burying ground remains. The charter members were: James Jones and wife (father and mother of Eliza Jones Phillips)

Micajah Phillips, John L. Sallee,
Frank Coffey, W. J. Kendrick,
Joshua Buster, Mrs. Juan Hall,
Dr. Jno. S. Frisbie, Sr., Peter Marshall.
Dr. Jno. S. Frisbie, Jr.,

After the Masonic Hall was built it was used for services until 1860 when the church on Columbia Avenue was built. Captain Tuttle, in his diary, says he spent the day " . . . . helping erect the framework of the church." The first resident minister of the church was William Simpson.

Later pastors were: Caleb Sewell, Joseph Ballou, John I. Rogers, James L. Allen, James Zachary, Roy L. Porter, A. H. Hope, William Stone, A. H. Baugh.

This recital would be incomplete without the mention of Rev. William Cooper. As a Baptist preacher, he left the imprint of his godly character upon the people of Wayne. Throughout the county he was known and loved. He was a familiar figure when he was well past eighty years of age riding horseback into Monticello. His erect, almost military, bearing never failed to call forth admiration. He left a long record of good work behind him.

Other ministers who preached and solemnized marriages were: Lewis Parker, about 1832; Isaac Powell, 1837; Abner Jones, 1840; William Cooper, for a long period beginning in the sixties; William Floyd and John Price were noted in Wayne in 1841; William Gooding in 1832; A. Davis and E. M. Bosley in 1835.

Dr. J. S. Frisbie was authorized to solemnize marriage in the late thirties. Captain Tuttle in his diary speaks of going to hear "Brother Moore" in the sixties.

J. W. Blackburn in the nineties can be well remembered. He was pastor of the Baptist church erected at that time, largely through the efforts of Mr. John H. Shearer, a well-to-do and prominent citizen.

The names of the churches in the county are redolent of a deep feeling of reverence, peace, and loyalty. They are not sectarian or denominational names. There are the names of the old Biblical sites with their sacred significance—Bethel, Bethesda, Salem, and Mt. Pisgah. Then there are Charity, Concord, Pleasant Hill, Pleasant Grove, with their suggestion of peace and harmony; and those of some faithful shepherds give names to Lockett's Chapel, Alexander's Chapel, and Roger's Grove.

These are the places of worship where real religion abounds and many a meeting has been held in each of them, sending out their congregations inspired to a life of devotion.

Bethel Church at Parmleysville was organized in 1810. The records have been preserved intact, one of those rare occurrences, and are in possession of W. M. Powers. There could be no greater privilege than that of having access to this early record book of Old Bethel whose names tell the story of a splendid God-fearing, law-abiding section.

We quote from the record book: "Bethel was constituted 3d Saturday in July, 1810, with 9 members." John Smith (Raccoon John Smith) was pastor for seven years. The first clerk was Philip Smith, brother of John Smith.

The first pastor to follow John Smith was William Rice. Then came Isaac Story, followed by Eben Fairchild, who was succeeded by Ephraim Bunyard. William Cooper, Elias Hopkins, Lewis Fairchild, Reuben Jones, and Wesley Denny were some of the preachers who served Old Bethel through the century and a quarter since its beginning.

M. W. Powers has been clerk for twenty-five years. There has been no more splendid congregation in the county than that of Old Bethel, for the citizenry that has gone to make the church was of that fine old stock that settled there, before, and immediately after, its formation in 1800. And these good Baptists of Old Bethel had doubtless met to worship in the homes of the members before John Smith formally organized the church in 1810.

## PLEASANT HILL CHURCH

Pleasant Hill Church was established on Carpenter's Fork of Otter Creek, June 12, 1841. In faultless penmanship, the old record book recites: "The Brethren and Sisters who were given up by Otter Creek Church of United Baptists and by the Clear Fork Church, being assembled, agreeable to appointment at Pleasant Hill Meeting House, were constituted a Baptist Church of Jesus Christ by elders acting as Presbyters to wit: Richard Barrier and Henry Tuggle."

The names of the charter members are as follows:

Henry Blevins, Emilla Blevins, Joel Bertram, Elizabeth Bertram, Elijah Bertram, Camealy Bertram, Ephraim Bertram, Laruhanna Bertram, Jacob Bertram, Louvena Bertram, Ahial Bertram, Rowena Bertram, Jonathan Bertram, Feroby Bertram, William Bertram, Sr., Nancy Bertram, William Bertram, Jr., Andrew Young, Eady Young, Lilly Brown, Benjamin of color, Eady of color, Martha Savage, John Koger, Rachael Koger, Louis Koger, Vicy Deering, Rhodes G. Rains, Nimrod Stinson. Received by experience Sallie Stinson, Serelda Kennedy, Esther Denny, Polly Deering, Jerusha Young, Nancy Lockhart; Henry Blevins, Moderator; Elijah Bertram, Clerk, pro tem.

At the next meeting Joel Bertram was chosen clerk and continued in this office until 1860 when William Bertram took his place. In 1871 another Joel Bertram came in as clerk remaining until 1884, giving way to Reuben Bertram, then James Bertram, then W. C. C. Bertram continuing until the present time. A Bertram for clerk for nearly a century.

Moderators were Henry Blevins, Henry Tuggle, William Bertram, Nimrod Stinson, James Abston, R. R. Dick, Ephraim Bertram, N. Albertson, Alvin Bertram, Wesley Denny, W. R. Davidson.

The Dalton family came into the community and into the church in 1842. Big Spring Church is referred to, with Abijah Fairchild bearing a letter asking for assistance.

The minutes of Pleasant Hill Church are a key to the character of the people of that section, showing a high moral standard of conduct, deep religious feeling, and a stern devotion to duty.

The list of members throughout its existence contains the names of men and women who have been identified with the life and development of the county and state.

In 1828, Daniel Shearer helped to build a church at "Pleasant Bend," now Cooper. A. N. Shearer, father of Miss Ala Shearer, then a lad of nine, remembered going with his father to do this. The Oatts, Coffeys, Vickerys, Alexanders, Shearers, etc., met there to worship. "Raccoon" John Smith, William Simpson, Brother Burdette were the early preachers. They called it the Church of Christ. In 1852, they organized and planned to build a church in Shearer Valley. The Civil War came on and this house was not completed until the war was over, but enough was done that the soldiers camped in it during the war. This house stands yet, and members of the Church of Christ meet there for worship. Jenkins Shearer, and later Daniel Shearer, preached in this church.

Matthew Floyd preached at old Beaver Creek Church and also in Old Salem at Frazer.

Other preachers of an earlier day were Reverends Rexroat, Matthews, Davis, and Wright.

The old "Union Church" was built in 1860, and used by all denominations until the end of the century. Absolute harmony prevailed during this period—an everlasting tribute to the real religious spirit of the people of the community, as well as the literal interpretation and acceptance of the terms of the Constitution of the United States. Such a situation could exist only among men and women of a high order of intelligence, with rare breadth and tolerance, in a period characterized by petty religious squabbles.

This was an experiment so unusual as to arouse interest. The whole population turned out to hear a visiting preacher, regardless of denomination, to listen with an open mind and sympathetic interest.

So far as is known this situation has not been duplicated anywhere. There have been other churches used in turn by different denominations, but none as an actual union church.

The children of adherents of different faiths attended the same Sunday School. There could have been no experience so calculated to develop the spirit of real religion.

## RACCOON JOHN SMITH

No preacher exerted a more powerful influence on the lives of the early inhabitants of Wayne than Elder John Smith, known as Raccoon John Smith. No more picturesque figure stands out in the annals of those days. With the zeal of the prophets of old he fought the good fight. More exactly, his was the voice in the wilderness proclaiming the word of God.

The older inhabitants who were living in 1900, or later, who had come under the spell of his fiery gospel, remembered him with profound feeling.

His life was romantic and exciting, with comedy and tragedy intermingled. He was born in Sullivan County, Tennessee (North Carolina at that time), October 15, 1784. When a boy of twelve with his father and older brother he came over the Wilderness Road to Crab Orchard, thence through Wayne to Stockton's Valley. The mother and younger children remained at home until a place could be prepared for them.

Needing meal and also needing the older boy's help in clearing the forest, John, the younger son was sent by his father one hundred miles on horseback through the wilderness to Horine's Mill. His clothes were ragged, his father not having completed his deerskin shirt and trousers. He returned in safety with the needed supplies. A band of Cherokees had camped near his father's cabin and John became friendly with them and learned their language as he sat at night around their campfire.

In 1799, Isaac Denton, a Baptist preacher, came to Stockton's Valley and built a meeting house on Clear Fork, the first church in this section. John came under the influence of this pious man and loved him.

Robert Ferrill, a wheelwright, a man who had for that day a good education, also settled there. He had some good books and started a school and it was from him that John Smith received most of his education. He visited Monticello frequently and married Anna Townsend there. She died in 1814 and he married Nancy Hurt of Wayne County. When the controversy in the church was at its height he preached sermons that seemed inspired, throughout Central Kentucky. In the early days, his cabin on Little South Fork in Wayne had been destroyed by fire, burning two of his children to death. His inward conflict over the eternal damnation of these infants disturbed him powerfully. His first wife, mother of the children, soon followed them. He died at the home of a daughter in Mexico, Missouri.

His life was one of ceaseless activity and much of it was spent in Wayne. He performed many marriage ceremonies there and we have record of the following:

    1815—James Bertram and Gilly Heaton

    1816—John Chrisman and Sallie Stone

    1817—Jacob Eads and Ada Norman
           Silas Young and Elizabeth Conaldson
           John Williams and Lavina Bertram
           Joseph Hurt and Polly Eads
           Joshua Buster and Julia Haden
           Silas Sheppard and Polly Stone.

Isaac T. Reneau, who had been educated to be a physician, came under the spell of Elder John Smith's convincing logic in 1831, in Wayne County. He very soon after entered the ministry and preached there. He was precise in manner and speech. He was quoted as saying, "I make no mistake in walking or talking" —with a definite New England accent. And immediately thereafter, strolling out in the night into the yard where he was being entertained at the home of Milton Mills, he stepped into the cellar. This was considered a joke on the man who "made no mistake in walking or talking."

## EARLY LAWYERS

The first attorney admitted to the bar in Wayne County was Samuel Brents, a young man who had been admitted shortly before to the bar of Green County.

Francis Emerson, who had also been qualified as attorney in Green in 1801, came before the Wayne Court to practice. There was a brilliant array of young lawyers in Green County at this time, men who were later distinguished, and many of these came to the Wayne Circuit courts. Among these were Allen Wakefield, first Circuit Judge; Samuel Brents, Benjamin Hutchins, John King, Richard Buckner, William Owens, William Adair, and Benjamin Burks. John Rowan and Ben Hardin went at an early date from Green to Nelson.

Rodes Garth, the young teacher, early qualified as attorney, and represented Wayne many times in the State Legislature, both in the Senate and House of Representatives. A list of early members of the legislature will be found in this chapter.

Micah T. Chrisman was clerk of the House, 1867-1873.

The legislature, June 3, 1865, appropriated money to erect a headstone at the grave of Milton Buster, who was State Senator at the time.

Of the early lawyers practicing in the courts of Wayne, the following article gives an account:

## OLD-TIME JUDGES AND LAWYERS

The lawyers of Kentucky whose professional lives began with that period which marks articulation of the last days of the second with the first days of the third constitution of the state are rapidly passing away. Indeed but few of them yet remain to connect the deeper learning of fifty years ago with the superficial training of the last decade. Their contemporaries of other avocations, except one here and there, are not. Singly and sometimes, it seems, in small groups they left—"each one," as our Scotch kinsfolk cautiously say, "for his ain place."

He whose life spans both epochs will find, in the characteristics which differentiate one from the other, food for rumination—profitable or not, pleasant or not, as he may use or abuse the opportunity. He will have more than a chance to indulge the reminiscential mood common and usually so pleasant to those whom age has but gently touched. More than a chance truly! The opportunity will seek him: for there is that affinity between age and retrospection which almost makes the twain one.

There are many now living who can recall with reasonable distinctness the bench and bar of the region of country bordering Green River and the lower Cumberland in Kentucky, when Judge Zack Wheat, of Adair County, was on the bench. He was the first elective judge under the Constitution of 1849-50. Through this long stretch of vanished time, one can yet see his portly form, his benignant face, his kindly mien—the air of candor and fairness which betoken a benevolent gentleman and a just judge.

His immediate successor was Judge Thomas E. Bramlette of the same county. He was elected in 1856, defeating Hon. A. J. James, of Pulaski County. At the same election E. L. Van Winkle, of Wayne County, defeated N. B. Stone, of Russell County, for Commonwealth's Attorney. In manner Judge Bramlette was thought to be somewhat austere. Deficient in suavity, approaches to him were not readily made by the masses of people: but it was understood by those more intimately acquainted with his temperament that despite a hasty temper and a haughty air, he had the impulses and the sentiments of a kindly disposed gentleman.

He was accounted an able and a just judge. He resigned his commission in 1861 to accept Colonelcy in the Federal army. Judge Durham, of Danville, was appointed by the governor to fill the unexpired term. His incumbency was of such brief duration, beside, civil affairs of that period were so greatly overshadowed by the engrossing events of the war, that but little is remembered of his distinctive qualities as judge. It, however, may be well assumed that the energy and strong practical sense which marked his career as a lawyer and subsequently as representative to Congress, gave tone and color to his judicial administration.

His successor was Judge F. T. Fox, of Danville, who was elected in August 1862 for the full term of six years and re-elected in 1868. By comparison with previous times his personality as a judicial character is well remembered. The history of Kentucky is luminous with the names of jurists whose just renown would have added luster even to English Courts.

Judge Fox was not the equal of many of them in professional learning, but in those higher qualities which left the brave and true judge beyond the reach of temptation he was fit associate of that great company. In that galaxy which the pride and affection of Kentucky have dedicated to the memory as their most honored officials, no name shall shine with purer ray than that of Fontaine T. Fox.

Judge M. H. Owsley was elected as the immediate successor of Judge Fox in 1874, and was re-elected in 1880, serving the two full terms of six years each. In astuteness of intellect and clearness of apprehension Judge Owsley stood pre-eminent. His elemental legal learning was neither extensive nor profound. He had never been a student of literature or of law, but he possessed the natural aptitudes of a lawyer. Barring a few minor shortcomings, he was an ideal trial judge—quick to discern the controlling issue in a cause, able to separate the relevant from the irrelevant, rarely afflicted with a confused understanding of a legal proposition and habitually leaping to conclusion with the rapidity and inerrancy of feminine intuition. With more self-denial and less sociability, more dignity and less disposition to secure public favor, he would have left a better if not a more enduring fame. He died in 1891, just at that age when usually the mental powers have reached their highest stage.

In 1886, Judge Morrow was elected in the old Eleventh Judicial district, serving until 1892 when the change of Judicial districts, under the present Constitution, went into effect. He has been twice elected in the Twenty-ninth district which embraces only three counties of the old Eighth. Owning qualities of a great judge, he is a worthy successor of the best of those who have preceded him.

But few attorneys who practiced before Judges Wheat and Bramlette are living—perhaps none who were at the bar in Wheat's day. The majority of them who practiced before Judge Fox and before Judge Owsley during his first term are dead: Cravens, Suddarth, Parker Hardin, Nat Gaither, T. C. Winfrey, and possibly Ed Butler and E. Dohoney, of Adair, long since entered their last appearance.

Wolford, Adams, and Fogle, of Casey; N. B. Stone, of Russell; William Moore, Virgil Moore, W. McKee Fox, A. J. James, and R. M. Bradley, of Pulaski; Sherrod Williams, F. P. Stone, Shelby Stone, Henry Taylor, Hiram Phillips, E. L. and J. S. Van Winkle and J. S. Chrisman, of Wayne, beside a number of younger members of the profession in each of these counties, have gone hence. At their respective homes they were well known to the public of that day, and the names of some of them will abide in local history. Several of these were men of undeniable mental force. Considering that they studied and practiced far from the center of commerce, when the character of litigation and amount in controversy stimulate the practitioner to greater study, their professional attainments were not to be ridiculed. It has been the consensus of opinion that F. P. Stone was the most intellectual, and taking into account only his natural gifts, the least successful of all those who have been named. Ill health and resultant misfortune assailed him before he had fairly reached the zenith of his power. Bereft of clear reason for fifteen years, the light of his great intellect flickered like a dying lamp until life closed amid the settled gloom of insanity.

There is yet living in Russell County one of the contemporaries of these older lawyers who was probably the youngest of that class, Hon. Joseph Elsie Hays. He still survives in honored age and comfortable independence at his home in Jamestown, Kentucky. A few years since he voluntarily retired from practice to enjoy the repose, which befits the closing days of a life of unremitting labor. It was one of the moral precepts of mythology that the gods should not bestow all the good on one. Colonel Hays was not a special favorite of fortune. He was not born with the traditional silver spoon in his mouth. Had the environment of his early life been less ungracious, it would be difficult to estimate the professional reach to which he might have attained. He came of the best Virginia blood, but his father in early manhood became so broken in health and as a consequence so decayed in fortune that the entire support of his family was devolved on his son Joseph before the lad had reached an age for such responsibility.—J.A.P.

## LATER LAWYERS

The following are brief biographical sketches of some of the later lawyers of Wayne County.

James Stone Chrisman, who served in the State Legislature, the Congress of the United States, and the Confederate Congress died in 1881. His colleagues passed the following resolutions on his death:

"The death of the Honorable James S. Chrisman, who died on the 29th day of July last at his home in Monticello, Kentucky, demands that his professional brethren who served with him and the officers of the Court where he so long and prominently labored should place on the records of the Court some expression of their sense of his worth and character.

"Major Chrisman's strong ambition and restless activity brought him into conspicuous notice before the Country for the last thirty-five years—years so full of historic events, of war and peace, of national troubles and progress. He filled with distinction many state and national offices of importance, having been a member of the Convention of Kentucky which framed our present Constitution, twice a member of the Kentucky Legislature, a member of the Congress of the United States and of the Congress of the Confederate States.

"In these bodies he was an active and prominent member, advocating his views with impetuous eloquence or opposing his adversaries with fiery vehemence. His professional life, for the most part, was spent in this Judicial District where he was generally known and ranked by his people among the foremost lawyers of his locality. He was an advocate of more than common parts possessed of declamatory power and feeling, unsurpassed by any of the many distinguished men whom he met in contests of the forum.

"He had many genial qualities and was companionable and oftentimes exceedingly fascinating to his associates. He had strong resentments and firmly noted friendships; his integrity in his public and private relations was above reproach. His loss to his family is grievous and irreparable and his disappearance from among us leaves a void that will long be noticed. We tender his family our sincere sympathy and ask that this paper may be spread on the order book of the Court, suitably published in the newspapers and a copy be made out by the clerk of the Court and presented to his bereaved widow and children.

"I. N. Sheppard, Secretary
"Jno. S. Van Winkle
"T. Z. Morrow
"John W. Tuttle
"Jno. L. Sallee"

Micah Chrisman Saufley was born in Monticello, Kentucky, on the thirteenth of May, 1842. He was a man whom to know was to honor, for in every relation of life he was found ever true to duty and to the trust reposed in him. In youth he acquired an academic education and his professional training was received in the Louisville Law School.

Kentucky has had her full share of prominent lawyers, and chief among them is Judge Saufley. He removed to Stanford after admission to the bar and was elected County Judge of Lincoln County in 1870. He rapidly acquired a considerable practice, and for ability, conscientious fidelity, and successful effort he was excelled by few. In 1880, he was elector from the Eighth Congressional District.

He entered the Confederate Army in November, 1861, as a private of Breckinridge's Brigade, but was soon made lieutenant in Morgan's Cavalry.

Soon after the war, in 1867, he married Miss Sallie Rowan of McMinnville, Tennessee, daughter of a distinguished lawyer and granddaughter of Governor Caswell. In 1888, he was appointed by President Cleveland Associate Justice of the Supreme Court of the Territory of Wyoming. In November, 1892, he was elected circuit judge of the Thirteenth Judicial District of Kentucky. His record on the bench was a brilliant one. His gift of oratory, his dignity, his fine sense of justice place him in the forefront of the Kentucky judiciary.

---

."Judge M. C. Saufley is out in the *Interior-Journal* with a short biography of Hon. Thomas Peyton Hill, which it is needless to say is well done. As the Colonel when a young man was a citizen of Monticello, we copy that part which refers to his life while here: 'With a law license in his pocket and a young wife by his side he moved to Monticello, Kentucky, to offer his legal services to those who were *inops consilii*. In the course of a short time he was appointed by the county court, under the law then in force, to the office of county attorney. He remained at Monticello but a few years doing but little good for himself or anyone else. A passion for fox and deer hunting had developed in him and he spent about all he made in buying and keeping packs of hounds. An old lawyer who discovered that he would make a better disciple of Themis than Nimrod very brusquely took him to task on account of his improvidence and with friendly peremptoriness ordered him to leave the town and locate in Somerset for the practice. Hill took his advice. Leaving his dogs and gun with his fellow sportsmen in Wayne, he gathered his mammon and impedimenta, which consisted of 25 cents to pay ferriage across the Cumberland, a pair of saddle bags and a woman's satchel, and with wife and baby he dropped down on James Griffin, a tavern keeper of Somerset.' "—*Wayne County Outlook.*

Ephraim L. Van Winkle, Secretary of State in Kentucky during the Civil War, was from Wayne County. He died before the expiration of his term and his brother, John S. Van Winkle, was appointed to fill the unexpired period. The *Louisville Daily Courier* of May 29, 1866, thus speaks of him:

"The following from the *Frankfort Yeoman* will in some measure enable our readers to form an idea of the great loss which the state has sustained in the death of the late Secretary of State:

" 'Ephraim L. Van Winkle was born July 20, 1827, in Wayne County, Kentucky. His father was Micajah Van Winkle and his mother was Mary Phillips. His grandfather was Abraham Van Winkle, the first of the name in Kentucky, and belonged to the Dutch family who came with Governor Stuyvesant in 1647. Ephraim Van Winkle was brought up in the mercantile business but early manifested a thirst for knowledge. He attended the Monticello Academy and was graduated from the Louisville Law School in 1850, with highest honors. He practiced with success in his native county until 1855 when he was chosen to represent his county in the State Legislature, which he did with distinguished ability. In 1856 he was elected Commonwealth's Attorney for the Sixth Judicial District and removed to Somerset. In 1860 he was elector for the State-at-large on the Bell-Everett ticket. He became distinguished for his logic, eloquence, and boldness in debate. In 1863 he was appointed Secretary of State by Governor Bramlette and removed to Frankfort. His official and social position, his mental and social worth, his distinguished ability as well as kindly personal relations, long sustained, demand extended notice.' "

He died May 23, 1866, and was interred at Frankfort.

At a called session of the Wayne County Court held at Monticello on Monday, May 28, 1866, Hon. G. K. Marcum, presiding, on motion of W. Simpson, Esq., John W. Tuttle, James L. Hardin, and M. C. Saufley were appointed by a committee to draft resolutions expressive of feelings of members of the bar on the death of E. L. Van Winkle.

Signed: John L. Sallee, Clerk; B. Mills, Sheriff; J. E. Vickery, Deputy Sheriff; W. Thornton, Jailer; Tim Sumpter, Coroner; J. Smith Frisbie, I. N. Sheppard, J. J. Garth, P. W. Hardin, William Simpson, Marshall Stone, J. S. Chrisman.

John S. Van Winkle was born March 8, 1829, in Wayne County, Kentucky. He was the youngest of six sons and four daughters born to Micajah and Mary (Phillips) Van Winkle, natives of North Carolina.

Micajah Van Winkle was born on the Yadkin River in 1792, and in 1798 was brought to Lincoln County, Kentucky. He was an active and influential citizen of Wayne County, to which he had moved with his parents. He served as magistrate and sheriff of Wayne for many years. In 1853, with his family, he located in Jasper County, Iowa, where he carried on farming until his death. He was a son of Abraham Van Winkle, a native of Maryland, who with his parents went to Virginia and thence to North Carolina, where he married Miss Charity Sallee. He moved to Lincoln County, Kentucky, in 1798, and thence to Wayne County, where he filled the office of justice and sheriff for a number of years. In 1837 he moved to Morgan County, Illinois, where many of his descendants still live. Some of his children were emancipationists. He died about 1845, at the age of eighty-five years. His ancestors came from Holland with Peter Stuyvesant.

Mrs. Mary (Phillips) Van Winkle was a daughter of Cornelius Phillips, who married a Miss Shores, both of North Carolina. They settled in Wayne County about 1800. Cornelius Phillips was an influential farmer and slave owner, served as magistrate and sheriff of Wayne County, and was of English origin.

John S. Van Winkle was raised on a farm, and received an academic education at Monticello. In 1852 he began the study of law with his brother, Hon. E. L. Van Winkle, and was graduated from the law department of the University of Louisville. He was licensed and admitted to the bar in 1854, when he opened an office and practiced in his native county. In 1861 he was elected to represent his county in the legislature. In 1863 he located in Danville and in 1866 was appointed Secretary of State by Governor Thomas E. Bramlette. At the expiration of his term, he resumed the practice of law at Danville.

James K. Polk Frazer who married Marietta, daughter of Cosby Oatts, came as a young man to Monticello to engage in the practice of law. His untimely death cut short his career.

Sam C. Hardin and Jack Saufley were young attorneys in the eighties. Saufley, a brilliant and handsome member of a prominent family, died early. Hardin removed to Clinton after his marriage to Miss Johnston of Lancaster. The *Monticello Signal* of June 3, 1886, publishes his card of announcement as a candidate:

"To the People of Clinton County:

"Some months ago I came into your county for the purpose of practicing my profession, and making Clinton County my future home. It is unnecessary to state that I have received a cordial welcome on every hand. I now feel that I am fully identified with the interests and aspirations of her people, and from these considerations, coupled with many solicitations from the citizens of the county, I have concluded to become a candidate for County Attorney. I therefore take this method of formally announcing myself as a candidate in the columns of the *Monticello Signal*, independent of any clique, caucus, or party. I am not the candidate of any ring, or individual, and make the race solely on personal merit and qualifications. I have no record as a public officer and can only refer the people of Clinton as to character and official fitness to the citizens of her sister county, Wayne, where I was born and raised. If I am elected to the position to which I now aspire, I promise the people to make them a faithful and sober officer.

"Very respectfully
"Sam C. Hardin"

Hiram Hays, who came to Wayne from Russell County, in his boyhood, practiced law in Wayne for several years. He was a good lawyer with an engaging personality that gained popularity for him. He served the county in different capacities and was always active in the life of the community. He was especially noted for his fine sense of loyalty. He married Miss Eva Owens and removed to Pulaski.

Two young attorneys in the latter part of the nineteenth century were E. T. Sanders and J. P. Harrison. Sanders died after a few years' practice.

An editorial in the *Monticello Courier* June 2, 1902, comments thus on Harrison as a candidate for Congress:

MICAJAH PHILLIPS, 1796-1883
*Father of the Public School System in Wayne County*

*Water mill on Elk Creek Owned by Micajah Phillips*

*Ruins of mill built by Joshua Jones on Elk Creek*

HOME OF MICAJAH PHILLIPS

*Built about 1830. The building to the right of the home is the "schoolhouse," where a tutor taught the children of the Phillips family and some others*

"J. P. Harrison, who was nominated for Congress by the Democratic convention, recently assembled at Corbin, having concluded to make the race for Congress, made his first speech at Albany, Kentucky, on Monday, the first date of Circuit Court. He will make quite a number of speeches throughout the district during the campaign. We take pleasure in saying in behalf of Mr. Harrison that his conduct, from boyhood up, has been without reproach and that he possesses ability, culture, and probity, and if elected to the high office to which he aspires, will reflect credit upon the district. He was admitted to the bar several years ago and has demonstrated all along the line much aptitude in his chosen profession. We feel assured Mr. Harrison will be able to present the principles of his party in the most satisfactory manner."

A picturesque and interesting figure in the social and political life of Wayne, in the "Stage-coach Period," was "Boss" Sheppard. He served for many years as County and Circuit Clerk, and it was as a sort of self-constituted custodian of the courthouse, that he received the title of "Boss." He was also Postmaster for many years in later life.

He was a Democrat of the old school, with intense prejudices and loyalties. In 1887, his friends urged him to become a candidate for the State Legislature, but he was defeated.

Judge Joseph Bertram, of the well-known family of that name, was born in Wayne County and was prominently identified with the political life of the community. He was a teacher in his early life while preparing for his chosen profession, the law. He practiced in the courts of Wayne and adjoining counties for some years, and was elected county judge in 1891 and represented his county in the legislature. He was a classical scholar and a man of profound legal knowledge.

Of some of the foregoing preachers, lawyers, and doctors the following letter gives an impression:

Mrs. Mary Cecil Cantrill,
Theobald Place,
George Town, Kentucky.

Dear Madam:

I must inform you that I have just arrived home from the old historic town of Greensburg and find your letter of November the 14th enclosing a check for two dollars for the "Hayden letter." I am sorry to part with such relics as old letters, yet as Mr. Hayden was your Grandfather I feel sure you will keep it in a safe place.

Some years ago I was in Mount Sterling and found an old letter written by Joshua Buster to Eld. Raccoon John Smith describing his visit to Danville in 1837 to hear Alexander Campbell preach, who was at that time making a preaching tour over Kentucky. He preached a Sermon in Nicholasville at that period and went on to Danville where he was met by more than five thousand people who heard him preach on the subject of "Christian Union Upon the Bible Alone." Your Grandfather Buster rode on horseback from Monticello to Danville to hear Mr. Campbell and his letter to John Smith speaks of Mr. Campbell as one of the greatest preachers he ever heard.

I have no collections of relics at home. I never married, and travel very often in the interest of the Filson Club. Your Father, Granville Cecil, was born in Montgomery County, in Southwestern Virginia about the year 1807 or 8. Mr. Kendrick was a native of Washington County and came to Wayne County about the year 1829. He was a very remarkable man and if his lot had been cast among such a money-getting people as the Yankees he would have been a *Millionaire*. I knew your father personally. I also knew Mr. Kendrick. I never could tell which was the smartest. Your father was quicker to jump to a conclusion than Kendrick, yet he seldom was wrong in his judgment.

Monticello, when I first visited the place in 1848, had as many remarkable lawyers in it as any town I ever visited. There were some extraordinary men in the little town. Littleton Beard, J. S. Chrisman, Ephraim L. Van Winkle, also John S., were all able men. But these men about the little town attracted my attention in those days more than all the lawyers in the place: Eld. Wm. Simpson, Joshua Buster, and Dr. Jonathan Frisbie. I have often thought about these men. Frisbie was born in Connecticut, came to Wayne County in 1819, died 1860, but I have no time to say more. Present my regards to Judge Cantrill.

SAM'L M. DUNCAN.

Nicholasville, Ky.
December 6, 1897.

## COUNTY DIRECTORY—1886

Representative .................................................... Hon. Jno. H. Shearer
County Judge ........................................................ Jas. A. Phillips
County Attorney ................................................... H. R. Hayes
County and Circuit Clerk................................... I. N. Sheppard
Sheriff ..................................................................... G. T. Ramsey
Assessor ................................................................ Jno. F. Goddard
Common School Commissioner .......................... J. W. Sallee
Jailer ....................................................................... W. G. Huffaker
Surveyor ................................................................ T. A. Dodson
Constable .............................................................. Jas. G. Hardin
Coroner .................................................................. G. K. Marcum

## COUNTY DIRECTORY—1897

County Judge ........................................................ S. H. Tate
County Attorney ................................................... J. A. Brown
County Clerk ......................................................... H. C. Kennedy
Circuit Clerk .......................................................... W. C. Rogers
Sheriff ..................................................................... J. C. Huffaker
Superintendent of Schools ................................. Mrs. Mollie Denney
Jailer ....................................................................... J. A. Goddard
Coroner .................................................................. Thomas Bates
Master Commissioner ......................................... John W. Tuttle
Trustee Jury Fund ............................................... Will M. Tuttle

## COUNTY JUDGES OF WAYNE, 1801-1938

E. N. Cullom, 1801-1805
James Jones, 1806-1810
Nicholas Lloyd, 1811-1815
Abraham Van Winkle, 1816-1820
James Jones, 1821-1835
Micajah Van Winkle, 1836-1840
James Oatts, 1841-1845
W. P. Hardin, 1846-1850
John L. Sallee, 1851-1854
Milton P. Buster, 1855-1859
G. N. Markham, 1860-1862
G. W. Mills, 1862-1866
G. R. Marcum, 1867-1867
Joshua Berry, 1868-1876
E. A. Haynes, 1877-1881
J. A. Phillips, 1882-1886
E. A. Haynes, 1887-1890
Joe Bertram, 1891-1895
S. H. Tate, 1896-1898
Charles McConnaghy, 1899-1902
W. R. Cress, 1903-1905
H. C. Kennedy, 1906-1910
Isaac Walker, 1911-1913
J. S. Sandusky, 1914-1918
J. C. Denney, 1918-1922
J. S. Sandusky, 1922-1926
Hobart Roberts, 1926-1930
Roscoe Dalton, 1930-1933
G. E. Roberts, 1934-1938

## MEMBERS OF LEGISLATURE FROM WAYNE, 1803-1877

SENATE:

Edward Cullom, 1809-1813
Martin Beaty, 1824-1828-1832
Rodes Garth, 1841-1844
Milton Buster, 1861-1865
Barton W. S. Huffaker, 1873-1877
(Wayne and Pulaski) John McHenry, 1833-1836

HOUSE OF REPRESENTATIVES:

Arch. E. Mills, 1803
Isaac Crabtree, 1806
North East, 1807
George W. Gibbs, 1809
Isaac West, 1810
Thos. Cooke, 1811
Rodes Garth, 1813, 1814, 1824, 1828

Lewis Coffey, 1815
Joseph Jones, 1816
Walter Emerson, 1817, 1819, 1820
George Berry, 1818
Joseph Rapier, 1822
Thomas Hansford, 1823
Moses Sallee, 1826, 1827
Sherrod Williams, 1829, 1830, 1831, 1832, 1833, 1834, 1846
Nimrod Ingram, 1835
J. S. Price, 1836
Shelby Coffey, 1837, 1838, 1839, 1842, 1843
Leo Hayden, 1840
Micah T. Chrisman, 1841
Littleton Beard, 1844
Milton Mills, 1845
Marshall N. Hudson, 1847
Martin Beaty, 1848
Joseph V. Warden, 1849
John L. Sallee, 1850
Isaac N. Sheppard, 1851-1853
Walter E. Hall, 1853-1855
Ephraim S. Van Winkle, 1855-1857
Joseph C. Belshe, 1857-1859
Shelby Coffey, Jr., 1859-1861
John S. Van Winkle, 1861-1863
H. W. Tuttle, 1863-1865
Barton W. S. Huffaker, 1865-1867
Thomas J. Eads, 1867-1869
James S. Chrisman, 1869-1871, 1871-1873
Pearson Miller, 1873-1875
L. J. Stephenson, 1875-1877

## EARLY PHYSICIANS

In the summer of 1819, Dr. John S. Frisbie, a graduate of Yale and of the Philadelphia College of Medicine, rode his horse into Monticello, tied him in front of Roger Oatts' tavern, glanced around the village of 200 inhabitants, and registered a determination to settle here in the practice of his profession. He had ridden over Central Kentucky and was more favorably impressed with Wayne than any other place visited. At any rate, he remained the rest of his life ministering to the sick, assisting the newborn into the world, and easing the last hours of the aged.

He was born in Litchfield, Connecticut, of Scotch forebears, about April 8, 1790. He married Hannah Jones, daughter of James Jones, about 1820, and his son, J. B. S. Frisbie, succeeded him in the practice of medicine, continuing until about 1885.

Thus for more than threescore years, the Frisbies concerned themselves with the bodily welfare of the people of Wayne, and "old Doctor Frisbie" in his later years turned to preaching and was authorized to solemnize matrimony by the court of Wayne County.

Samuel Duncan, of Nicholasville, speaks of him in a letter written in 1848. He says he visited Monticello that year and he found more remarkable men than in any other town in proportion to the size. Among them he mentions Dr. J. S. Frisbie, the elder.

He is the first physician of whom we have any record in Wayne, though it seems safe to assume that among the settlers from Virginia there might have been one or more. Marshall Hudson, born in 1816, died in 1858, became a doctor, but he died comparatively young.

Dr. Edmund Bryan is mentioned in the court records as being in Wayne in the thirties. Dr. Richardson is frequently referred to in Captain Tuttle's *Memoirs* from 1861-1867. Later Dr. John Hall, a promising young doctor, died about 1875. Dr. Jones at Mill Springs, Dr. H. A. Phillips, and Dr. J. F. Young bring the list up to 1900.

No record of Wayne County doctors would be complete without the mention of the Cooks. There were four in one family, sons of Edmund Cook. They were Dr. John Cook and Dr. Littleton Cook, who went to Lincoln County, and Dr. Will Cook and Dr. A. S. Cook, who remained in Wayne. They were of that great body of physicians of that day who rode horseback over rough roads, regardless of the hour, the weather, or their own convenience, to minister to the sick—a group consecrated to service.

A well remembered figure was Dr. A. S. Cook on his horse, riding to the remotest corners of the county in the service of his fellow men.

Dr. J. W. Castillo was a contemporary of the Cooks, practicing in Wayne for many years.

Dr. James Buster, son of Joshua Buster, preceded them.

# EDUCATION—EARLY SCHOOLS—COMMON SCHOOL SYSTEM

## CHAPTER VI

In 1799, Robert Ferrill, a wheelwright, came over the Wilderness Road into what was shortly to become the new county of Wayne, and settled in Stockton's Valley. He built a mill there and opened a school. He was a well educated man and had some good books. He had few pupils, as settlers were far apart and the work of clearing the land and tilling the soil claimed the time of the youths.

But young John Smith, later to become a famous preacher, had just come into this section with his father, and Ferrill found him an apt and interested pupil. This was probably John Smith's first school, and, undoubtedly, the first in the environs of Wayne.

The first school in Monticello of which we have any record was opened in 1807 by Rodes Garth. He taught "Roman History, the Scriptures, orthography, and pronunciation." This young man was referred to by Micah Taul as "a young man of probity and worth."

He was later admitted to the bar and served several terms in the legislature. His diary of the War of 1812 gives us an idea of his knowledge of English composition. It was indeed a happy beginning of the educational undertaking of the town to have a teacher of such qualification as the first schoolmaster.

"It was a good school," says John Augustus Williams in his *Life of John Smith,* and John Smith, who had moved to the Little South Fork, walked fourteen miles from his home to attend the school, walking back home at the end of the week. This school continued some years and in 1819 John S. Frisbie, a graduate of Yale, came into Monticello and began to teach a school. Michael Huffaker is the first teacher mentioned in the records of the county, in the thirties.

The Monticello Academy was established in 1830, under the provision by which the revenue from the Seminary lands could be used for that purpose. John Lankford was the headmaster. It languished for a time, but Professor Mullins revived it. He was succeeded by William Burton, a superior teacher and a well educated man, who left an impression upon the life of the town and county to be felt to this day. His knowledge and thoroughness provided an educational foundation unusual in that day. He was precise in speech and manner, a product of the best New England schools. From the county around students came, and the better speech of the hills, in Wayne, is credited largely to him.

In 1837 an act to establish Common Schools in Kentucky was introduced in the State Legislature, to be wrangled over for ten years before it was finally adopted. But by the time this law became effective, Wayne County was organized and the law was accepted. The Academy then became a necessary adjunct to the system, as a teacher training center for the county.

When the Education Act was proposed, commissioners were appointed to take charge of the Seminary lands. The court records show that at the November term of the Wayne County Court, 1837, "Micajah Phillips, Micah Chrisman, Joshua Buster, Braxton Carter, Chas. E. Mills, Martin Beaty, Henry R. Saufley, William Simpson, and James H. West were appointed trustees of the Wayne Seminary Lands." Micajah Phillips was Secretary of the board and the minutes kept from November, 1837, to November, 1843, tell the complete story of the organization of the county into common school districts. From these minutes it is easy to visualize the struggle of the citizens of Wayne County, who were eager to see the opportunity to acquire an education extended to all.

The commissioners, Micajah Phillips, John Rousseau, Martin Beaty, and Francis Goddard rode horseback into the remotest corners of the county. The roads were often almost impassable. The Common School was rejected in some districts, at the first meeting, but the commissioners patiently returned and, on reconsideration, the law was accepted by the majority of the voters. Finally, the Secretary was able to announce to the Superintendent of Public Instruction that Wayne had voted to accept this revolutionary measure in its entirety. Micajah Phillips wrote "Finis" in his minute book September 26, 1843. It had taken six years to organize the county, yet that was accomplished before the law became effective.

Jonathan S. Frisbie, John Lankford, and Littleton Beard were the first examiners for the county—one was a physician, one a lawyer, and one a teacher. The examinations were oral. The candidate for a certificate was required to read aloud a selection from some English masterpiece chosen by the Board and to exhibit a specimen of his handwriting. Skill in the solution of mathematical problems guaranteed a high rating. Some questions were asked, but the candidate could "talk himself into a job" if he talked well. The pay was pitifully inadequate and the teachers were expected to "board among the scholars."

August 31, 1840, B. B. Smith, the Superintendent of Public Instruction, made the following report to the county:

Department of Education

Augt. 31st, 1840

To the County Court of Wayne:

Agreeably to the provisions of the 9th Section of the Act of 1838 for the establishment of Common Schools in the Commonwealth of Kentucky, you are hereby informed that the proportion of the income of the School fund for 1840 which falls to the share of Wayne County is $709.20 or 40 cents on 1,773 children payable on the 16th day of Jany. 1841.

The draft must be upon the superintendent of Publick instruction, by the County Commissioners (Sect. 11) in behalf of those districts only which have actually organized (Sect. 40), and upon evidence of their having adopted the System, appointed trustees, provided a School house and agreed to assess themselves toward the support of a teacher (Sect. 18). The balance will remain to the credit of the County, until such time as the provisions of Sect. 40th are complied with.

B. B. SMITH
Superintendent of Publick Instruction for the Commonwealth of Kentucky.

By 1842 there were a dozen school houses, a few of the "pole" variety. They were in the following districts:

No. 1—One mile south of Monticello.
No. 2—Three miles north of Monticello.
No. 3—Just west of Monticello, at Mt. Zion where William Calfey had been conducting a school.
No. 5—Near Lockett's Chapel.
No. 7—Frazer.
No. 11—On Cumberland River near the home of Giles Lloyd.
No. 15—On Otter Creek.
No. 17—Upper part of county near the home of Solomon Tuttle.
No. 23—On Big South Fork—Rev. Richard Barrier, Trustee.
No. 24—Little South Fork near Robert Parmley's.
No. 25—Little South Fork.
No. 26—On Van Winkle's Road, leading from Jamestown, Tennessee, Road.
No. 28—Shearer Valley, Teacher, Daniel Shearer.
No. 29—Powersburg.
No. 31—Near Gregory.
No. 32—On Clinton County Line.

Among the early teachers, before the Civil War, were Mrs. Amanda McGee, William and Thomas Simpson, Joseph Ballou, later a minister, and Marcellus Baugh who taught at Number One School House in 1860. This was his son's first school. The son was the father of the Rev. A. H. Baugh of Hustonville.

The dates of these teachers' work have not been exactly determined.

Of the many splendid public school teachers it is impossible to speak in too high praise. In rude log houses they struggled for a pittance, and it can be assumed that they were actuated by a passionate love for the work. Mr. James Littrell, who had completed fifty-four years of service in 1930, tells of the first school in his district, according to Professor Young:

"It was known as a 'pole building,' located a mile south of Powersburg. These were rudely constructed of poles in an upright position. The first teacher was Virginia Hurt, the second

James Frost and the third, Jacob Hurt. Another near Pleasant Hill Church at Sunnybrook was first taught by Jeremiah Catron." William Littrell, brother of James, was his first teacher.

It was said of James that he knew "everything in books and everything outside of them."

Textbooks in the early schools were scarce and, according to Professor Young, the same were used as in other sections at that period. They were Dilworth's Spelling Book, Murray's English Reader, and Murray's English Grammar.

By 1860, the Goodrich Readers, edited by Noble Butler, and Butler's Grammar had taken their place. Then came the series of McGuffey's Readers.

In 1849, Micajah Phillips was still Secretary of the Board, as we find this letter directed by him:

Monticello, Ky.
Jany. 31, 1849.

Robert J. Breckinridge,
Superintendent Pub. Instruction

Dear Sir:

In your annual report to the legislature of the state of Ky., you report the teaching districts of Wayne County to contain 1,237 children of the lawful school age and the school com'rs of said county entitled to receive $432.95 cents. By adverting to the report of the school commissioners made to you for the year 1847, and also published in yr. annual report, you will perceive by a correct addition of the number of school children contained in the teaching districts that they will amount to 2,400 children of the school age between 5 & 16 years of age. That number, at 35 cents per scholar, the rate of your former calculation, will give the Com'rs of Wayne County $840.00, distributable among the teaching districts of Wayne, according to the no. of children in each. I thought it my duty to call yr. attention to this error, expecting thereby, in conjunction with the other Com'rs of Wayne, to draft upon the 2nd Auditor, in behalf of the teaching districts of Wayne, for the amount due them in order that it might be corrected. If the error should not (be) corrected by yourself, in all probability the order of the Com'rs of the County for the correct amt. due them, would be dishonored. You will have the hearty thanks no doubt of every friend of the cause of Common School instruction, for your very able & zealous efforts to promote the objects of the institution—and particularly for your efforts to rouse up the representatives of the people to redeem the sacred pledges of the State, the good people of this state, who when properly informed upon this great subject will surely sustain you. If I am in error in regard to the amt. coming to Wayne, please inform me.   Micajah Phillips, Sect'y

Smith's *History of Kentucky* says, "To the County of Wayne belongs the honor of having been the first county in the state to adopt the entire system." And this was largely due to the efforts of Micajah Phillips, Secretary of the Commissioners, who has been called the "Father of the Common School System of Wayne" by Prof. Harry Young. The first county school superintendent was Robert McBeath, member of a family noted for their intellectual qualities.

Interest in education was of necessity abated during the Civil War, but in 1866 William Kendrick who had become prosperous and was interested in the education of his large family, erected a good building and Milton Elliott was brought to Monticello and made principal. This was known as Kendrick Academy and until the building burned in 1872, ranked with the best academies.

Before the establishment of the Common School System, William Calfey conducted a private school at Mt. Zion Meeting House, and was probably the first teacher duly elected by trustees under the new law in Wayne County.

During this period when there was great disorganization due to war there was an effort to carry on some educational activities. Some families, where it was possible, engaged tutors. Micajah Phillips had built a schoolhouse in his yard and brought a young man from Bethany, Virginia, as a tutor for his children.

"Subscription" schools were common in the county before the public schools were organized. Mr. B. C. Berry remembers that Robert McBeath had a good school in a building on the Berry place. His son, Thomas, followed him. They were good

WILLIAM SIMPSON
*Clerk of the County and Circuit Courts for a half century*

JUDGE M. C. SAUFLEY

*Chief of Kentucky Lawyers of his day*

CHRISTIAN CHURCH IN MONTICELLO

*Built in 1860 and used by all denominations for half a century*

LAST STAGE-COACH USED IN THE UNITED STATES

*Owned by the Burton Family, Monticello, Kentucky*

teachers, "especially in arithmetic" and he was sorry when he had to go to the public school.

In 1887, Professor Thompson conceived the plan of rebuilding the academy. A company was formed with stock of $10,000.00. W. J. Kendrick agreed to donate the land. The incorporators were: J. W. Tuttle, H. L. Phillips, J. B. Kendrick, W. J. Kendrick, and T. L. Thompson. The project did not materialize.

Marion Huffaker taught a school near Monticello at No. 1 Schoolhouse in the early sixties and Marshall Stone one in town.

The first schools were taught in the homes of the teachers, and when the number of the pupils justified a log house was built. The first schoolhouse in Monticello was just around the corner from the old Fuston Tavern. The Shearers and Huffakers were families of school teachers. Miss Ala Shearer, a veteran, was accounted a power in the schools of her day. In the eighties and nineties, there were Lucy and Amanda Taylor, Sallie and Eula Kendrick, Emma Kelley, Fount Cooper, William Sandusky, Tobias Huffaker, Mrs. Mollie Denny, who became the very efficient county superintendent, and many others who contributed to the intellectual and spiritual uplift of the county.

In 1879, Mrs. Roxie Buchanan began a private school that was in every essential a Dame School. She taught in the old house referred to above. She was well educated, having attended Loretto Academy. The children of that period owe her a debt of gratitude for her thorough and painstaking efforts. William Bradshaw succeeded her.

In 1885, a Classical High School was opened by W. T. Chafin in the Masonic Hall. The curriculum was full and the teaching thorough. He brought T. Leigh Thompson and T. C. Job, college graduates, to assist him, and for a few years there flourished here a school with no superior in the state.

Higher mathematics, ancient and modern languages, the sciences, history, and English were taught. Mr. Thompson succeeded Professor Chafin and Miss Georgia Brock, of Lexington, was added to the faculty. Mr. Chafin returned later, remaining until about 1890. With Miss Oakley and Miss Graves, he had established, for the first time, a trained kindergarten and primary teacher.

The *Monticello Signal* of June 6, 1885, carries an advertisement stating that the "object of our literary department is to teach thoroughly everything necessary to fit boys and girls to enter the best universities." Signed: W. T. Chafin, Principal.

The same paper on January 4, 1887, announces the Spring Session of the Monticello High School, T. Leigh Thompson, Principal. "The motto of the principal is to give a thorough, practical English education."

In 1889, Prof. H. C. Jones was chosen principal of the Monticello High School. He was a college graduate and a good teacher. His health prevented his continuing longer than one year. Hayden Grubbs of Danville succeeded him. He was a brilliant young man, graduate of Centre College, and a superior teacher. He left to enter West Point. Professor Chafin returned for a short time and he in turn was succeeded by Mr. Ballard, bringing the chapter on education in Wayne up to the end of the century.

The program of the meeting of the County Teachers' Association in 1886 is interesting. It shows that these teachers of Wayne were ahead of their time in realizing that education is concerned with things more vital than the three R's.

TEACHERS' ASSOCIATION AT LOCKETT'S CHAPEL, JUNE 5, 1886.

| | |
|---|---|
| An Address on Education | Z. W. Wilborn |
| Method of Teaching Grammar | J. D. Shearer |
| History | D. S. Powers |
| What Makes a Good Teacher | Miss Lucy Taylor |
| Rural Teaching | Jas. L. Littrell |
| Select Reading | W. T. Chafin |
| Primary Arithmetic | W. A. Simpson |
| As Is the Teacher So Is the School | Miss Nannie Ingram |
| Beautify the Schoolroom | Miss Lucy Jones |
| Geography | A. Fairchild |
| Education Library, Discussion | Prof. Chafin, Joe Bertram |

Noon Recess

| | |
|---|---|
| A Lecture to Primary School Teachers | Z. W. Wilborn |
| Dull Pupils | Miss Sallie Hatchet |

How Should We Prevent Whispering............................J. A. Brown
How to Interest Children in Studies..................Mrs. Bettie Taylor
Formation of Character........................................Miss Nettie Kelley
How to Secure Attendance in a Country School..Sherman Denney
The Trials of a Teacher........................................Miss Ala Shearer
Time for Reading.................................................Miss Nannie Bates
Government of Schools............................................J. W. Guffey
Is There Any Limit to Girls' Accomplishments
                                                  Miss Sallie Kendrick
Early Impressions............................................Miss Mollie Huffaker
Limits to Study...........................................................J. F. Young
A Practical Talk to Teachers.......................................J. W. Sallee

We have included a great many teachers and persons interested in education, and we do hope they will accept the part assigned to them.

                                                  Josie Duncan,
                                                  Emma Kelley,
                                                  Eula Kendrick.

WAR BETWEEN THE STATES—JAMES
S. CHRISMAN—E. L. VAN WINKLE—
CAPTAINS ROBERTS, SAUFLEY,
TUTTLE, STEPHENSON

## CHAPTER VII

THE QUESTION OF REVISION of the State Constitution had been considered for some time and by 1849, when a convention was called at Frankfort for that purpose, it became a contest between the pro-slavery and emancipation elements.

James Chrisman was chosen delegate from Wayne. He was thirty-one years of age at that time, handsome, brilliant, and an able lawyer. He ardently espoused the rights of the slaveholder. There were many slave owners in Wayne and many who felt that the institution of slavery was unsound, yet agreed that the slave owner had certain rights.

This was James Chrisman's position, yet he thought the question of slavery should not obscure all others in the convention. He felt that the older delegates to the convention had small patience with the opinions of the younger men and so expressed himself.

He was elected to represent his district in Congress at the next election and served from 1853-1855. By this time feeling between the pro-slavery element and the emancipationists had reached the point where an explosion was inevitable. When a convention was called at Russellville, in 1861, to consider the secession of Kentucky, Wayne was one of sixty-five counties that responded by sending Mr. Chrisman as delegate. The convention went through the form of declaring Kentucky a member of the Southern Confederate States and Chrisman was placed on the executive council of the convention. This council divided the State of Kentucky into twelve Congressional districts. On a designated day an election was held in all counties within the lines of the Confederate army, and Chrisman was elected a member of the Congress of the Confederate States at Richmond.

There was great excitement in Wayne, as there was in the rest of the country. Everything was forgotten but the burning question of war.

There were hot-tempered Rebels, cooler Union men, and those who hoped to remain neutral. A company had been recruited for the Southern army, and there were recruits for the Union. Captain Tuttle's diary tells of the "parade of the blue cockades" and of the retaliation of the "Yanks." Even the children were taking sides. Company H was organized with Captain Shelby Coffey, First Lieutenant Lewis Coffey, First Sergeant Mike Saufley, a gallant, fearless young Confederate.

In the rolls of Confederate soldiers published by the State Adjutant is this note:

"Co. H. 6th Reg. Cav. known as Co. G.
The Old Roster calls this Co. 'H'
The rolls on file are marked 'B'
The correct letter is 'H'

(Signed) M. C. SAUFLEY, 1st Lieut."

Company G was partly organized in Wayne. It was in the Battle of Fishing Creek. It was first commanded by Shelby Coffey, who died of wounds received in Clinton County. It was reorganized at Burnsville, Mississippi, with N. B. Stone as captain. It was in the Battle of Shiloh. Captain Stone resigned and was succeeded by B. E. Roberts. It was in the Battle of Murfreesboro. The roster follows:

Capt. B. E. Roberts
1st Lieut. Lewis Coffey
2nd Lieut. Samuel Cowan
1st Sergeant Mike Saufley

Privates

John Coffey
James Coffey
Andrew Coffey
Seaborn Crutchfield
John Copenhaven
James Conley
F. Cowan (M.D.)
Charles Conley
Martin Colyer

John Dawes
Constantine Durham
Henry Ferguson
Jesse Flinn
William Fritz
William Gresham
James E. Gramar
James Gabbert
R. H. Philpott
Thomas Oatts
Thomas Sheppard
Robert Belshe
Green Gresham
Nat Gaither
Andrew Hays

William Hunter
Woods Hines
William Hutchens
James Hughes
Arch Hatchett
James Hardwick
Marshall Stone
James Carrigan
Curtis Hunt
Wesley Johnson
Alben S. Jones
·Frisbie Mercer

James Pratt
John Silvers
T. J. Silvers
William Smith
Bryan Stone
John Wray
William Weaver
Samuel Blackwell
N. B. Johnson
Samuel Barnett
John R. Caldwell
William Grizzard

In 1863, Major James B. McCreary's Regiment, Eleventh Kentucky Cavalry, was camped for a time near Monticello. This organization was composed of some of the finest flower of Kentucky's young manhood, recruited from Madison and Wayne. Those on the rolls of Company F in this division, from Wayne, were:

James Cochran
Samuel Meeks
Silas Pearce

Granville Troxell
Ezekial Woolcott
O. F. Wright

Major McCreary's diary gives the following account of Morgan's Cavalry in Wayne:

"On the morning of July 2, 1863, General John H. Morgan's division of cavalry, twenty-eight hundred strong, rose at the break of day. A few miles apart, the two brigades composing the division had spent the night on the bank of the Cumberland River, in Wayne County, Kentucky. The stream was full from shore to shore, and great nests and piles of driftwood, interspersed with thousands of logs, floated by on their way to the ocean. A thrill of joy stirred every heart and quickened every fiber when the order came to these expatriated Kentuckians to turn their faces homeward.

"The Federals on the north side of the river, quieted by the tremendous currents that flowed in the stream, were less vigilant in their watch. When these hardy Kentuckians, these men of brave hearts, rode down to the edge of the stream, some unsaddled their horses, drove them into the swift currents and forced them to head their way for the other side. There was small opposition to prevent these newcomers from landing. The Federals were not sure where General Morgan's men would cross, and so, peacefully, unsuspectingly, they slept in their tents, trusting to luck and high water to hold back these daring invaders.

"The Eleventh Kentucky Cavalry was in the Second Brigade, then commanded by Adam R. Johnson, of the Tenth Kentucky Cavalry. James B. McCreary, then Major, was acting as Lieutenant Colonel of this regiment. The stream was half a mile wide. A small ferryboat and a few canoes constituted the means of transportation across the turbid stream. The ferryboat could at best carry a small portion of the soldiers, and a large majority of them, flinging their clothes into the ferryboat, hung onto the sides; others, holding their horses by the manes and tails to prevent being swept down by the swift tides, essayed to cross and overtake the horses that had passed on before in this perilous swim.

"As the first detachment of the second brigade reached the opposite bank, the Federal picket stationed on the north side undertook to resist the landing. Some of the Confederates who were in the ferryboat and in the canoes rushed into line, while those who were naked and had swum, despising the role of laggards and not stopping to dress, seized their muskets and their cartridge boxes and rushed at the foe. The strange sight of clothesless men engaged in combat paralyzed the enemy. They had never before seen soldiers go into conflict clothed only in nature's garb, and it seemed to them that warriors, fully grown and armed, were just born into the world and must have come down from some spirit land, weird and strange, to rush to combat.

"Among scenes like these began the thousand-mile march which constituted Morgan's Ohio raid . . . .

"The 11th Kentucky was a magnificent regiment. It had been recruited in Madison, Clark, Estill, and Wayne counties, and was filled with men of courage, ambition, patriotism, and loyalty to the Southern Cause . . . .

"On the thousand miles which marked this raid of General Morgan, through Kentucky to Indiana and Ohio, his

(McCreary's) conduct as Colonel had elicited the admiration of General Morgan, who assigned him important duties . . . .

"Amongst the prisoners captured at Buffington's Island, was Colonel James B. McCreary, with a large number of officers, including General Duke, Commander of the first brigade. The prisoners were transferred down the Ohio River in steamboats, carried to Cincinnati, and then later transferred to the Columbus penitentiary . . . .

"Nine-tenths of all the officers of Morgan's men were from Kentucky. Their families were well to do and they supplied them an abundance of money which they spent freely. Some of the captives had managed to bribe their guards to get knives, which were case knives, and when well ground down they became formidable weapons; and among those who had gotten the knives was Colonel James B. McCreary.

"After General Morgan's escape the cells of all these prisoners were searched and Colonel McCreary was found in the possession of a knife. The demand was made that he should give the name of the person from whom he had received it, either by gift or by purchase. This the gallant young officer flatly refused to do, preferring any punishment to the betrayal of the man who had helped him in his extremity. It was in the midst of winter and the Ohio penitentiary in those days not altogether comfortable, was cold and dreary. The officer urged Colonel McCreary to surrender this name, and he promised him, if he should do so, that he would escape punishment. Firmly and flatly the Confederate refused to divulge the name of the giver of the knife. He was told that if he persisted in this course that he must suffer solitary confinement in an underground dungeon, fitted up for the most hardened criminals. To all this he responded: 'You may kill me if you will, but I shall not betray the man who gave me the knife.' Under guard, and in the roughest manner, he was hurried away to the dungeon, without fire, without any convenience or comfort—no bed, no cot, no blanket. There in darkness and stillness in these awful surroundings he awaited the orderings of what seemed to him to be a slow living death . . . ."

Captain Bolin E. Roberts' company of gallant Confederates from Wayne had joined Morgan at Lexington where there was great excitement. Wolford, with his Union men, including some from Wayne, was also there. The Confederates seemed in dire danger of losing their all-too-meager supply of arms.

Captain Roberts' gallantry had earned for him the confidence of General Morgan, and Winston Coleman, in his little volume, *Lexington During the Civil War,* tells of Roberts being the leader of a group selected to slip out of Lexington at night with the guns in two wagons loaded with hay.

Captain Roberts and others of the Wayne Countians were captured and taken to Camp Chase, and his account of their experience is interesting as it corroborates Major McCreary's in every detail.

## PRISON LIFE IN THE PENITENTIARY AT COLUMBUS, OHIO, IN 1863-4

*Written for the Signal by B. E. Roberts, Captain Company H, 6th Kentucky Cavalry, Morgan's Brigade, C. S. A.*

Tuesday evening, the 23rd of February, was set apart for the strike for liberty. The second range men when brought in from dinner, instead of being turned loose in the hall as had been the custom, and as we expected, were returned to and locked in their cells, after which the third range was taken out, but when brought back were treated in like manner, so our plan was "nipped," and instead of us having them in the cells they had us, as usual. We at once suspected we had been betrayed in the "house of our friends," but could only "wait and watch." We were not kept long in suspense, for Scottie, Dean & Co. came blustering in and began at the beginning. Without a word of explanation they unlocked the cells as they came to them. Standing the occupant of each, one at a time, out in front of the cell on the balcony, they "went through him to the bone." Some searched the man while others searched the cell.

The grand object of the search was soon discovered to be the contraband articles we had received through the air chamber from our friend over the way. The first one found was handed to our pious old Brother Dean, who, holding it up in his hand, remarked: "It is a good thing to stick a sheep with." Brother Dean charged the "sheep-sticker" in a book he had brought in for the purpose to the cell where found, and the one occupied by Captain Thos. H. Shanks. I had two of the "sticker" family in bed with me at the time besides an old horseshoe rasp—all in my little straw bed—and of course I counted myself as "gone up the spout" for once, but when my turn came I was subjected as the rest to a close examination. About the first pass the fellow made at the bed, he brought out the old rasp, but failed to find the "stickers." Finding nothing contraband on my person they hustled me back into my cell and, locking me in, passed on to my next door neighbor, Captain W. Brent Perkins, charging a "rasp" against cell No. 9. Perkins occupied cell No. 10 and with him they found an old case knife he had had for butter spreading purposes in camp, and it had passed muster in and out of prison over at Johnson's Island and at this prison when we came here first in August last. They took it away from him and Brother Dean charged it in his book against him, although it was further off than a third cousin to the "sticker" family. After all had been searched, knives of the "sheep-sticker" pattern were found with Captains Ed. Rochester, Thos. H. Shanks, Ralph Sheldon, Sam Taylor, and Ben S. Barton, Major Wm. Bullitt, Colonel J. B. McCreary, and Lieutenant John B. Cole, making eight out of twenty-eight we had, while Captain Perkins was charged with the case knife and Captain B. E. Roberts with a "rasp."

In a short time after the search was over the names of all these parties except Capt. Roberts were called by Dean from his little book from below, and, as called, the cells they were in were unlocked and the occupants marched down and out to the "Hole." The stillness of death reigned throughout those gloomy cells, halls, and corridors, broken only by the clanking of the heavy bolts in the locks, the receding foot-falls of our friends and the ox-like "tramp, tramp" of the guards and jailers. The monotonous sounds of their retreating footsteps having died away, Captain Bob Logan broke the stillness by calling out from his cell in the 2d range: "Did they take Roberts?" I told Robert, or

Capt. Logan, to curb his curiosity or anxiety for a while, as such an inquiry before such a tribunal would be taken as prima facie evidence of guilt and they would come back and take me, and I had no desire to explore that dark abode; and yet, if being in possession of the knives constituted the guilt, I was certainly the guiltiest man in the house, as I had two of them in "my little bed," and the twenty-six which had been given out came in through my cell, and had all passed through my hands.

Poor Capt. Perkins was in a low state of health and was wholly innocent of any hand or part in the plot, not that he was not brave enough and true enough, for he was all this and more too. We had refrained only from mentioning the matter to him lest in his delicate state of health the excitement naturally arising from such a desperate venture would work to his injury. Had we had the least idea that any confession we could have made would have saved him we would have gladly done so, but our whole experience taught us the lesson that we would have only involved ourselves without saving him. He was doomed to the sacrifice— to remain just as long as his weak and enervated system could indure the torture.

We were kept in our cells all the time now with an abatement of all our former privileges, which though scanty and seemingly very niggardly, we could the more fully understand and appreciate when taken from us. We felt we were harshly dealt with. We could have behaved better perhaps, in any other sort of a prison, and when we consider our own rudeness and our stubborn refractory dispositions we cannot of right complain much.

On Thursday, the 25th, Capt. Combs and Lieut. Jos. Crockston, or Croxton, were taken out from among us. We could only conjecture as to "why," and "wherefore," and all felt uneasy and troubled for their fate. Soon after, and while we were speculating in our minds as to the fate of these men, Capt. Merian and all his force came in. Our cell doors were unbolted and we were invited out and down into the hall where we were ordered to fall in marching order, prison regulation, single file, and were conducted out and around somewhat in the same way, partly along the same route we had at first been brought into the quarters we were now leaving. And as we had been ordered to take up our baggage, grip-sacks, etc., we did not know but they were going to either send us away on exchange, or to some other prison where we would come under the regulations of the military department exclusively. But we had not gone far before we turned into a low, dirty corridor which led us into a dirty, ill-ventilated hall along a range of cells, and in what was denominated the "Old Block" of the prison. This block and these cells had long been occupied by the Negro convicts.

The cells were very much smaller than those we had left in the "New Block" and taking them all in all it would hardly have been possible for them to have found a place on the Globe more loathsome and filthy. The odor rising up from the dirty, greasy, slimy cells, a noxious, poisonous vapor which stunk in your nostrils, was formed from a stinking compound of scents composed of Nigger, chinches and the accumulated filth of a long period of years. The poor Niggers had been moved out to make room for us—the filth and the chinches remained to cheer and comfort us; the latter, like the Devils of the olden time, might with propriety be named "Legion," for indeed they were many, fat and well fed. They had grown up like calves of the stall on the blood of the luckless Negro. Well, we had risked all and lost. Our jailors "dropped on to our little racket" just in time, and we could but expect hard usage; but it seemed we were to enjoy just a little more than we contracted for.

On the 26th Colonel McCreary was the first to be brought in from the "Hole," having reached, in the cold calculating judgment of Captain Merian, next to his last "inch" of life; feeble, enervated, relaxed, he could scarcely walk or stand alone. The day following, poor Perkins, with Captains Shanks and Rochester were brought in with every evidence of the most intense suffering written in step, in face, and in eye. These were followed the next day, the 28th, by Major Bullitt and Captains Sheldon and Taylor. They came tottering and staggering in like drunken men, or men trying to walk on stilts. The last installment, Captain Barton and Lieutenant Cole, were brought out on the 29th, having been confined some two hundred and fifty consecutive hours, longer than any one else of our party had been or perhaps could have been confined. Their eyes, bloodshot and swollen, looked like they would burst from their sockets. The blood had burst from under the finger nails of Barton. There could not have been more than "seven-eighths of an inch" of their lives left in their bodies when removed from the "Death Trap."

We were inclosed in this small ill-ventilated hall, and so full of offensive odors that they thought no doubt 'twould be impossible for us, while we remained here, to compose our minds sufficiently to plot any more escapes; and in the shady nooks of this ambrosial hall, we were graciously permitted to luxuriate some two or three hours each day, and while it was bad, it was better than our cells and we made what we could of it. When loose and together in the hall we could talk, play games—checkers, chess, and some played cards, and, our unfortunate friends last from the "Hole" getting up and onto their feet again, we settled down as best we could into a quiet, HAPPY family.

---

Major McCreary's diary during this period speaks of meeting "the lovely Juan Phillips at Mrs. Hall's." He named his camp "Camp Juan" for her. He also tells of driving the Yankees back from the home of Juan, "the house, where, in pleasing dalliance I had spent many happy hours and where I had reason to believe those who liked me lived, became the rampart, behind which those seeking my life fight."

He tells of taking tea with Miss Emma C. (Coffey) on her birthday.

Again: "This rainy day was spent with fair Juan. Ah! How unlike the day is her sunny face and sparkling eyes. The hours flew by on angel's wings and on the morning of the 30th [May 1863], sad yet happy I tore myself from these endearing scenes, it may be forever, and again sought the rugged scenes of the forest bivouac."

Many times has the story been told of how the two Oldhams were saved by Miss Juan Phillips. Jonathan Truman Dorris in his recent book *Old Cane Springs* tells the story again as given to him by Milton Elliott, her son:

"Micajah Phillips, a prominent and well-to-do citizen, lived at Monticello, Ky. His home was hospitable and the officers of both Union and Confederate armies frequently visited him. When the Oldhams [Othniel and Thomas, Confederate soldiers], who had been guests of Mr. Phillips, determined to return to Madison County, they notified Miss Juan Phillips, the daughter of their host, of their intention and indicated that if caught they would say they were cattle buyers. If this story did not effect their release, they wanted her to know exactly why they were going and it was because of illness in their family.

"They were captured shortly after leaving Monticello. Soon thereafter two Union officers, a colonel and a lieutenant, came to the Phillips' home where Miss Juan overheard the lieutenant say, 'Colonel, what will be done with those two men?' The colonel replied: 'They seem like fine men but they were caught within our lines without a pass and will probably be shot as spies.'

"Miss Phillips said: 'Pardon me, Colonel, but were those men Othniel and Thomas Oldham? I know they are not spies. They are gentlemen and if you permit them to be executed you will have innocent blood on your hands.'

"The Colonel sent a courier to have the execution delayed until further investigation."

On January 19, 1862, the Battle of Mill Springs, or Fishing Creek, was fought, bringing gloom to the Confederates. General Zollicoffer was killed in the battle and a monument marks the spot where he fell. During the period preceding the battle, General Zollicoffer had his headquarters at the Metcalfe home, where a table is still shown as one he used in writing. Company G, 6th Kentucky Cavalry, partly recruited in Wayne County, took part in this battle. The Brown home at Mill Springs still shows a door through which a cannon ball passed.

*A History of the Confederacy* gives this account of the battle: "General Zollicoffer's command was transferred to Monticello early in 1862, placing him in closer touch with General Johnson and for the better protection of the right flank. His force was increased by Major Crittenden's division. The Cumberland River had been made navigable by winter rains. A serious disaster occurred on General Johnson's right flank in the defeat of General Crittenden at Fishing Creek in Pulaski County on the 19th of January, 1862.

"Mill Springs is a hamlet in Wayne County on the south side of the Cumberland, just above Fishing Creek. On the 17th General Crittenden was occupying Mill Springs. Across the river at Beech Grove were several battalions. General Thomas was at Somerset and there were five regiments at Columbia. Having learned that the Columbia force was camped at Logan's Cross Roads and was attempting to join the Somerset force, and that this would be retarded by the high stage of the water, Crittenden determined to attack before this junction could be effected.

"Generals Zollicoffer and Carroll marched northward hoping to surprise the Federal soldiers, but this was not effected. Rain was falling and the morning was so dark that Zollicoffer, mistaking a Federal regiment for one of his own, rode into it and was killed as General Crittenden said 'within bayonet reach' by a pistol shot of a Federal officer."

April 29, 1863, a detachment of Morgan's Cavalry was camped at Monticello when General Carter, with Wolford's 1st Kentucky Cavalry and the 7th Ohio, came upon them and after heavy skirmishing drove them out of town. On May 11 there was a brisk engagement at "The Narrows," in Horseshoe Bend of the Cumberland River, between 480 of Colonel Jacob's 9th Kentucky Cavalry and 800 of General Morgan's Confederate Cavalry. The former were successful at first but finally had to fall back across Greasy Creek. Federal loss in killed, wounded, and missing after this engagement was 42, while Confederate loss amounted to 32, according to General Duke's report.

On June 9th there was again heavy skirmishing along an eight mile line near Monticello, and General Pegram's Confederates retreated before General Carter.

There was skirmishing at different times in and around Monticello and sickness and death in the camp. The rolls show John Benton died March 25, 1863, at Monticello, of brain fever. Cabell Chenault died at Monticello. John Spiller, a private, died at the home of Micajah Phillips.

But the devastating lawlessness that beset Kentucky from guerrilla raids caused the greatest bloodshed in Wayne.

Champ Ferguson and his band of "bushwhackers" kept the people of Wayne terrorized throughout the war. They would bring their victims into the town of Monticello, riding in at breakneck speed, cursing, shouting, and shooting.

Early morning was the favorite time for entry. A cry, "Ferguson's coming" would send women and children into cellars to cower and tremble in the dark for hours.

One morning, early, a messenger galloped in yelling for the citizens to close windows and shutters, pull down shades, remain indoors, and under no circumstances see what was being done, or attempt to take any part in it. The order was obeyed, but a curious woman peeped and saw the three Bostons tied on horses that were urged forward by the band, shooting as they came. They led them into the middle of the square in front of the old courthouse. There the victims fell and lay throughout the day, dead and dying, no one daring to go to them.

There was no feeling of security, as the mothers put their children to bed at night. Stock was all taken. Crops were scant and food was very scarce. There was no flour; cornbread sufficed. There was no coffee, a substitute of parched wheat being used. Molasses took the place of sugar, except in rare instances. The land swarmed with robbers, cutthroats, thieves, and malefactors of every kind, a motley horde—guerrillas who, under reckless and ruthless outlaws, brought Kentucky to such a pass that Lincoln put the whole state under martial law in 1864, adding to the confusion and despair of the citizens.

General Burbridge ordered that all persons enlisted in the Confederate Army, who were found in parts of Kentucky in possession of Union forces, be treated as spies and punished according to usages of war.

This order caused untold suffering by execution of innocent men, and Burbridge, who was stationed at Danville at this time, was thoroughly despised. He must have felt this for he left Kentucky at the conclusion of the war and never returned.

Though Wayne was almost completely Southern in sentiment and action, the county furnished some distinguished Union men, notably Captain John W. Tuttle, a brave and gallant officer. He enlisted in Company H, Third Kentucky Infantry, U. S. A., as First Lieutenant (Captains Henry Taylor and William Hudson) was promoted, himself, to Captain, with First Lieutenants James M. Bristow and Harrison Carter; Second Lieutenant William Bramlette; Sergeants Calvin Jeffries, James Francis, Richard Bristow, John C. Jarvis, Charles Carter, Alfred Wright, Michael Buster; Corporals Josephus Wood, John H. Petty, Samuel Hull, Martin Richardson, Allen Smith, John Warren, George Pults, John White, Joseph Griffin, Charles Kearns; Teamster George Warren. Captain Tuttle sustained a serious wound which caused lameness that he kept through life. John W. Tuttle was a man unusually gifted. He was a good lawyer and mathematician. He was an artist and had superior literary abilities. He was both historian and antiquarian.

Captain Tuttle kept a diary from 1861-1867, covering his service in the Union Army. He belonged to a family with many branches of distinguished ancestors.

Captain John W. Tuttle was born in 1838, in Wayne County and died there in 1927. He was the son of William Henry Tuttle, born in Litchfield, Connecticut, in 1808, classmate of Henry Ward Beecher and Harriet Beecher Stowe. He married Courtney Metcalfe, daughter of John Metcalfe and Frances Norton Baylor. They lived at Mill Springs where he operated the old mill. William Henry Tuttle was son of Jason Tuttle of Litchfield, Connecticut, a Revolutionary soldier who was son of Jabez Tuttle also a Revolutionary soldier. Frances Norton Baylor was daughter of Walker Baylor and Jane Bledsoe. Walker Baylor was son of Colonel John Baylor, Revolutionary soldier, and Frances Walker. The Bledsoes were with the Long Hunters, 1770-72.

Captain Tuttle married Miss Mollie Milton of Oldham County.

The following are some extracts from Captain Tuttle's Diary, 1860-1865:

## EXTRACTS FROM DIARY OF CAPTAIN JOHN W. TUTTLE

Thursday, August 2, 1860: Dr. J. B. S. Frisbie, W. A. Haskins and myself were sitting in the porch when all at once a meteor of the most intensely brilliant character arose in the S. E., rising in its course at an angle of about 20 degrees, and moved with an apparently slow motion towards the N. W. Its light was of a peculiarly white character more brilliant perhaps than that of the sun. It completely blinded, for a moment, all who beheld it.

After the meteor had disappeared I walked down town to learn the sentiments of the people generally with respect to the strange visitor. The matter was being discussed freely and many opinions expressed with regard to it. The savants differing among themselves displayed a depth of research into the hidden mysteries of physical science truly astounding. Illustrious examples shining forth from the page of history should have taught them the folly of attempting to tamper with the staid orthodoxy of the common mind to popular opinion. The theory finding favor with the greater number was that the "last day" of the existence of this little ball of dirt had most certainly arrived.

Some minutes after the disappearance of the meteor a sound, deep and unnatural, not unlike the rumbling of heavy thunder, in the distance, when near the earth but partaking of the roaring nature more like the roaring of a whirlwind. The sound continued for several minutes and gradually died away greatly to the relief of those regarding the sound as the herald of an earthquake or judgment day.

Monday, August 6, 1860: I am this day 23 years of age. Was elected Lt. Col. of the Ky. Militia for Wayne County . . . .

August 23: John T. Sanders and Eliza Frisbie married. Waiters: Miss Mary E. Hardin, G. C. Haden; Miss Joan Phillips, Joshua Berry; Fannie Coffey and George Noland. Took charge of J. S. Frisbie's school while he attended his sister's wedding. They left for Mammoth Cave.

Tuesday, August 21, 1860: We had a fine rain this morning for the first time in several weeks.

Started to Squire Powers' about 8 o'clock. I was overtaken by a very hard rain but having an umbrella and shawl I managed to keep tolerably dry.

When I reached the residence of David Powers, Esq. the trial of Privett had just commenced. Thomas Pile, Esq. my man of June 20th was the associate justice. I regarded his connection with the case as the most ominous feature in it but as it happened I got along with him very smoothly. Two or three witnesses for the Commonwealth had given in their testimony when I arrived. I immediately entered into the case. At the close of the proof I arose and addressed the court for about 20 minutes and submitted the case.

After brief consultation their Honors acquitted my client. When they announced their determination in the cause, I exclaimed with apparently earnest enthusiasm, "And a most righteous judgment, too, your Honors have rendered," though as well satisfied of his guilt as of my own existence.

Thursday, October 6, 1860: Assisted in raising framework of new church.

Monday, November 12, 1860: Spent the morning reading law. Received letters from J. M. Saufley and John A. Middleton, both of Louisville. Devoted the greater part of the evening to reading the news. Considerable excitement prevails on account of the threatened secession of South Carolina, Georgia, Alabama, and Florida.

Monday, December 17, 1860: Accompanied Miss Sallie home this morning. The trip was a highly interesting and agreeable one to me. On the way agreed to exchange a miniature of hers which I had had in my possession for about two years, for one she had taken last summer. As there was no fire in the parlor we went into the family room. As Mrs. Coffey was present I felt sorely perplexed as to how the exchange of miniatures could be effected without her knowledge. At length, recollecting having loaned Miss Sallie Irving's Sketch Book I asked her if she had finished reading it. She said she had and went into the parlor to get it. I followed and made the exchange of miniatures. I cared nothing for the book *then* but in order to keep up appearances brought it home.

Saturday, December 29, 1860: This morning Gen. B. F. Coffey and Dr. J. W. Bell paraded the streets with blue cockades on their hats, the badge of secession. C. W. Buster, Pa, and I, held a consultation for the purpose of devising some appropriate rebuke and finally concluded to get a few bolts of blue ribbon and have cockades fastened to the hats of about a dozen negroes. This plan was forthwith put into execution. The negroes were caused to march through the streets several times. The General and Doctor were highly incensed at having their cockade-wearing burlesqued. Their discomfiture however was in no wise calculated to detract from the enjoyment of the ludicrous spectacle by the crowds who thronged the streets and doors and windows to witness it.

Friday, January 11, 1861: Received a letter from M. B. Perkins requesting me to raise a company of State Guards in this county. Received by mail notice of secession conventions having organized in Ala., Fla., Miss., also of the assembling of two Union Conventions at Louisville of the supporters of Bell and Everett and of Douglas and Johnson. The Louisville *Journal*, received by today's mail, is out in a leader proposing the temporary erection of a central Confederacy in case it should be impossible to maintain the Union entire as it has heretofore been.

Wednesday, January 16, 1861: Read the *Dutch Republic* as much as I was permitted during the morning. My partner, James S. Hardin, returned about noon. Says it is rumored that the Star of the West was fired into off Charleston by the Secessionists.

February 28, 1861: Played euchre for homemade sugar nearly all day. Won 14 pounds.

March 30, 1861: Dr. E. Richardson returned from N. Y.

Sunday, June 16, 1861: A report was in circulation today that about 20 Secessionists intended to arm themselves and compel Mr. Hardin, in his speech tomorrow at Mill Springs, to answer the questions propounded to him by Jack Garth and Ike Sheppard yesterday. Considerable bustle among our boys on this account. They were determined to defend Mr. Hardin against them.

Monday, June 17, 1861: Went with 15 or 20 to Parmleysville where I was gladdened by sight of the Star Spangled Banner floating on the breeze. Hon. S. Williams, Secessionist, and Hon. E. L. Van Winkle, Unionist, spoke. I could not rid myself of the idea that those whose views do not coincide with mine on the great question are either fools or traitors.

Tuesday, June 18, 1861: J. A. Stephenson, G. K. Noland, N. D. Ingram, and I went to Josh Berry's and stayed all night. We held a meeting and unanimously adopted the following preamble and resolutions:

"Whereas our beloved County of Wayne is and for some time past has been infested with an unconstitutional number of juvenile ministers of the Gospel with lustrous eyes and shining locks who are waging war upon our dearest interests by endeavoring to persuade our sweethearts that none but Divines are worthy of them; therefore Resolved: that we the much injured and too little appreciated 'bohoys' of the proud County of Wayne do ordain and declare that we will submit no longer to these grievances 'already too long endured' to which end we hereby warn all unmarried ministers of the Gospel (not too old to muster) who may now be or hereafter come within the limits of this County to depart immediately.

"Upon motion of Brother Tuttle be it further Resolved that the benefits of this Ordinance be extended to all the young men now living in the County of Russell whether preachers or not; that Bro. Stephenson be and is hereby appointed a committee of six to carry the foregoing Ordinance into vigorous execution. Upon motion the meeting then adjourned."

Sunday, June 30, 1861: Spent the day except as herein otherwise specified in writing the following lines in Miss Mollie Sallee's album:

> No poet am I as well you know,
> If of my skill you've seen a trial;
> And if you've not these lines will show
> That such is true beyond denial.

When quite a youth I did, sometimes,
Invoke the Muses' inspiration,
And perpetrate some silly rhymes
For want of better occupation.

But since that time, some wiser grown,
I've from the list of bards retired;
And 'yond my reach the Muse has flown,
By which my fancy was inspired.

So now, I hope you'll not expect
A poem from my humble pen,
By all the poet's rules correct,
And all the rhetorician's ken.

Then, dearest friend, in homely phrase
Your kind remembrance I would ask
And pray that you, throughout your days,
In Fortune's smiles may ever bask.

And on your heart I would impress
The truth of what I now declare;
That for your lasting happiness
You have my warmest heartfelt prayer.

I also made a picture in the album of a broom, shovel, and a pair of tongs and wrote beneath them "Armed neutrality, to be used only in case of extreme necessity."

July 2, 1861: Bro. White held prayer meeting at Dr. Frisbie's. Snowden Worsham went out alone to meet Champ Ferguson's Bushwhackers and dispersed them. Noted for bravery.

Saturday, July 27, 1861: . . . . We arrived at Albany about 10. The first thing we saw upon arriving at the top of the hill overlooking the town were the Stars and Stripes gaily fluttering to the breeze above the tops of the houses. On entering town we met a procession with 34 ladies in front on horseback, one of whom carried a National Banner followed by about 60 cavalry and 500 infantry. They presented quite an imposing appearance.

About two thousand persons were in town. After dinner a procession was formed which marched out about a half a mile from town where they were addressed by Hon. Thos. E. Bramlette in a speech of something more than three hours duration. He made a most thrilling appeal in behalf of the Union and called upon the loyal citizens of Clinton Co. to join a regiment he is raising for the purpose of aiding the Union men of E. Tennessee. About 30 enlisted in the service under him and 87 cavalry, to compose a part of a regiment destined for the same service, now being raised by Frank Woolford of Casey Co. The feeling for the Union here is very strong and the most intense enthusiasm prevails. A Secessionist is not allowed to open his mouth. The people of this county are apprehensive of an invasion by Tennesseans. They have picket guards stationed out at every pass. The alarm was spread about an hour by sun yesterday evening, and from three to five hundred armed men gathered from various parts of the county and stayed in town last night.

Sunday, July 28, 1861: I received authority in writing this morning from Col. Bramlette to raise a company of volunteers in Wayne....

Saturday, August 3, 1861: Was engaged this morning in endeavoring to raise a company for the U. S. Service under Col. Bramlette. After dinner a procession was formed which marched to Buster's. This occupied nearly the whole evening.

A call was made for volunteers and one man besides myself enlisted. John S. Van Winkle made a short but stirring address. On my return to town I obtained two more names to my list. A little before sundown it was announced that a company of cavalry from Clinton Co. would be here in a few minutes. Several hundred sallied forth to meet them. The band went down as far as M. Phillips and met them with National airs and escorted them to town. They were welcomed to the hospitality of the citizens of Monticello, through Col. Bramlette. He was responded to by Capt. J. A. Brents on behalf of the company. The company was then distributed out among the Union friends and entertained for the night. Their arrival created a desirable enthusiasm and enabled me to obtain seven more volunteers.

Sunday, August 4, 1861: The cavalry company started soon after breakfast enroute for their encampment near Crab Orchard.

I started to Albany about 8 this morning and arrived a little after dinner. My object in going was to ascertain the number of the company being raised by S. Taylor about which I had heard conflicting reports, also to report the number I had on my list and number I expected to get and to make arrangements for uniting my squad with his. Saw Taylor, made all necessary arrangements, called at his house where he and I remained something upwards of an hour after which I started towards home ....

Monday, August 5, 1861: Soon after breakfast started for Monticello where in due time I arrived. Met a young man whom Taylor had sent to see me upon the same business about which I went to see him. Spent the day enlisting. Succeeded in augmenting my list of names to about twenty .... The election passed off quietly in Monticello. Mr. M. N. Stone made a speech requesting the Southern Rights (?) men to assemble in Monticello on Friday next for the purpose of organizing a company to fight against their country.

Tuesday, August 6, 1861: Was busily engaged winding up my business preparatory to entering into the service of my Country. Went over home this morning and spent an hour or two. After dinner continued my preparations to start to war. About 4 P. M. went down to Mr. C. T. Hall's in company with Dr. Cox and Richard Burnett for the purpose of meeting the Ky. and Tennessee companies, now on their way to Camp Nelson near Crab Orchard, Ky. Stayed all night with Josh Berry. The Clinton Boys stayed there also.

Wednesday, August 7, 1861: Started to town this morning and arrived about 10. The Volunteers came in about an hour afterwards. About 2 P. M. Mr. C. S. Taylor made a speech of some length calling for volunteers. Col. Bowles also made a harangue. About a dozen came forward and enlisted. The company then elected C. S. Taylor, Capt., myself 1st Lieutenant, J. M. Bristow, 2nd Lt. and J. C. Southerland, 3rd Lt. We then adjourned to listen to a speech from Hon. Robt. Bridges. I do not hesitate to pronounce it the best speech I have yet listened to upon the great questions of the day. Have been engaged until now (near midnight) in making preparations to take my departure in the morning.

[Diary here departs from daily notations and begins narrative.]

More than three months have elapsed since writing the above, since which time I have been in the service of the U. S. It is impossible for me to chronicle all the events which have transpired in the meantime in chronological order but I shall endeavor to do so as much as I can, after which, if time and circumstances permit, I design resuming the diary system ....

We left Monticello on the morning of the 8th of August and reached Capt. A. R. West's about noon. This estimable gentleman had dinner prepared for us on our arrival of which we partook with a hearty good will doing ample justice to the abundant, well prepared substantials set before us after which we resumed our march. We reached the residence of J. S. Denny just on the top of the Cumberland River hills about sunset where about half stayed all night. The other half of those with us including the Tennesseans under Capt. Bowles went to a neighboring house. I went home with Mr. J. N. Brown and remained over night .... We were supplied with a few sides of bacon and light bread by Mr. J. R. Ingram and some other good citizens of Pulaski while on our march from the river to Somerset. When about four miles beyond the latter place on the Crab Orchard road we halted at a small spring in the woods on the left hand side of the road where we made our dinner on raw bacon and bread. We crossed Buck Creek about sunset and repaired in small parties to the neighboring houses where we put up for the night. Having collected our forces the next morning we set out for Camp Nelson where we arrived about 3 P. M. We found between three or four hundred men at this place who received us with presented arms and hearty cheers. This camp was situated at the old Bryant tavern stand, about a mile and a half from Crab Orchard on the Somerset Road. Capt. King who had arrived in camp some days before us turned over his quarters, arm, etc. to us. We were received into the service by Lt. Col. Gilmore, commanding post. We had no commissary stores at this place but boarded at Yantiss'. The whole of us ate at the same table which consumed about 3 hours to each meal. This caused great dissatisfaction among the troops and all were anxious to leave....

On the 21st day of August a dispatch was received at headquarters stating that a quantity of arms had been seized by the Secessionists at Lexington which had been shipped from Cincinnati for Camp Dick Robinson.

Early next morning about 300 cavalry under Lt. Col. Letcher set out for Lexington. Col. Bramlette started for Lexington for the purpose of ascertaining particulars concerning the seizure. Gen. Nelson, perhaps getting uneasy lest the cavalry should be overpowered, ordered 500 Infantry to march to their support. The Gen. went in person some time during the day. About 7 in the evening the Infantry took up its line of march under command of Col. S. S. Fry. I joined part of the company under my command to Capt. McKee's company and went as 1st Lt. We reached Nicholasville about 3. It rained on us from the time we left camp. Upon our arrival at Nicholasville, we found the wagons containing the arms the Secesh had seized. The Gen. commended in high terms the conduct of the cavalry.

Upon the arrival of the cavalry at Lexington, the Secesh became greatly alarmed and the Arch Traitor, John C. Breckenridge, who had taken a leading part in the seizure and detention of the arms, addressed a note to Col. Bramlette stating that if he (Bramlette) would withdraw the troops from the city he would use his *influence* to have the arms given up. Col. Bramlette sent him word to go to h—— with his influence, that he had come for the arms and intended to have them on his own terms, even should a resort to arms be necessary. The Secessionists then blew a bugle for the traitors to rally under arms. At the same time the cavalry formed and the Home Guards came out at the ringing of the Courthouse bell. The Secesh finding our boys were not to be scared and thinking the probability of whipping us rather remote graciously condescended to give us our property. The arms were put in wagons and brought to Nicholasville under escort of our cavalry.

From the time of our arrival at Nicholasville until daylight I slept in a commissary wagon across the tops of three empty barrels. We divided into parties and took breakfast at different houses in town after which we took up our line of march for Camp Dick Robinson, where we arrived some time in the afternoon, much fatigued with our long, wet, muddy, and sleepless tramp.

Nothing of particular interest occurred for some days except an occasional alarm in which cases the men always came out on the color-line with great promptness and evinced a perfect willingness to fight any number of Secessionists that the Devil should be pleased to send.

At this time we were but a few hundred strong, undrilled and poorly armed. We had assembled in open violation of the "Armed Neutrality" policy of the State and in direct opposition to the will of our Secession Governor. We were in constant apprehension of an attack from State Guards with whom, His Excellency, Beriah Magoffin threatened to disperse us. We were also looked upon with much disfavor by men professing to be loyal who yet clung to the doctrine of "Armed Neutrality."

Notwithstanding this many sided opposition to our course we lived and prospered. Our numbers soon swelled to thousands and we were soon in such a state of organization that the Secessionists no longer threatened us.

. . . . On the 9th of Sept. I left Camp Dick Robinson for Monticello on a recruiting expedition . . . . I got three or four men and went into the court house late on the night of my arrival and took every lock and bayonet off of forty six muskets with which the secessionists had been drilling. We put them into a bag and took them out to the country where we concealed them. We should have taken the guns also but had not the means of transporting or concealing them without involving great risk of discovery—and we were particularly desirous of avoiding discovery for many reasons, not one of which was correctly assigned in a letter written upon the subject a few days afterward by some of the Secesh to the Frankfort *Yeoman*. We were apprehensive lest they should fall into the hands of a party of Secession Guerrillas who were then hovering on the Southern border of our country.

It was with feelings of deep sorrow that I marked the sad changes that had taken place in Monticello in the short space of six months. When I left (8th Aug. '61) to make my home in the tented field, none save the twelve who were with me had joined in the internecine strife, just then beginning to shake the foundation of our once peaceful and happy society, and hundreds of friends crowded around to extend a parting hand and a thousand good wishes; but at the time of my visit I found but a slender few remaining. They had either gone to the war or fled before the tide of revolution whose fiery waves threatened soon to burst across our mountain girded borders. Of these many have gone to their last account while the remainder are so scattered that I can hope to meet but few of them upon the "Old Stamping Ground" when the roll of the battle-drum shall have become silent and the "War Bugle" ceased its fierce wild clangor.

Narrative—1862:

On my return to camp (Feb. 12th) I had a remarkably Quixotic adventure the denouement of which mortified me prodigously. While riding along about a half a mile beyond Allcorn's (from Camp Green) I looked out into the woods and beheld a horseman approaching the road at an angle of about thirty degrees. The first thing that attracted my attention was his riding in the deep wood where there was no sign of a road and, secondly, his equipment and general appearance. He was riding a packsaddle, had a halter on his horse, and crutch in his hand. The crutch I mistook for a short gun and the packsaddle and halter for the accoutrements of a trooper's horse. I at once concluded he was a trooper and as he did not wear the livery of Uncle Sam, I sat him down as belonging to the rebel cavalry. This conclusion was strengthened by the fact of his having on a low yellow hat such as the rebel soldiers wear. In fact the illusion was perfect. My first impression was that one of the guerrilla bands, that about that time were prowling around through the hills, had gained information, from some of the Secesh about Monticello, of my intention to return to camp on that day and that this fellow was either conducting me into an ambuscade or, in concert with others, was closing in on me with intent to kill or take me prisoner. I thought if that was their game I would not go into any such an arrangement. I had no particular desire to die except in a regular battle where my friends might learn that I had fought bravely and died gloriously and I still less relished the idea of spending the summer in a Southern dungeon.

I stopped my horse and looked about me, on all sides, seeing no one else approaching from any other direction. My mind being relieved upon that point I began to consider what course I should pursue in reference to the chap approaching the road. As his attention did not seem directed to me as particularly as it would likely have been, had his object been what I at first suspected, I determined to give him battle and if possible take him by surprise.

In the execution of this design I rode up to within about forty yards of the place I expected he would emerge from the wood into the road, and drew up behind a little clump of bushes. I then took out my Colt's Navy, shortened my reins and prepared to make a charge the moment my supposed enemy should make his appearance in the road. When he entered the road I drew my "Rosinante" back upon his haunches and dug both heels in his flanks. He plunged forward at a tolerably respectable gallop and in a moment brought me within short range of my intended victim. I was almost in the act of firing when I discovered my error. He proved to be a little old lame man and when I bore down upon him in furious charge, he turned upon me with such a look of horror as I shall never forget.

As may be easily imagined, I felt no slight mortification when I came to realize what an enormous ass I had made of myself in the affair, but then he looked so much like a Rebel I could justify myself in what I had done. My disappointment was such as to convert me to the belief that there must have been some truth in the opinion entertained by Don Quixote de La Mancha that wicked enchanters *do* sometimes through envy transform giants, knights and indeed enemies of all kinds into simple country peasants. But even though the enchanter may not in this particular instance have exercised his diabolical art, yet I hope I am almost as excusable for my mistake as was the soldier of

DR. J. B. FRISBIE, JR.

*With his father, Dr. J. B. Frisbie, he ministered to the sick in Wayne County for sixty-five years*

JOHN L. SALLEE
*Prominent citizen of Wayne*

*Captain John W. Tuttle and
Mollie Milton Tuttle*

*Ephraim L. Van Winkle, Secretary of State, 1863-1866*

the first Kansas when he mistook a hog one dark night for a Secesh.

On the evening of the Twentieth of March, a fleet of six steamers landed at the mouth of Greasy Creek for the purpose of conveying our regt. and the Sixth Ohio Battery to Dixie Land. The next day was spent in embarking which was completed about 4 p. m.

The steamer May Duke, upon which our Company (H), Captain King's Company (F), a part of Captain Marat's Company (I), and a part of the battery was embarked, ran up the river opposite the residence of Mr. J. H. Meadows, to wood. I was sent with a detail of twenty men to throw wood over the cliff. The night was dark and the hill very steep. A part of the men succeeded in gaining the top but I did not. The next morning we started for Nashville. Our flotilla did not keep together but we were continually passing each other during the whole trip. We all arrived without accident at the City of Nashville, about 11 p. m., March 17th. We disembarked the next morning. Lieutenant Bristow and I went down to where the river bridge stood before the exit of the thieving rebel, General Floyd, where we saw one of the gunboats that figured at Forts Henry and Donaldson after which we went to the State House. We ascended to the Observatory and climbed out on top. Here we had a fine view of the city and surrounding country, but the great height, together with the motion of the boat, being still in our heads and the dizziness, occasioned by climbing the spiral stairs, we were compelled to get down in a hurry. When we again reached terra firma we explored the basement story, also saw the stone vault within the wall where the remains of the architect of the building were interred. Having satisfied our curiosity with regard to that noble structure we repaired to the wharf where we found our regiment (and the 21st Kentucky which came down on our fleet) ready to march. We marched about $3\frac{1}{2}$ miles out on the Nolin pike where we encamped. While here we were visited by the paymaster who paid us two months wages. We were attached to the 20th Brigade commanded by Colonel Harker. I was appointed Ordnance Officer of that Brigade and acted in that capacity for some days but, my regiment having in the meantime been detached from that Brigade, I resigned and went back to my former position (1st Lieutenant Co. H, 3rd Kentucky Vols. U. S. A.).

April 5: We resumed our march and came within about 11 miles of Waynesboro. On the next morning we pursued our weary journey. About 9 a. m. we heard heavy cannonading apparently somewhat south of Savannah though what it meant none of us knew. General Hascall commanding our Brigade received a dispatch from General Wood to press vigorously forward as a battle was in all probability going on and our services might be needed. The cannonading was kept up all day without intermission. We marched 23 miles that day and much exhausted pitched tents a little after sunset. I walked out beyond the noise and confusion of the camp and could distinctly hear the heavy booming of cannon.

We took up our line of march before sunup and pressed forward with all the speed the mud and swollen streams would permit. We found the roads obstructed by wagons for fifteen or twenty miles and were compelled to leave our trains behind. When within about eight miles of Savannah we halted and drew three days rations which the men deposited in their haversacks and again struck out for the scene of conflict, the noise of which had by this time become one continuous, heavy, sullen, terrible roar—fearfully distinct to us. We heard various reports when within a few miles of Savannah with regard to the progress of the battle. Some of them were to the effect that Beauregard had the rebel army of the Potomac on the ground and was cutting our men all to pieces—another that the rebels were giving way and our victory certain, and numerous details and statement with regard to the numbers engaged, those killed and wounded, etc., upon each side. We reached Savannah a little after dark. The town was filled with the dead and wounded brought from the battlefield. Our regiment was put on the top of the boat and was exposed to a drenching rain during the trip—reached Pittsburg Landing about 10:30 p. m.

We had just disembarked when the rattle of musketry was heard in front, which we supposed to be a recommencement of the battle. For a moment everything appeared to be in a state of wild disorder, thousands of men were hurrying to and fro working in and through each other like a disturbed swarm of bees, and a moment after, the most perfect order prevailed throughout the vast sea of human beings that met our view. Companies, regiments, brigades and divisions were formed with perfect military precision and soon the immense dark columns were moving rapidly to the front. When we reached the front we formed our lines of battle and stood under arms during the entire day but no enemy came.

The first view we had of the battlefield of Shiloh, as it is called, was not at all calculated to steady one's nerves. The dead men were scattered all over the field, some in groups, others in heaps, and the wounded, of whom all had not been gathered up, were crawling about through the deep mud presenting a most piteous spectacle. Dead horses and mules, shattered wagons and gun carriages, trees slivered and torn by shot, shell, grape and canister told how terribly destructive had been the work of the artillery, to the music of whose roar we made the last two days march to the field.

The next day after our arrival I spent about half a day rambling about over the field examining the dead with the expectation of finding some with whom I was acquainted but found none. It is a notable fact that the dead Union soldiers retained a remarkably natural appearance while the dead rebels were almost universally very greatly bloated and black in the face.

On the next day some little skirmishing took place between our pickets and those of the enemy. This boldness with which they approached our lines in various places upon our front together with some other circumstances induced us to believe that the whole rebel army was advancing upon us. The longroll was beat and in a few moments our whole army was in battle array. We advanced about half a mile and awaited their coming until late in the evening when, being satisfied from the reports of our picket scouts and the skirmishers we had thrown out that no attack was likely to be made upon us, we fell back to our place of occupation upon the field. That night our Brigade was ordered out on picket duty. We slept upon our arms all night and observed the utmost silence. Our slumbers were not disturbed during the night and the next morning we marched back to our former position.

We bivouacked upon the field for nine days and nights without shelter. It rained on us almost the whole time. The dark dismal swampy woods in which we were stationed, the heavy black clouds that hung over us, the deep mire through which we waded and in which we slept, the want of every article of comfort, convenience or even necessity, the insufferable stench of the carcasses of dead men, mules, and horses rendered this a picture of "darkness" to which Poe or Byron could do no more than justice. Our food was dry crackers and water.

But the most complete avalanche of oaths the writer ever heard was that day uttered by General Wood and hurled and showered upon the Captain who had allowed his men to fire off their guns upon our front. It was a masterpiece of profanity, faultlessly rendered. Our much beloved little division commander had no equal in that line in the army and perhaps none in the navy. General Nelson would have turned green with envy if he had heard him.

When fully assured that the rebels had no intention of attacking us we returned to our former place of bivouac. We remained upon the field of Shiloh for ten days and nights without shelter of any kind. The bad, impure and even filthy water we were compelled to drink, rendered our sojourn there anything but cheerful or pleasant. After the rations the men had brought with them in their haversacks gave out we had nothing at all to eat but dry crackers, commonly known as "hard-tack" until within a day or two before we left there when we obtained a small quantity of pickled pork and coffee. The men carried boxes of crackers on their shoulders from the landing, a distance of five miles, by the route they were compelled to go, in order to avoid the deeper parts of the mire. The mud had deepened considerably since our arrival.

Bullet-proof Vests: While there (near Shiloh) a benevolent young man came around with bullet-proof vests for sale. They were woven of a stiff, tough wire and looked as if they would ordinarily turn almost any bullet. The line officers, however, all declined to purchase on the ground that they might get shot through the head and be found dead on the field with a badge of cowardice on their bodies. He next concluded he would try to sell one to Colonel Bramlette. We thought he was taking his wares to a bad market but did not tell him so. On the contrary, if the truth must be told, we rather encouraged him in the idea. We expected the Colonel would kick him out of his tent and two or three of us innocently sauntered around to headquarters, one at a time, to see the fun.

Greatly to our surprise, however, the Colonel treated him with the most winning affability. He examined the vests, asked a great many questions about them, evinced a deep interest in what the young man said about their efficacy in preserving many valuable lives to the country's service, said he had a great desire to *try* one of them. He asked the young man to put one of them on and step off about ten steps at the same time taking a large army pistol from his holster that swung to his tent pole and working the cylinder around to see that it revolved all right.

That was not exactly the way the young man had construed the Colonel's desire to *try* one and as he had no desire himself to have his vests tested just that way, he began to make excuses. But the Colonel answered all his excuses and insisted on the trial he had proposed. The young man would not agree to it. He however, had a thick hide and thicker skull, and still persisted in his efforts to sell one of them to the Colonel. The Colonel said he did not think he wanted one of them just then but did not know how soon he might and asked if he had one that would fit him. The young man selected one he thought was about the right size and asked the Colonel to try it on. The Colonel took it and made two or three rather ludicrous attempts to adjust it upon his person when the young man said, "Oh, Colonel, that is not the way. You have it fore part behind." The Colonel turned upon him and in a withering tone said, "Young man, I think I know what I am about. When I get to be such a d—d coward as to want one of these things (at the same time holding the vest between his thumb and fore-finger and eyeing it contemptuously) I will want to wear it in such a way as to protect the part of my person likely to be most exposed to the enemy."

The young man snatched the vest from his hand, gathered up the others and hastily disappeared from our camp.

Bivouacked near Corinth: May 10th, a heavy force, of which our division constituted a part, was thrown around to the left and front. Having settled into position, the writer was sent forward with his Company about three miles on outpost duty, differing somewhat from the picket service afterwards adopted by the army.

Time, place and occasion concur in bringing to mind an incident mentioned by Captain Thos. Speed in his well written history of the 12th Kentucky Infantry which he alludes to as "a clear case of making matter for the newspapers" and was possibly the same occasion referred to by another writer belonging to that regiment upon which "a certain officer sought a little cheap notoriety by skirmishing upon them from the rear." The writers may not have meant either, but there seems at least to be such a coincidence as to justify explanation.

The way of it, so far as we were concerned, was this: We were informed that we were a part of the line of extreme outposts of our army and were instructed to keep a vigilant watch from that position and if too strongly attacked we were to skirmish back to our line of battle holding the enemy in check as long as we could.

Through the whole night we heard men coughing and horses snorting and neighing almost directly in front of our line in the direction it was posted. We supposed it was a body of rebel cavalry on picket but did not know. As soon as daylight began to appear the writer sent a note back to Colonel Bramlette informing him what we had heard and asking him what it meant and what we must do. The Colonel probably not relishing a disturbance of his slumbers at that hour sent back the somewhat curt reply that ". . . . Captain Tuttle should inquire at the front and not at the rear." The writer accordingly selected eight or ten men and proceeded to "inquire" in the direction indicated.

We slipped quietly and cautiously through the woods for something over a quarter of a mile when greatly to the relief of our highly strained nerves we came upon the 12th Kentucky Infantry instead of the body of rebel cavalry we had expected to find. We were at a "ready" with cocked pieces but did not fire at random or anything else and did not "drive 'em" though we may perhaps be said to have skirmished upon the rear of our very good friends of the 12th. They were not, however, in camp or even in regular bivouac as might be inferred from one of the accounts but were, like ourselves, on outpost duty. The position was new and the lines had not been adjusted. The direction of their line and that of ours if extended would have formed something less than a right angle and all were faced in the same general direction so that we really approached them from their rear although our position was almost, if not quite, as far advanced as theirs. After a pleasant chat with Captains Crozier, Ham, Collier and others, the writer returned to his company. . . .

On the Fourth of May, 1862, I was commissioned Captain of Company G . . . .

Monday, September 8, 1862: Rejoined the regiment about daybreak and marched six miles in the direction of Gallatin and bivouacked. The principal incident of the day was the demolition of a formidable nest of Yellow Jackets. I planned the attack and Captain Taylor "did the work for them" in handsome style. Under my direction the gallant Captain sent forward his Aid De Camp with about ¼ pound of powder which he himself in his own proper person followed at about the distance of three paces with a shovel full of coals and hot embers. When my forces reached the earthworks of the enemy the van-guard *charged* the fort and the Captain immediately emptied the content of his shovel upon the citadel. Immediately there was a tremendous explosion and the brave little garrison "went up." Our loss was but two wounded. Captain Taylor had his face badly burned with powder and embers and (Drum) Major Cruzan, who was asleep on the ground near by, had his face bruised severely by a stump Colonel Scott's "haven took" with him when he rather hastily retired from the scene of action.

[The intervening period before the next entry is partially covered by the preceding "narrative."]

Wednesday, August 26, 1863: Spent the morning reading *Littel's Living Age*, etc. In the evening was appointed Field Officer of the Pickets for the Brigade.

While at one of the posts giving instructions to the Lieutenant in command, the horse I was riding suddenly and without apparent cause commenced rearing and plunging. He first fell nearly straight backwards with me upon a stack of loaded guns which he scattered in every direction, then reared straight up and came back against a tree by which process my left thigh was broken and then took a fair fall of his own of which he had the exclusive enjoyment.

Those on duty at the post picked me up promptly and sent for a surgeon. Two or three presently came with an ambulance but I was suffering too much pain to be hauled in so they sent for a litter and had me carried in to our regimental hospital. My leg, which had only been temporarily splinted and bandaged, was then dressed by Dr. Rhoann and Dr. Todd, our Brigade Medical Director. I suffered the most excruciating pain and was delirious part of the evening and night.

Thursday, August 27, 1863: Dr. Blair, Division Medical Director, Dr. Todd, Brigade Medical Director and Dr. McMahan came to see me this morning. They concluded my leg had drawn up too much so they made a big splint and lashed my leg to it after stretching it about an inch and a half. The process was almost as painful as the first breaking. I suffered very much in course of the day and night. Every kindness and attention that could be thought of was shown me by those in immediate attendance upon me and the officers and men of the regiment generally.

Monday, November 23, 1863: Divided the morning between reading *Lalla Rookh* and listening to the casual cannonading from Moccasin Point and Fort Wood and the occasional replies of Lookout. There was some musketry on the other side of Lookout but we are not informed of what is going on over there.

About noon our bugles sounded to arms and looking over our vast encampment I saw the whole army of the Cumberland was falling in. Stationing myself upon a hill just above the camp of my regiment, I witnessed the formation of companies, and companies into regiments, and regiments into brigades. In a very few minutes all in three heavy columns were moving to the front. Looking over towards the rebel encampment I saw they were rapidly marshaling their forces in battle array to meet our advancing columns. It was truly a grand and imposing spectacle to see these immense bodies of men moving out and forming in line of battle with the precision of regimental maneuvers. The 11th A. C. moved past where I stood and formed itself to operate as a grand reserve for the left wing.

When our columns had well cleared the outer encampment they deployed into line, threw out their skirmishers and advanced a considerable distance, when the right and center halted and the left pressed on. Soon upon the extreme left a shot was fired, then another, and another, until the entire skirmish line of the left became engaged. A few minutes sufficed for them to drive in the rebel pickets when they were met by the rebel skirmishers whom they in turn drove back upon their outer line of rifle pits. Our line of battle on the left pressed forward, and after a sharp conflict of an hour's duration, drove the enemy from their rifle pits, killing and wounding several hundred and taking upwards of two hundred prisoners. It gained and held Orchard Point and a ridge of considerable strategic importance running parallel with Missionary Ridge along the entire front of our left.

The rest of the evening was spent in cannonading at various points along the line, the Infantry remaining stationary. Our forces are engaged tonight fortifying the positions gained and in advancing our picket lines. Our wounded are being brought into camp tonight and well cared for.

Tuesday, November 24, 1863: Sharp firing commenced on the west side of Lookout Mountain early this morning growing warmer as it continued. About 9 A. M., Moccasin Point opened furiously upon the rebels with shells. At about 11 A. M. we saw the rebels sweeping around the end of Lookout next to the river retreating towards their fortifications, pursued by the 12th A. C. and a part of Sherman's command all under General Hooker. The rebels made a stand at a fort and line of earthworks on the mountain. Hooker fought them about an hour when he charged their works driving the rebels out of their works and causing them to retire a considerable distance in great confusion. Here they made another stubborn stand either from heavy reinforcements or another line of works. A sharp skirmish was kept up until midnight when the rebels retired. The flash of guns could be distinctly seen from my tent forming two sparkling lines from the bottom of the hill nearly to the summit.

Wednesday, November 25, 1863: Early this morning I took my position just in front of Fort Wood to witness operations on their left it being expected that the greater part of the fighting of today would take place in that quarter, the rebels having evacuated their position on their left and massed a heavy force on their right. I could distinctly see long lines of rebels moving in that direction on top of Missionary Ridge when I took my position. Our forces shifted to our left to meet this movement of the enemy. About 8 A. M. General Sherman opened a severe cannonade upon the rebel right and in about an hour charged upon the heights occupied by the rebels. I saw line after line climb the hill and from the heavy roar of musketry knew they were struggling nobly for the position. For some time I thought they had gained the heights but after a little while I saw our forces retreating down the hill. Heavy musketry was now heard on the rebel left which drew a considerable portion of the rebel force in that direction when Sherman's columns again ascended the hill. After a terrible struggle of more than an hour's duration, Sherman succeeded in gaining a foothold on the north end of Missionary Ridge.

About three o'clock P. M. the fighting became very heavy on the extreme rebel left and while the attention of the enemy was attracted in that direction the Army of the Cumberland with all its batteries moved up all along in front of Missionary Ridge. All the field batteries and also the heavy guns in Fort Wood opened upon the rebels on Missionary Ridge. This continued for near an hour when the Army of the Cumberland broke by heads of Demi-Brigades to the front and charged the enemy's rifle pits on the side of Missionary Ridge. We were just then peppering the side and top of Missionary Ridge with shells from every cannon that could be brought to bear and the rebels were showering down bombs from the top of the ridge upon our charging columns all together presenting one of the grandest spectacles ever seen.

Our charging columns plunged through the shower of death-dealing missiles hurled upon them and carried the rebel rifle pits.

They were proceeding to climb the hill when they were ordered back. They formed again and this time gained the summit taking the rebel batteries which poured a galling fire of grape and canister into their ranks.

Just as the sun was setting, the banners of our charging columns were planted all along on top of Missionary Ridge and the rebels were in full retreat.

The Third Kentucky had 56 enlisted men killed and wounded and seven officers wounded, one of whom, Adjt. G. D. Hunt, mortally.

Saturday, November 28, 1863: Our Division and other troops marched from here this evening to the relief of General Burnside now at Knoxville, threatened by overwhelming numbers of the enemy. Spent the day reading and cutting letters on head boards for the graves of those of our regiment who fell on Wednesday. Am in command of camp.

Sunday, May 8, 1864: Our regiment marched about a mile around on the left flank of Rocky Face Ridge and occupied a gap. Three forward skirmishes and soon brisk firing broke out all along the line. The 125th Ohio went out on a recognizance and succeeded in gaining the top of Rocky Face with the loss of four men killed and about twenty wounded. Colonel Opdyke sent word back that the rebs were thick in his front and advancing. The 79th Illinois was sent to his support. The 23rd A. C. joined on our left. Three or four of their Generals came to see us.

A little after noon, our regiment and the remaining regiments of our brigade marched up on top of Rocky Face. Here we had a fine view of the country for many miles on both sides. Saw three rebel forts and a number of lines of fortification which appeared to be occupied by rebel cavalry pickets only. Toward night however, the whole rebel army marched out of their camps about Dalton and bivouacked in Crow Valley down to our left. The camp fires of the two armies presented a spectacle magnificent beyond description. A little before sunset our regiment was sent on picket though relieved a little after dark, not being its time for picket.

Rebels fired a volley into us during the night and, though the balls pattered around us, none of us were hurt. Received a letter from Dan Collier. Glorious news from Grant's operations in Virginia.

Monday, May 9, 1864: When I awoke this morning, they were clearing a road to bring two pieces of artillery up the hill to batter down the fort in the ridge in front of us. Our brigade moved forward about sunrise. Heavy skirmishing was kept up all day by our advance, of which four companies of our regiment under Lieutenant Colonel Bullitt and Major Brennan constituted a part. Colonel Dunlap and I, under orders from General Hooker, remained with the six companies in reserve. Balls sang over us all day long, wounding a few of the reserve.

About noon, the 23rd A. C. moved in line of battle down Crow Valley and connected with the left of our Division. Our artillery was well handled though one of the pieces was so exposed to the enemy's sharp shooters it could not be used a great deal.

About 5 P. M., we received orders to the effect that General Wagner should charge a line of rifle pits on the side of the rebel fort next to Crow Valley and if he succeeded in carrying them, our Brigade (Harker's) was to charge directly on the fort. Our advance consisting of detachments from our regiment and the 64th Ohio and probably from another regiment or two of our Brigade were to take the lead when they saw us coming. Through some misunderstanding, Colonel McClain of the 64th started on the charge before we in the rear were ready for the assault. Our regiment and the 125th Ohio were to charge by the flank on top of the ridge, the 125th in advance of us, but as Colonel McClain and those with him had started, we were compelled to support them immediately. Our regiment happened to be nearest ready and started forward at once in double quick time following the charge of our advance detachments and followed by the 125th Ohio.

I brought up the rear of our regiment and pressed forward with all my might. I thought at the time I was nearly to the fort but found afterwards I did not get there by nearly one hundred yards. Met our men rushing to the rear and tried to rally them but, failing in that, joined them in the retreat. Some of our men got within thirty yards of the fort before they were repulsed. Wagner made a feeble demonstration on our left and fell back. Wood came up bravely on our right but was repulsed.

Left my haversack nearly as far up as I went towards the fort being too much exhausted to carry it. Received a painful stab in my right leg with a bayonet during the scramble on the charge. I, with some others, jumped over the bluff and returned on the west side in the retreat. Being crippled in both legs, I could not have gotten along very well had my retreat not been facilitated by some rebel sharp shooters in trees who made the balls sing about my ears. Thought the rebels would pursue and did not know how far our men would fall back so considered my chance for a berth in Libby pretty fair, but looking up the hill I saw the Stars and Stripes waving and made for them. Got nearly to the top of the hill when I sank entirely exhausted. Some of my men came down and helped me up the hill. Rested a few minutes, drank some coffee, and returned to the regiment (or the main body of those who remained together). Found they had only fallen back about 200 yards and were behind some works we had thrown up in the morning and were still pegging away at the rebels. Lieutenant Colonel Bullitt was very seriously wounded, Captain Bristow slightly wounded, though badly bruised. Four enlisted men were killed and 26 wounded out of our regiment. The Brigade lost thirty-one killed and 113 wounded. We were relieved a little after dark and retired about where we went into bivouac for the night.

Thursday, September 8, 1864: The train in charge of Lieutenant Worsham moved out to Decatur this morning. Bid Phil goodby and returned to my quarters. In the afternoon I walked to see the rebel works in front of the position we occupied while investing the city and after examining several forts and lines of works, I went over to the picket line which, from the twenty-second of July to the twenty-fifth day of August, was the scene of so many advances, dashes, demonstrations, sallies, etc. Found the trees cut up into splinters and minnie balls. Grape and canister and pieces of shell covered the ground to a depth of about a foot. This may seem a little extravagant to some people but it is necessary for them to see a piece of ground over which balls pattered like hail for thirty-three days and nights before they can form any just ideas of the traces left behind.

When I visited this spot it was lonely and deserted and an awful stillness prevailed. I visited many spots where I had seen many noble comrades fall dead or wounded and where I had stood myself in agonizing terror amid the roar of cannon, the crash of musketry, the hissing of minnie balls, and the shriek of huge shells that came with a mighty crash through the woods. I continued my lonely ramble musing upon the many thrilling scenes which had been there enacted and night came on before I was aware. It was with some reluctance at first that I turned my steps towards the city but all at once a feeling of superstitious horror came over me and I almost expected to see the fierce combatants spring up and resume their work of human slaughter. Alone in the dark woods with an imagination crowded with scenes of horror which every spot upon which I turned my eyes suggested, I began to feel about as uncomfortable as Ichabod Crane did when he found it necessary to whistle in order to keep up his courage and I was as truly glad to get away from there as ever I was upon any one of my former visits.

Returned to the city—got lost in the streets and met guards at every crossing some of whom detained me some time and each one giving different directions with regard to the direction of my quarters so I did not find them until late bed time. Found a plateful of sweet potatoes sitting in my window which I soon dispatched and laid my weary frame down to rest.

1864: A band of marauders under one Preston Huff, numbering 7 to 9 came to Monticello on the twenty-second of November. They first got beastly drunk then prowled around attempting to kill a number of citizens and greatly abusing a great many others.

After dark they obtained axes and went about town breaking open the doors of the stores and groceries. Merchants abandoned their stores to the mercy of these fiends in human shape who helped themselves to more than a thousand dollars worth of goods and destroyed much more. They prowled about the streets like demons, shooting at every man that showed himself until late bedtime, when they drew up in front of Mr. Huffaker's brick building and fired more than hundred shots at it, mostly at the windows of the corner room occupied by Mr. E. Layton. They were trying to kill Mr. L. P. Baker. After this, left town promising to return soon. Nearly every man in town procured some kind of weapon, prepared to act in concert, but they never returned.

Saturday, April 15, 1865: Left Stanford on stage this morning and proceeded to Danville where I took breakfast at the Chiles House after which took stage for Nicholasville, thence the cars for Lexington where I took dinner at the Phoenix Hotel, after which took the cars for Frankfort my destination, the purpose of my trip being to superintend the mustering out of Companies C, D, and E of the 30th Kentucky Mounted Infantry.

At Camp Nelson heard the report that President Lincoln had been assassinated at a theatre in Washington last night but did not believe it. Upon arriving at Nicholasville heard the same report and some discussion as to its probable truth. It was not until my arrival at Lexington where I heard the whole matter talked over that I could bring my mind to a realization of the magnitude of the crime that had been perpetrated.

Sunday, April 16, 1865: Spent the day examining and arranging the papers of the 30th Kentucky except an hour or two spent with Mr. E. L. Van Winkle during which time we took a walk up to the cemetery. The death of President Lincoln is fully confirmed and the deepest feeling is everywhere manifested.

Monday, April 17, 1865: The Capitol and other public buildings as well as most of the principal business houses and offices in Frankfort are draped in mourning and the deepest sorrow seems to prevail everywhere. I was very busy all day working on the rolls of the 30th.

[Here ends the diary of Captain Tuttle.]

---

Captain Tuttle is eulogized by a friend, in the following article in the *Kentucky Courier*, Mt. Sterling:

"Outstanding among the many prominent and older citizens of Monticello was Captain John W. Tuttle, a well-known and respected officer of the Federal army in the Civil War, and later studied and practiced law as his chosen profession in life. Captain Tuttle was well educated in the best schools and colleges of the country, a ready and versatile historian and literary genius, a fluent speaker and writer; progressive in the business affairs of his town and county, and a citizen of most commendable civic pride, using his time and talents willingly for the upbuilding of his own community, and for ideals which would advance his county, state and country. Captain Tuttle was also the friend to all young men, struggling for an education and start in life. It was through his efforts, influence and management, that the names, heroic services and sacrifice of the young men of Wayne County who lost their health and lives in the World War have been honored and remembered by the erection of a worthy and fitting Doughboy Memorial at the cost of $5,000, which stands in the center of the Public Square at Monticello. Prominent in the councils of the Republican party, high in the esteem and confidence of the National Administration when of the party, Captain Tuttle held positions of trust and responsibility with his State and Government, which necessitated frequent trips to Washington City, even in his old age. (He was our friend in our earliest boyhood.)"—J. W. Hall.

Ephraim L. Van Winkle, Secretary of State in Kentucky during the Civil War, was from Wayne County. He died before the expiration of his term, and his brother, John S. Van Winkle, was appointed to fill the unexpired period. He was an emancipationist, believing the institution of slavery a blot on the nation. The following letter to a relative in Monticello gives his views on the subject:

Frankfort, Kentucky,<br>Decr. 27th, 1863.

Dear Juan,

I rec'd your very kind letter several days ago and have to say in reply that I was happy to learn of you that you were all well & that my hopeful son was at school doing well. I don't know how to send him a present as there is no way of getting it to him. I bought you an album as requested, quite an elegant

BATTLE OF MILL SPRING, KENTUCKY, JANUARY 19, 1862

one for the price & am sure you will be pleased with it. Tuttle had no way of taking it or it would have reached you ere this. I will if I have an opportunity, place the photograph of your humble servant in front. I think, however, to have it well done I will have to wait until I go to Louisville as this operator here is not first rate as I understand.

I have placed the photograph of Mrs. Douglas in the album which you can remove if you wish. I indexed her for No. 2 which will place her on the same leaf with mine, tho on opposite sides. I can get you a number of Major Generals if you like it, yet I fear they will not suit you, not because they are military men, but because they have had something to do with the establishment of "Abrahamic Sins." What a pity it is that St. Paul was not the friend of slavery. If he had been doubtless many who have imbibed prejudices against that institution would not have had their moral sensibilities shocked by its presence in our good country. Did it ever occur to you that there are many good people, earnest and honest, that differ with us radically upon many questions of Statesmanship and that we always allow them an honest difference until we reach the great question of slavery at which point we burst forth with indignant denunciation of rascal, scoundrel, hypocrite and "Abolition Dog." Why is this—Is slavery of such a doubtful and uncertain moral right that we fear discussion; does an opinion, honestly entertained, that it ought to be abandoned degrade the mind and moral nature of the man who so regards the true policy of the country? If so, to entertain the opposite opinion ought to elevate and ennoble human nature. Jefferson Davis *et id omne genus* will soon reach the point of human perfectability and a grateful country will in due season deify the great apostles of "A more refined civilization" and to secure the permanent elevation of our morals and manners, we will turn our great Navy into slavers and make the ocean groan with captives from the coast of Africa & upon the sand coasts of that benighted region we will hold high carnival around the bloody altars of "Dahomey." What boots it if we do tear asunder husband & wife, mother and child & fill the air with the lamentations of human woe? It matters not, they are but poor ignorant negroes. Mark you, whenever I become the aider and abettor of the extension of human bondage, may a righteous God strike me with his wrath as a cumberer of the Earth and as one who has lost all high and manly views of right and given over to judicial blindness, etc.

Well, Juan, I have said more than I ought to have done about politics, yet I felt tempted by your remark about "Abrahamic Sins" to run the thing down and see at whose door rested the great load that now hangs down my beloved country, and now that I have placed it upon the right head, I will pass to more agreeable topics. I have had quite a merry Christmas considering that my engagements have been very burdensome. Have been at three dinner parties, one at the Governor's, and one at Crittenden's, and another at my under secretary's, J. R. Page. At each place was assembled the youth and beauty of the Capitol; gayety and festivity as a matter of course was the order of the day. At the Governor's, I had to act as assistant host and you may imagine it was no light task. I, however, got through like a French dancing master, or worse, and have in the end to count quite a number of new and agreeable acquaintances, male and female, as the result of my labors. Up to this time, however, have seen but few of the unmarried part of our population. Next week they will all be at the Governor's when I will take notes and give you the result of my judgments upon the most conspicuous. Miss Locky Malone is spending the winter with the Governor. I have made her acquaintance and have taken her round to several places. She is not the gay, dashing widow I had supposed her to be, but quiet, retired, modest and not fond of strangers or gay company.

I wish you could be here and take a whirl with us during the winter. Next winter you can do so without doubt and I will try and have made a sufficient number of acquaintances to aid you in getting a good start, unless you take a foolish notion to marry before that time rolls around. If Bennet could get out I really believe it would be a gone case with them from the horrors of this war. I would let the American people drive the atrocious scoundrel into the ocean but this reparation cannot be made and I therefore go for conservative measures for the purpose of obtaining the return of *law* and *order* and the *repose of the nation.* It is for this I am a conservative, not that I wish to help the cold-blooded conclave who have deliberately involved in ruin the homes of millions in order that they might open the seas to the traffic in human souls & perpetuate the spread and growth of human slavery. I am not the man who would interfere with slavery. I am for law and order but .... more anon.

Yours Truly,<br>
E. L. VAN WINKLE.

The above letter was written to the young sister of Van Winkle's wife who had died sometime before the foregoing letter was written.

John Castillo, a young soldier in the Union Army, in his letters to friends at home, very clearly though unintentionally, expresses the average soldier's feeling about war and its utter futility. All he wanted was "to meet his rebel friends in peace." From three letters the following extracts are made:

Wilmington, North Carolina<br>
March 3rd, 1865.

Dear Cousin,

I am sorry that I could not answer your letter sooner but you must not think that it has been carelessly neglected, for I have written two letters and could not send them until they were too old to send, for our mail is not regular now and there are but few chances to get our letters off. But, cousin, I have but little news to tell you for we have got clear out of the world at last, or at least out of the civilized part of the world, for North Carolina is not inhabited by anything now but alligators and Negroes, with a few crocodiles. The country around Wilmington is nothing but a swamp. In fact, the whole state is nothing but swamps and sandy plains with no timber except pines. It is just the place to get lampblack. I wish you could have seen me the other day, for we had been on the march for several days through the swamps and at night lay down by a pine fire in the sand. I don't know but I guess you would have taken me to be an American citizen of a foreign descent, and I expect that we will be on the march again soon in the direction of Goldsboro, for our brigade has been released from post duty here by a brigade of the 24th Corps. Cousin, it looks like we are getting the Rebs in a terrible close place and if you don't do something for the Confederacy, it will go up the spout soon I think. I wish something could be done to stop the war and it will not stop until the Confederacy has played out and I fear that will be some time yet though at this time the prospect looks well for a speedy end to this war . . . .

> Camp of 12th Ky. Vols. Infry., 1st Brig., 3rd Div., 23rd Army Corps, Goldsboro, North Carolina, March 23rd, 1865.

My Dear Cousin,

This morning affords one the time and opportunity to answer your kind letter which I received the other day, but being under marching orders I could not write until our march was ended which was completed the 2nd day. We arrived here on the night of the 21st, General Sherman on the 23rd. On the arrival of the latter 15 guns were fired and three big cheers given them by the boys of the 23rd Corps and at 4 o'clock P. M. on the same day had a general review of the 23rd Corps. The talk is that our Division is to remain here for some time. I would be glad that it would be the case for I am tired of marching so much for I lost my pony as we came here and I have been afoot on all the marches since we have been in this state and we have traveled 200 miles; but I intend to get me a critter before long, then they may go when they see proper. I will not mind the march then unless they march at night. I don't like to march after night. I had always rather sleep 2 nights than march one. When we leave here I suppose we will go towards Richmond unless Mr. Lee starts us back towards Wilmington. I don't think that he can do that and hold Richmond for we have got a big army here now; the cars are running from here to Wilmington. A train has just arrived and I am looking for some mail from some of your Wayne folks . . . .

April 9, 1865.

.... I will this evening try to write to you as this will be the last opportunity I will have for a few days as we will set out on another campaign tomorrow. I have no news that would suit you, that is of any importance for I know that the downfall of the Rebel Capital and the capture of 23,000 prisoners with 500 cannons would not be very interesting to you. General Lee is making for Danville, Va., where Jeff. Davis and his cabinet are. His men are deserting by thousands and going to their homes. General Grant is in pursuit. General Sherman will now wake up Mr. Johnson who is lying here close at hand with a good big fire.

You never heard the like of cheers as was given last night by our army. They kept it up all night. Shooting off guns and beating of drums, shooting sky rockets in the air. Brigadier General Riley left us for his home yesterday. He came to the Brigade, the regulars all got in line and he bade adieu to his old command. The brigade gave him nine cheers. I had almost forgot to tell you about us having preaching this evening. It was the first sermon I had heard for many a day. We will have preaching regular now as we have a chaplain in the brigade. His name is George W. Johnson. He is from Maysville. I expect that I have told you enough about the war for one time but I can't think of any thing else to write about. You say the Wayne Rebs are all exchanged. They had better stayed North awhile longer for they stand a good chance to be recaptured now. It may be that I will get to see them down here. I would like to see them very much if in peace but I don't want to see them other wise ....

August 9, 1865.

.... I will continue my letter over another sheet of paper as it was my good luck to get a letter from you last night.

I had just written you a letter yesterday and had it sealed and ready to send you this morning and as I got your letter last evening, I concluded to answer it and send two together. I have got no news to write and so I will just answer your questions as nigh as I can.

Well, in the first place, you want to know if we have Atlanta yet. I will answer, no, and we ain't working much at it. We are trying to cut off the Macon Road; and are getting very close to the road but it may cost us more to go that short distance than it has to go several miles. I can hear the rebs cuss this morning very plain. They seem to be doing something; they are either leaving or reinforcing. I don't know which. For my part I wish they would leave for I am getting very tired of this campaign for it is the longest one I ever saw. I have been in it nearly two months and I am getting very tired of it and some have been in more than three months. In the second place, you want to know if we have any Negro Regiment down here. We have one that I saw. I don't know of any other. We have none in our department and I hope we may never have. You say that Uncle Abe has called for 500,000 more men and you want to know what we want with them as we have most got them whipped. Well, for myself, I don't think they are whipped and more than that I don't think they ever will give up under the present administration and all the hope I have is that McClellan will be our next President. You must vote for him for me and do all you can and if he is our next President I think all will soon be right again, but if we have an abolition president I don't believe we ever will have peace if we had every man in the North called out . . . .
—J. Castillo.

---

When the dread tocsin of war had echoed through the land, it struck two hearts in different keys. Two brothers said, "Goodbye," and one took his way to the North. The other went South. The mother watched them go with sadness in her heart, fearful yet hopeful that both would return. They did. When the bitter struggle was over, William McBeath came back in the resplendent uniform of a Major in the Federal Army. His brother Anthony trudged home in the tattered outfit of the defeated Confederates.

William arrived first, and as good a dinner as could be provided was prepared to celebrate his return. While they were seated at the table, they looked out and saw Anthony approaching in his rags, with what was known as a "taterhill" hat on his head. This was too much for his sister, Susan. She burst into tears and ran, weeping, from the room.

These two young men symbolized the great struggle of brother against brother, that wracked the land for four long years. William was made Commandant of a fort in Wyoming, to guard against an Indian uprising. Anthony took upon himself the task of rehabilitation of his mother's farm.

Wayne County suffered lightly in comparison with some other sections. Some of the gallant lads, both Union and Confederate, never returned, but time passed, the horror was forgotten, life went on again in an even, uninterrupted stream.

There was no bitterness. Captain Tuttle, as long as he lived, jocularly referred to his friends who were Southern sympathizers as "Secesh," and their children were greeted humorously and hospitably as "Rebels." The Unionists, by the more rebellious Confederates, were cheerfully denominated "Damyanks." But a more harmonious community would be hard to find, where common ties soon adjusted the differences of "the North and the South."

# STAGE-COACH DAYS IN WAYNE

## CHAPTER VIII

*"No d—d bullock shall obstruct the United States Mail."*

THUS LARKIN DECATUR EDGE, with a fine disregard for his pious upbringing, flourished his whip and sent the coach rocking into a drove of cattle that Messrs. Cecil and Kendrick were sending along the Monticello-Burnside road to points north to market. Lark Edge was a scholar and a wit as the above quotation proves. He was familiar with Roman history and his drolleries relieved the tedium for many a passenger on the five-hour ride to, or from, Burnside to Monticello. He came of good Quaker stock in Pennsylvania, but the exigencies of life in the backwoods had somewhat tempered his forbearance.

Through cold and snows of winter and summer's rains and heat he came daily bringing the United States mail and an occasional passenger. He rose at unseemly hours to get off in the morning in time to catch the train going north, at Burnside, and, remaining to get the mail from the southbound train, he was often very late returning, bearing the news from the outside world before the days of telephone and radio. He was an expert driver and there was showmanship in the way he went around the hairpin curve down to the ferry at Burnside, the timid passenger holding on with closed eyes, expecting to find himself in the Cumberland River when he opened them. But his skill took them safely around and no accident ever occurred. His rugged weatherbeaten face was always pleasant and the laughter wrinkles at the corners of eyes and mouth betrayed his sense of humor. Yet it was good-natured humor and he knew the drovers could easily assemble their scattered drove again.

He was employed by J. W. Hall, whose advertisement appears in the *Monticello Signal*, 1884 and 1885:

## Monticello & Burnside Mail Stage Line

Stage leaves Monticello daily at 6 a. m. and arrives at Burnside at 11 a. m., returning, leaves Burnside at 1:30 p. m. and arrives at Monticello at 7 p. m.

J. W. Hall & Son, Proprietors.

By this time the road had been macadamized from Burnside to Monticello with the exception of a stretch, about four miles, between Frazer and Bronston, which, in bad weather, was almost impassable. This must have tried Edge's patience as much as the Stanford-Somerset road over which he drove the stage in the seventies.

According to Mr. Coleman, the Stanford *Interior-Journal*, of February 5, 1875, quotes him thus: "Larkin Edge says a man can't drive a stage from here to Somerset and be a Christian. The mud is so deep and the road so long that a Christian man would lose all patience with himself before he got to Waynesburg. After he reached that point, Job, himself, would get out of heart before he reached his destination."

After the Halls came the Burtons—Mack Burton, the most obliging man imaginable and later Charlie Burton, the most polite and efficient. He owned and drove the last stage-coach in use in the United States, a museum piece today used only on such occasions as the opening of the new Burnside bridge. This coach was loaned to the exposition at Detroit but the Burton family will not sell it.

Droves of cattle, horses, mules, sheep, and hogs could be seen any day along this highway always going north, under their own power.

This was an industry that throve without railways. Sheep raising was carried on extensively in the vicinity of Monticello. The Phillips family had grown prosperous with this as one line of endeavor, and the "Sheep Lot" still identifies a tract on the old Micajah Phillips farm just south of Monticello. Here the sheep were assembled for driving to Burnside after the old Cincinnati Southern had been extended that far in the 80's. Before that the nearest railroad point was Stanford or Lexington.

The Oatts Brothers developed a thriving trade in horses and mules, sending them to Augusta, Georgia, for the southern market.

Messrs. Cecil and Kendrick had a prosperous mercantile business by 1830. Merchandise of all kinds was hauled by wagon from the Louisville wholesale houses. The Cecil of the firm was Granville Cecil who moved to Boyle County and amassed a fortune. The Kendrick was William, affectionately known as "Uncle Billy," who died in Wayne leaving a vast landed estate. Some of the elder Phillips's also had a mercantile business and Joshua Berry long carried on a trade in general merchandise. These all flourished in spite of difficulties of transportation that made prices high. All merchandise was brought by wagons from Louisville.

Jefferson County records for 1810 show that Jacob Shearer was licensed as common carrier, with Christian Shearer as partner. Thereafter he operated a wagon train from Louisville to Monticello until about 1840 bringing merchandise, farming implements, furniture, etc. It was a laborious undertaking requiring hardihood and intelligence, and the people were indebted to the Shearers for many necessities and luxuries brought from the metropolitan markets.

The following extract from the *Signal,* January 13, 1887, is an index to the value of the horse and mule industry in Wayne County:

"During the last two weeks eleven carloads of stock have been shipped from this county. They were mostly two and three year old mules. There were some extra saddle and harness horses.

"The Oatts Brothers shipped three cars to Augusta; Dr. Phillips, Rucker Kendrick and J. P. Ingram shipped three cars to Atlanta; Granville Duncan, Shelby Ragan and the Miller Brothers, shipped three cars to Atlanta; Lewis Coffey and B. C. Berry shipped two cars to Atlanta. These eleven carloads would have averaged over $100 per head on the market here. There are several carloads of stock in the county to be shipped yet and the total sales of the mule market will amount to over $100,000."

An account book purchased by Micajah Phillips for recording minutes of the first Common School Commissioners cost seventy-five cents in 1837. In these days of mass production and easy transportation it could be bought for ten cents.

At that time coffee was fifty cents per pound, sugar equally high. A calico dress pattern was worth five dollars.

Even with these prices prevailing, the ladies kept themselves dressed in the style of the period.

A letter from a young lady of eighteen visiting in Crab Orchard (known to old inhabitants as "the Orchard") to her sister back in Monticello tells of the fashions of the day:

Crab Orchard,<br>August 4, 1866.

".... There is so much excitement up over the success of the Democratic Party. They have kindled a bonfire and have been speaking and yelling. Oh, you never heard the like.

"There is a crowd here dancing downstairs and two or three have been up after me . . . . two or three more have come after me so I must go down and I'll steal time to finish after awhile . . . .

"It's 2 o'clock and the ball has just closed. They are still whooping and yelling out in town on account of the election. I've been very busy. Made me a calico dress. Aunt Sarah helped me. Made me a beautiful Bishop lawn, two ruffles round the skirt a finger length wide and a ruffle across the shoulders. It is so pretty. It is open behind. So many dresses open behind and ruffles on everything, one, two, and three and five . . . ."

In those early days it was the custom for young couples to ride horseback to Mammoth Cave on a wedding journey. In a letter written in 1853 by Emily Worsham Hardin she says:

"All that is talked about here [in Monticello] is weddings. I will tell you who are going to marry the 1st of September and start to Mammoth Cave. It is Julia Frisbie and Mr. Burton, Gord Hayden and Tine Frisbie, Harriet Phillips and John Frisbie and Mary Mills and Doctor Hall. Vi Long married the little Buckner that lived at Mr. Hendersons . . . . These are such scary looking times. We will not raise more than enough corn to bread us. Some will not even do that . . . . I have had four blankets wove. They weigh a pound to the yard. Pink and Jim [Mr. and Mrs. Jim Oatts] stayed all night with me the other night. They are going to be close neighbors. They have bought Mr. Allen's farm, Negroes and all. Ellen [Mrs. Braxton Carter] is staying at the tavern now. I have not seen her for some time. Gran and Betty [Mr. and Mrs. Granville Worsham] are going to start south in about three weeks.

"Leo [Hayden] has gone to Texas. He went home with Billy Crisp. You ask whether we are going to move away from the farm. We came very near selling to Mr. Will Meadows this spring . . . .

"It has been very dry. All the neighbors come to our spring for water. Father's spring is nearer dry than it was ever known to be . . . .

"The children and black ones all send their love. Di says tell you she had one beau since you left but she did not have her hair slicked up and did not have on her 'Sundays.' Little Martha is learning to spell at home, she can spell very well in four letters . . . ."

By 1860, M. D. Hardin had sold his farm and come into Monticello. He had bought the tavern which stood on the southeast corner of the square. After the war, about 1870, he bought from Major Neal the house near the courthouse and kept a tavern there until 1889. This house, a log structure that had been weatherboarded and had a wing added, burned in the fire of 1897.

In the 60's and 70's, Monticello was a village of 300 inhabitants. There were more families of distinction in proportion to population than any other town in the state. These families produced men of exceptional qualities. In addition to the numerous descendants of Joshua Jones, that fine old pioneer, the Cecil, Kendrick, Phillips, Saufley, Chrisman, Buster, Cullom, Van Winkle, Tuttle, Stone, Huffaker, Ingram, Cooper and other families already named, produced some distinguished men. Here was no rude frontier life, but an urbanity surprising to outsiders. In a letter from Samuel L. Duncan, of Nicholasville, to Mrs. Mary Cecil Cantrell, copied in an earlier chapter, he names some of the men of this period. Three outstanding men, to him, were Doctor Frisbie, Elder William Simpson, and Joshua Buster.

The lawyers of this period are discussed by Judge James A. Phillips in an article in a previous chapter. Some of these were distinguished. James S. Chrisman was delegate to the Confederate Convention at Russellville. He was also Confederate Congressman. He had been a member of the United States House of Representatives and a delegate to the State Constitutional Convention of 1849. He had married Lucy Bell, descendant of Dr. Ephraim McDowell. His sister, Emily, was the mother of Judge M. C. Saufley of Stanford. Hon. Shelby Cullom had moved to Illinois where he was governor and later United States Senator. John Catron had moved to Tennessee where he became Judge of the State Supreme Court and later was appointed a Justice of the Supreme Court of the United States by Andrew Jackson. Captain John W. Tuttle, a superior lawyer, literary man, and gentleman in every sense of the word gave conspicuous service in the Union Army. Sherrod Williams, a brilliant but erratic man, moved to Mississippi. Tom McBeath, a man of great ability, moved to Florida, where he became president of the Florida State College. Mark McBeath was long National Committeeman from Mississippi. Robert McBeath was Superintendent of Schools for Wayne County.

In an article *Stage-coach Days in Kentucky*, J. W. Hall gives a picture of life at that time:

## STAGE-COACH DAYS IN KENTUCKY

"It was in the mild October weather of 1875, when we left the old home in Wayne County, Kentucky, destined for some point in the famous bluegrass region, in pursuit of better educational advantage and opportunity, and where the ambitious, anxious and willing student could work his way in school. The distance from the old home to the nearest railroad point, Maywood, on the L. & N. near Stanford, was about 75 miles. This, the first part of our journey, was made in a two-horse, covered wagon, belonging to a wealthy uncle, merchant and farmer of the home county. 'Uncle Jim,' the colored driver and former slave of the rich uncle, was quite pleasant and agreeable, had made many trips to this railroad, shipping point, hauling goods and merchandise, and was familiar of course with the country and roads through the woods and hills. So, armed and equipped with a little black valise, containing a few items of clothing, a testimonial from the citizens of Monticello, a very little money, and a box of cooked ham, some sweet cakes and pies, and plenty of sugar and ground coffee, which our Mother and Aunt had so kindly prepared, 'Uncle Jim' and I were slated to leave on a certain day. The trip to Maywood by covered wagon means of transportation, required about three days. We camped at night on the road, convenient to some spring. 'Uncle Jim' made good coffee, prepared the meals, set the table, and otherwise made the trip safe and pleasant. We slept comfortably and cozily together in the covered wagon, among sacks of ginseng, boxes, chestnuts and the pelts of fox, raccoon, opossum and other fur-bearing animals. It is true that this improvised and unique sleeping room was not saturated with the perfume of geranium and the attar of roses, but when you come to think about it more seriously, it was simply the best we could do, and why should we now complain?

"The familiar scenes surrounding the old home, the view of mountain range, densely wooded valleys, forest-covered hills, sparkling streams of rivulet and cascade, the gorgeous and panoramic pictures of autumnal colors through which we had traveled for three days, are all left behind. On reaching the depot and railroad station at Maywood, the outlook and aspect of all nature had now seemed changed to a new world. This point was just a short distance from the well-known Hall's Gap hill, overlooking a wide area of Bluegrass fields and farms. Here again, we became intensely interested on seeing our first railroad passenger train, and perhaps no more so, than all others, who at some time in life, had seen their first railroad train. Here, too, we bid goodbye and good luck to 'Uncle Jim' and bought a ticket for our first 5-mile ride in a passenger coach, from Maywood to Stanford in the month of October, 1875. Besides being a very great improvement on the ox-cart and horse-drawn covered wagon of the early day, this first experience of the new method of travel is now worth relating. This first 5-mile ride in a passenger coach produced even a greater thrill perhaps than the first airplane flight of some people in 1931. But we can not now speak from experience of airplane travel, yet we must here confess, that while riding the first 5 miles in a passenger coach, we caught ourself actually 'leaning up hill' when the train was swinging around sharp curves. This, of course, was very thoughtful on our part, to give the train the advantage of our weight, and thus prevent it from turning over at the curves. Well, now, that was a truthful experience, and we are willing to stand the expense of the joke. We all have to learn, and partly from just such embarrassing and trying experiences. In 1875, airplane travel, vitaphone music and radio communication were not even dreamed of by the most visionary.

"If we remember correctly, Stanford was reached late in the afternoon. Our old, colored friend, 'Uncle Jim' was on the return homeward, and we began to realize that we were out in the cold world among total strangers, farther from home than we ever had been; that we had but very little money, and that 'traveling' away from home meant expense and a heavy draw on this small amount of ready funds. Under these circumstances we must think quickly and honorably, plan for the best and wisest course, then proceed and act accordingly. So, we thought of the name of a good farmer, living on the Danville pike, just two miles out from Stanford, who was an old friend and former neighbor of our father in Wayne County. We decided to go out to his home and spend the night. Then, loading the little black grip on our shoulder, we started out afoot on the old turnpike road, and coming surprisingly to a pole across the pike, the first 'toll-gate' we had ever seen, and believing it meant 'pay' we stopped, set our grip down, and asked the lady gate-keeper what we should pay to pass under the pole or through the gate. She replied with a sympathetic smile, 'nothing at all, for one traveling as humbly as you, there is no charge.' But here let us speak again in self-defense, for honest simplicity, the unsophisticated, genuine quality of innocent character will show itself, even in these modern days of the smart set of young thieves, social sheiks, murderers, and highwaymen, who would laugh in scorn at the reading of these lines. The trouble with this class of young men of the present age and generation is the want of real principle, as a basic and sure foundation on which to build real character. They neither study nor work, for either an education or a living. They want money to spend foolishly and unwisely in the many ways of idleness and frivolity, but not honorable, willing and independent enough to work for it. Too many idlers and non-producers among both sexes of this modern generation.

"After a short visit with Mr. Hubbard at his home on the Danville pike, our former friend and neighbor from Wayne County, we returned to Stanford for our second train ride. The line of the Knoxville branch of the L. & N. railroad extended probably, and was completed no farther than Livingston in Rockcastle County, but our 20-mile route was over the Richmond branch to Paint Lick, thence 4 miles by mail-hack to the village of Kirksville, Madison County. This point then, was our first objective in prospect and pursuit of scholastic advantage and opportunity, for Kirksville at that time had a real High School, an Academy for both sexes worthy of the name. Here we made our first business deal in the way of school work, with the principal, Prof. Milton Elliott, one of Kentucky's greatest teachers in his day. In the trade with Prof. Elliott, his terms of agreement and contract were binding, but generous and liberal in favor of the young man, who was strictly honest, anxious and willing to work for an education. He very kindly assisted us here in securing a nice boarding-place with a wealthy farmer, who lived only one-half mile from the school building, where we could pay the full account for board expense by working mornings, evenings and Saturdays. This new job meant the doing of chores about the home, cutting stove wood, making fires, milking the cows, feeding mules and other stock about the barns, and on Saturday, driving a wagon and hauling corn and pumpkins from the farm. At night we had a large comfortable room, good lights and books, and plenty of time for study in preparing our lessons for class next day. Many of the older citizens of Madison County, and elsewhere in the State, where he conducted fine schools, will most kindly remember Prof. Milton Elliott, not only for his strict

discipline, remarkable and exceptional ability as a teacher, but for his high sense of honor and integrity, justice and obedience, and for his lofty dignity and high standing as a Christian minister. Those pleasant and profitable school days under his direction and management and happy associations are well remembered."
—*J. W. Hall.*

---

Life was pleasant in those days with neighborly attentions in sickness and distress, and graciousness in social contacts.

These were free high-spirited people quick to resent a slight yet generous to forgive, and disagreement was often settled summarily by a fight, ending in a handshake. Captain Tuttle tells some amusing stories of those days.

James Hardin, a young attorney, partner of Tuttle, was an exuberant young fellow. Standing one day with some other young men on the street, he saw a barrel of salt lying near the side door of a store. Jumping up, he turned somersault over the barrel, landing on his feet on the other side, a feat of great agility.

He looked around for the applause to follow. Dr. C. A. Cox said, "that's nothing, a cow could have done it." Hardin retorted: "A jackass couldn't." Said Cox: "A jackass did." Whereupon Hardin was at him and they fought with fists until, satisfied the insult was avenged on both sides, they shook hands and left in complete friendliness.

On another occasion says the Captain, I played cards till far into the night, winning straight along. The next morning I called upon my opponent for a settlement.

"You treated me in a very ungentlemanly manner last night," said this opponent, M. D. Hardin. "You're a liar," said the Captain. Whereupon "Mr. Hardin knocked me down and we fought, gouging and kicking each other until we were tired. Then we shook hands and forgot the whole thing."

These were gentlemen of the old school and this was a sort of *code duello* by which satisfaction was secured.

But tragedy stalked into the county on more than one occasion. In 1886 the whole county was horrified by the story of Prewitt's crime. He had held a grievance against a man named Jarvis for some time and going to Jarvis's home in the eastern part of the county he brutally slaughtered both Jarvis and his wife. Their son, a child, escaped and ran a mile to a neighbor and spread the alarm. He was quickly apprehended and trial with conviction followed. It cannot be doubted that Prewitt was criminally insane. The *Monticello Signal* of January 13, 1887, gives an account of the hanging from which the following extract is taken:

"The hanging of Granville Prewitt brought the largest crowd to town to-day that has been here for many years. It was estimated at 4,000 persons and probably this was too small. They began to come in last night and the hotels and livery stables were crowded. This morning strange faces were seen on the streets by sunrise. They came from all over the County and adjoining counties. Some even from Tennessee were present. A more excited and anxious throng was never seen. The crowd was surging and pushing each other from one side of the town to the other all day. Whenever any little commotion would arise the whole mass of surging humanity would rush thither with eager expectation of seeing the doomed Prewitt.

"The gallows was erected in the rear of the court-house yard, around which was an enclosure, rising two feet above the platform. Everything was visible to the eager spectators until after the trap was sprung.

"The beam to which the rope was fastened was 16 feet high and the scaffold 7 feet high and 8 feet square. The fall was 4 feet and the rope with which he was hanged was $7/8$ of an inch.

"There was scarcely a standing place unoccupied for 30 yards around the gallows. Every tree, house-top and fence was covered and so thickly that one barn-top was completely crushed in.

"Only 60 were permitted to enter the enclosure; tickets for which were at a premium, selling at $5.00 . . . .

"Since the organization of the county only four men have suffered the penalty of judicial execution within its borders. The first was David Gibbs convicted of the murder of Roger Oatts, an old and respected citizen of the county. Gibbs shot Oatts from an ambush in the woods.

"He was convicted upon purely circumstantial evidence. One of the incidents tending to his conviction is often referred to as showing that 'murder will out.' Upon the ground near the scene of the crime was found a piece of half-burned red cloth, which had been used as wadding in the gun that fired the fatal shot. It was then remembered by some one, and upon the trial proved, that on the day of the killing Gibbs had purchased in town some red cloth known as turkey red, and of this the scorched wadding was found to be a sample. One witness testified to hearing the shot and exclaiming, 'There's Dave Gibbs's old musket, he must be hunting.' These incidents with others, confirmatory and corroborating in their nature, convicted Gibbs.

"He was driven in a wagon to the place of execution and the wagon was stopped immediately under the gallows. The rope being adjusted around his neck, the wagon was driven from under him. Just before he lost his footing, he sprang into the air, succeeding, as he intended, in breaking his neck.

"A negro about 21 years of age was the next victim of the gallows in the county. He was convicted of raping a 12-year-old daughter of one John George Hubbard, a carpenter who formerly lived in this place.

"The assault was committed under circumstances of especial and peculiar atrocity and well merited the severest penalty known to the law.

"William Ayres next atoned—in the feeble measure which an assassin's death can atone—for the brutal murder of a young man named Daffron, son of 'Uncle' Hayne Daffron, of this county. Daffron had returned home from the Confederate Army with a disabled arm, which had withered away until he was unable to use it, as the result of a gunshot wound.

"Ayres was a member of a band of Union guerrillas and together with a man named Jesse Bell, went to the home of young Daffron and cruelly murdered him. Daffron, with his one arm grasped the gun of the murderer and averted its muzzle for a short time while he prayed for his life. His prayer was without avail, and he fell the victim of as bloodthirsty a spirit as ever expiated a life of crime upon the gallows.

"Ayres left this immediate country at the close of the war. The father of the murdered man learned, six or seven years afterward, that Ayres was in Bowling Green, Ky. Going thither, he recognized him upon the street, had him arrested and brought here, where he was tried, convicted and executed.

"His companion, Bell, was also arrested and would have suffered the same fate had not Ayres after conviction and sentence sawed through the bars of the jail and made his escape.

"He was gone several months, making his way as far as Peoria, Illinois, at which point he was arrested and brought back. During his absence Bell was tried and the County Attorney, believing Ayres had made good his escape and disliking to take the life of Bell, who was but a principal in the second degree, while the chief offender went unwhipped from justice, told the jury he would be content with a verdict of 21 years in the penitentiary which verdict they returned. Thus Bell escaped.

"The execution of Granville Prewitt yesterday completes the dark chapter."

John Bartleson, a splendid citizen, was killed June 8, 1889, in an argument with Thomas Bates who was intoxicated. His son, Emerson Bates, running up to protect his father struck Mr. Bartleson, killing him, bringing gloom and sadness to the whole county.

March 3, 1865, an act of Legislature authorized the County Court of Wayne County to sell the courthouse.

This courthouse was in the center of the square. It had been built of logs in 1801 and a brick courthouse had later been added in front facing north. The courthouse was sold but it was not until 1876 that an act was passed that enabled the county to raise funds by sale of bonds to build a new courthouse.

In that year Milburn and Milburn, architects, drew plans for the building which burned in 1898 where the present courthouse stands.

On February 3, 1818, the Legislature had passed an act to establish a bank "to be denominated the Monticello Bank, in Wayne County with a capital stock of $100,000 to be divided into 1000 shares of $100 each, and books shall be opened in the town of Monticello on the first Monday in April next under the direction of George Berry, Hardin M. Weatherford, Abel Shrewsbury and Thomas Heaven, and books shall be kept open sixty days unless the stock shall be sooner taken." As far as it has been possible to learn nothing further was done toward establishment of a bank under these provisions but the effort bears witness today to the enterprise and indomitable spirit of the citizens.

Just after the Civil War a branch of the Commercial Bank of Kentucky was organized at Monticello through the efforts of William Kendrick. It was superseded by the National Bank of Monticello with M. S. Wilhite cashier. This continued from 1872 to 1877. After this Mr. Kendrick operated a private bank for a short time.

From that time, citizens of Wayne transacted business through the Somerset banks until 1894 when the Monticello Banking Company was organized.

The first newspaper published in Wayne County was the *Monticello Signal*.

In 1882, George Ringer, from Michigan, came to Monticello bringing the equipment for a newspaper plant, and with himself as publisher, and James A. Phillips as editor, the paper was launched. In 1886 T. Leigh Thompson became editor and shortly thereafter Mr. Ringer who had married Miss Lee Coffey returned to Michigan. Mr. Thomas became the owner and publisher as well as editor for a few years, the name having been changed to *Monticello News*. In 1897 Judge Phillips again became associated with the paper as editor with H. S. Douglas as publisher. Shortly thereafter Kirk Boone of Somerset became publisher and the name was changed again to *Wayne County Record*. In 1899 the name of *Wayne County Outlook* was adopted and in 1904 Mr. James Simpson, the present owner, became editor and proprietor.

Of Judge James A. Phillips, who was the moving spirit of the Wayne County paper for twenty years from its beginning, the *Louisville Times* had this to say:

"The *Wayne County Record* published at Monticello, edited by J. A. Phillips, and which has long been an independent paper, has come out strongly for Bryan and Democratic success. The editor in making the announcement says:

" 'We heartily indorse every plank of the Kansas City platform. The platform is an inspiration, embodying the historic principles upon which our Government has rested from its foundation and meets the exact requirements of the country upon the issues that have sprung into existence growing out of the encroachment of capital and the un-American ideas of imperialism. We fear that the old ship of State has been strained from the course outlined by the fathers of the republic and the purpose of the Democratic party is to swing her back into the old paths. We have done well and will do well by adhering to the policy of Washington, Jefferson and Jackson to avoid entangling alliances with the old world. Bryan and Stevenson stand for this and that is why we stand for them. We are opposed to the spirit of conquest, and subjugation, because it is repugnant to the spirit of liberty, which has been and is the very foundation of our national life. We have thus far avoided the scramble of the spoliators, but if we follow up the new-fangled ideas that have been seized upon the present Administration we shall most certainly be embroiled in the conflicts that are lowing up in the Twentieth century.'

"The *Record* also strongly advocates the election of Gov. Beckham.

"Editor Phillips is one of the brightest writers in the State. He was born in Wayne County, December 14, 1845, admitted to the bar in 1878, was elected County Judge in 1882, was elected County Attorney in 1891, became editor of the *Monticello Signal* in 1882 and of the *Monticello News* in 1897."

Certain names are associated with particular sections of the county. There are the names of Barrier, Bell, Bertram, Burnett, Cooper, Kennedy, Fairchild, Denny, Parmley, Hurt, Littrell, Powers, Ryan, etc., in the southern section. Coffey, Ingram, Oatts are names of Elk Spring Valley families. In the northern part of the county were the Jones, Lanier, Henninger, Metcalfe, Weaver, West, Tate, and Kelly families. In the western section were found the names of Eads, Bartleson, Jones, Chesney, Ramsey, and Rankin. Just south of Monticello were the Hall, Back, McKechnie, Duncan, Rector, Huffaker, and Shearer families.

In the immediate vicinity of the town were, in the period best remembered by the writer, the Phillips, Tuttle, Duncan, Kendrick, Chrisman, Saufley, Huffaker, Sallee, Tuggle, Frisbie, Simpson, Berry, Ramsey, Rogers, Wilhite, and Haynes families.

OIL—TIMBER—FARM PRODUCTS
—STOCK

## CHAPTER IX

After Martin Beaty's discovery of oil in 1818, no practical development of the industry was attempted in the county until 1865. The Drake well in Pennsylvania revived interest in Beaty's well, and the Wayne County Beaty Oil Company was formed. Three other companies were boring on Otter Creek by this time and all through that year excitement about petroleum was very high.

Captain John W. Tuttle went up Elk Creek trying to locate oil leases without much success. He finally secured a lease on the G. Ryan farm and later others in nearby territory; but interest lagged until 1888 when William Strube bored a well at the mouth of Bear Creek, striking oil. Captain Geary then acquired an interest in Strube's enterprise and there was much excitement when a good flowing well was brought in at Cooper. Colonel A. H. Hovey, a picturesque figure, about this time appeared upon the scene. He had been a hotel clerk in Chicago and being a fine figure of a man, handsome, even distinguished in appearance, had engaged the affection of a wealthy widow who married him. She died and left him some estate with which he began oil operations in Wayne which lasted for several years. Mr. Alfred Murray was operating here at the same time as well as McTeer from Pennsylvania. Mr. Williams also became interested. The Bradford Oil Company, Bradford, Pennsylvania, operated extensively during this period.

In 1900 Captain Geary brought in a gusher in the Sunnybrook field. Excitement reached a high peak. Other wells came in rapidly and the Wayne County field seemed to bid fair to become boom territory. A pipe line was laid to Somerset and a refinery built in Oil Valley. There have been sporadic strikes since, but Wayne, while producing steadily, does not show the quantity for a big oil business.

Probably the first producing well in Wayne County was on the Morgan Farm in the Slickford field. The oil was hauled to the Cumberland River and shipped by boat to Nashville.

A pipe line was laid from the Sunnybrook field somewhat later by the Standard Oil Company and the oil was piped to a refinery at Parkersburg, West Virginia. A refinery was built at Oil Valley about 1909 and a macadam road built from Monticello.

The Cooper district held some of the early producing wells on Beaver Creek. In the Parmleysville district are the Mt. Pisgah, Griffin, Sinking, Barrier, and Rocky Branch fields.

At Steubenville and Mill Springs strikes have been made.

The New Dominion and Vulcan Oil Companies have the controlling interest now in the production of oil.

"No county in the state is so favored by equal distribution of farming and mineral land," says Collins.

Coal is abundant and easily mined in the hills while the valleys are productive. Corn and wheat are the chief crops. There is some tobacco grown. Timber is still abundant though much of it has been cut over. Earliest lumbering consisted in cutting the most valuable and easily floated timber in the valleys of the rivers. This was chiefly poplar and oak. The walnut has long since been nearly wiped out.

In 1867 there was great interest over the proposed extension of the Kentucky Central Railroad from Nicholasville through Danville and Somerset to Knoxville. Wayne voters that year pledged themselves to subscribe $50,000 in stock. Joshua Berry, L. J. Stevenson, and others were prime movers in this enterprise.

It is easily comprehensible that there should be the greatest interest in a railroad that would come as near to them as Somerset. The nearest railway point of contact was Stanford and there were no macadamized roads between the two points. When at last a railroad did pass as near as Burnside and a toll road was built to meet this road, transportation became much easier.

That year witnessed a tremendous excitement about oil production in Kentucky. Oil companies were incorporated in almost every county.

Early in the year the Monticello Oil Company was incorporated by act of the Legislature with M. E. Ingram, W. S. Sheppard, L. M. Flournoy, W. McKee Fox, and F. F. Sheppard as incorporators.

In the same year the Beaty Oil well was incorporated by William Lanphier, William Senior, John G. Wells, Robert J. Miles, L. Barney, and E. L. Van Winkle, the object being to develop "petroleum, rock and carbon oils, iron, coal, copper, zinc, other minerals, lumber and vegetable resources on the Big South Fork."

The people of Wayne felt so keenly the need for railway transportation for the continued development of the resources of the county that by 1880 definite steps were taken to this end. The Legislature had passed an act entitled:

"An act to aid in developing the agricultural and mineral resources of Kentucky, and to that end to provide for an exhibit thereof at the Southern Exposition at Louisville, Kentucky, and at the World's Industrial and Cotton Centennial Exposition at New Orleans, Louisiana."

Leaders in this movement were L. J. Stephenson, J. Berry, and John W. Tuttle. The Executive Committee chosen was composed of L. J. Stephenson, J. F. Young, J. J. Shearer, James Tuggle, and Lewis Coffey.

A copy of the *Monticello Signal* of June 13, 1889, gives a recapitulation of what had been done:

"As the time is drawing near for an earnest and businesslike consideration of matters connected with our railroad enterprise, we publish this week the documents upon which its organization is founded as a matter of convenience to those who may have frequent occasion to refer to them.

"As many will remember, the movement originated in a call for a meeting of the citizens of the counties lying on the west side of the Cumberland Mountains, to be held at Tullahoma, Tenn., on the 28th day of Aug. '86. Seeing an announcement of that meeting, some of our citizens issued a call for a meeting of the citizens of Wayne County, and, on assembling, sent John W. Tuttle as their representative to Tullahoma. At the meeting at Tullahoma an organization was effected and county organization recommended. Pursuant thereto railroad committees were organized in all of the counties lying immediately west of the Cumberland Mountains, and their continuation, from Pulaski County, Kentucky, to Madison County, Alabama, and a general route proposed and discussed. After a number of other meetings at Tullahoma to further organization, delegates were sent to Cincinnati and other places to endeavor by means of statistics and representations to enlist capital in the enterprise. The enterprise was then in too vague and indefinite a shape for any definite arrangement with capitalists to be made, but the way was paved for future success.

"Then followed the organization of three railroad companies on a connected line in the states of Alabama, Tennessee, and Kentucky under separate charters from each of those states. The Kentucky division was organized under the chartered name of the 'Cumberland River and Tennessee Railroad Company.'

"Then followed one or more surveys by each company and an estimate of the cost of the entire line.

"After several meetings for the purpose, and the settlement of a great number of details, requiring amendments to the various charters and a complete organization thereunder, the three companies were finally consolidated into one company bearing the name 'Kentucky Division' and acquired by amendment to its charter. In the meantime, the counties of the state of Tennessee voted subscriptions to the capital stock of the company, proposing to build a railroad along the proposed line, and the citizens of Alabama raised a satisfactory amount by private subscription, and an Act was passed by the Kentucky Legislature authorizing the counties of Wayne, Clinton, and Pulaski to take stock in the proposed railroad under certain conditions, to issue bonds therefor and provide payment of same by taxation.

"The charter, amended charter, articles of consolidation and enabling act are here published for the information of the people. As now contemplated application will be made to the Wayne County Court at its July term 1889 to submit a proposition of subscription to the people of Wayne County, to be voted on sometime in September as may be fixed by the court. Preparations are made for Clinton and Pulaski counties to take similar action about the same time.

"Respectfully,
"L. J. Stephenson, Chairman."

The following article by Prof. L. G. Kennamer is a comprehensive report on the resources and development of Wayne:

## RESOURCES AND DEVELOPMENT OF WAYNE COUNTY

"Perhaps no county in the state has a more romantic history and geography than does Wayne County, the 21st of our series of Kentucky counties on parade and the 43rd county, chronologically, in point of creation. The state legislature in 1800 created only one new county and named it after General "Mad Anthony" Wayne, a distinguished Revolutionary soldier and Indian fighter. This great Pennsylvanian ranked in success and prominence as a military leader and commander next to Generals George Washington and Nathaniel Greene. His military campaigns on behalf of the thirteen colonies extended all along the Atlantic Seaboard from the stormy heights of Quebec to the Piney Woods of Georgia, and his Indian battles were climaxed in the Battle of Fallen Timbers, where he defeated the British and Indians in a very decisive victory in the then Northwest Territory. This genius of Stony Point, Germantown, and Yorktown succeeded General Washington and General St. Clair in command of the Colonial armies and died in 1796, four years before Wayne County in Kentucky was created.

"This great pentagonally shaped Commonwealth waits the rise of a historian and archeologist to interpret its prehistoric past and write its historic lore. Here lived and hunted the great tribes of Indians who supplied their needs from the game of forest and stream. Here early hunters, trappers, pioneers, and settlers lived and partook of the wealth of its landscape and resources. Their records are yet to be written. What a thrilling story would it be to have related the experiences of the great caravans of the pioneers who crossed the confines of Wayne County on their way to Middle Tennessee. The great groups of people who touched the banks of the Cumberland in Wayne County as they floated to the unknown and undeveloped southwest. The stories of courage and daring events that are untold about Mill Springs, Steubenville, and Windy would make a thrilling chapter in Kentucky history. Think of the historic association connected with the name of the county seat, Monticello. This county capital was named after Monticello, the home of Thomas Jefferson, which in point of construction and the modern convenience it possessed, was far ahead of its time and age. This county seat bears the honored name of one of America's great shrines, revered in the hearts of all Americans for the great statesman and philosopher who resided in its environ. Every boy and girl in Wayne County is thus surrounded by an atmosphere of courageous statesmanship and patriotism.

"This little Commonwealth is located in the southeastern part of the state and borders the two counties of Fentress and Scott on the Tennessee line. It was carved out of Pulaski and Cumberland counties. In 1912 it yielded a large part of its area to form the baby county of Kentucky, McCreary. At present this little empire has an area of 478 square miles which is about one-third the size of the state of Rhode Island and about seven times the size of the District of Columbia. This region supports an almost pure Anglo-Saxon population of 17,000 or about 36 people per square mile. More than three-fourths of the county's area has been taken into farms, and one-fourth thus remains unimproved. For every three acres of croplands there are three acres of pasture and six acres of woodland.

"The topography may be divided like all Gaul, into three parts, for it is at this county that the three regions of the Kentucky Mountains, the Knobs and the Pennyroyal meet. The southeastern triangle of the county with its highest elevation of 1,550 feet atop Sulphur Springs Mountain is a part of the Kentucky Mountains, a region possibly more familiarly known as the Cumberland Plateau or the Eastern Coal Fields. This area belongs in its natural and cultural landscape to Eastern Kentucky. The second region is a wide belt that runs through the central portion of the county in a northeast-southwest direction. This central area is an upland of knob lands and rolling limestone plains. Its surface is marked by many typical Karst formations, such as swallows, sinkholes, ponds, sinking streams, caves, and springs. Here are found some of the loveliest farms in the whole state as the rolling landscapes are dotted with fine homes, large barns, and the fields and pastures yield large increases of grains and livestock.

"The third region is that of the Pennyroyal or Mississippi Plateau, a triangle of cavernous limestone lands that are located in the northwestern corner of the county. This area is deeply incised by stream courses of the Cumberland River and its tributaries. Thus the whole area here is varied and picturesque because of the beautiful palisades and the lovely meandering courses of the streams. Along this beautiful Cumberland River, thousands of early pioneers poured into Tennessee and for many years regular steamship service from Burnside, Kentucky, to Nashville and Paducah served Wayne County as a commercial outlet. There is genuine beauty to be enjoyed each season by anyone who will take a trip down the Cumberland River or a drive over her state and county highways.

"Each of the three regions of the county abounds in thick growth of virgin timber, and much of it is underlaid by rich deposits of coal. The principal mineral resources, however, are limestone and petroleum. The limestone occurs in large quantities, is widely distributed, and sufficient for any reasonable demand for road building, urban or rural needs. The oil pools are widely scattered over the areas which bear thousands of barrels of oil each year and provide large quantities of natural gas sufficient to supply all local needs. The mining of coal is a domestic enterprise and only serves a very small region, inasmuch as the county possesses no railroad facilities, and all coal must be marketed by truck. The building of excellent state highways has connected Monticello, the county seat, and the other towns with the leading arterial routes of the state and nation.

"Previous to the World War, the Cumberland River provided some transportation for the county, but the use of the river had declined to a very negligible degree. Wayne is one of the many progressive counties of the state that has built a fine municipal airport, and thus it is making up for its railroad deficiency by the liberal use of roadways and airways. One important arterial highway is the "Lookout Mountain" airline, a short route connecting the North and South.

"Although the surface of the county is much broken with knobs and hills, the valley lands are very fertile and productive, and the soil is very generally based upon limestone. The value of the farm crops approximates a million dollars a year, and the production of livestock equals that of the farm crops. The principal farm crops are corn, wheat, oats, potatoes, while the orchards produce sufficient quantities of apples and peaches. The value of the livestock produced each year and exported to the surrounding counties include cattle, horses, sheep, swine, dairy products, and poultry. Thus the people of Wayne County have been blessed with an abundance of oil, hardwood timber, and coal resources, and by a wise use of their farm lands by which they are able to produce an abundant yield of farm crops and heavy exports of livestock. All this richness of resources is reflected in the good homes, fine schools, and in the excellent cultural advantages of education and religion. Thus there is translated through these institutions good citizenship on the part of its youth. Wayne County is progressive in the utilization of its resources and in the overcoming of its handicaps."

BIOGRAPHICAL, GENEALOGICAL
AND MISCELLANEOUS NOTES

THE FIRST MARRIAGE BOOK
OF WAYNE COUNTY

BIBLIOGRAPHY

## CHAPTER X

## THE JOSHUA JONES FAMILY

THE FAMILY OF JOSHUA JONES emigrated from Wales at an early date. They took part in the Welsh settlement of Pennsylvania. Edward Jones and Katherine, his wife, bought 3121/2 acres of land from William Penn in 1683. Their son, Edward, had a son Richard who married Jane Evans. Their son, Evan, was Joshua's father. His mother was cousin to Evan and his grandmother an Evans.

Joshua Jones was born in the Quaker settlement of Bucks County, Pennsylvania. He early evinced the adventurous spirit that had led his forebears across the stormy Atlantic. With his brother, Jonathan, he went into Virginia as a surveyor and in 1763 they surveyed lands for the state.

Joshua made the first survey of the lands on the Holston and Clinch rivers. He surveyed and entered 273 acres on One Mile Creek. Then he returned home and married Hannah Todhunter. With her family, she had left the Quaker meeting in Pennsylvania and come to Loudoun County, Virginia, and there in July, 1767, they were married at Fairfax Monthly Meeting of Friends, to the despair of "Friends" at her "outgoing" in marriage.

Though Joshua had come of good Quaker stock, the rigors of his life had been such that he had been forced to abandon his Quaker belief in non-combativeness to protect himself from savages in the wilderness. Hannah Todhunter's family and "Friends" wrestled with her "to no avail." Her grandfather, John Todhunter, the English Quaker, had left England in 1687. He had become a Quaker, refusing to pay tithes and taxes to the Church of England and had been excommunicated for "conscience's sake." He married Margaret Hoopes (widow of Abram Beakes), daughter of Joshua and Isabella Hoopes, from Yorkshire, England. The son of John Todhunter and Margaret Hoopes, John Todhunter II, married Margaret Evans, daughter of Thomas Evans, who was son of Evan Evans from Merionethshire, Wales. In 1776, Joshua Jones enlisted in the militia of Virginia battling "British, Tories and Savages."

After the Revolution, Isaac Shelby was sent by the governor of North Carolina to assist soldiers in locating bounty lands. Joshua Jones came with him as surveyor. He surveyed and entered 400 acres on Elk Creek in what later became Wayne County and began operation of an iron furnace at what is still known as Furnace Mountain. This was referred to by the Legislature of Kentucky, in 1800, as being in "great forwardness." He returned to Virginia in 1794, sold his interest in the ironworks there and returned bringing his wife.

Hannah Todhunter's brother, Jacob, who had been a Revolutionary soldier, had come to Lexington, Kentucky, and established himself as an attorney and married Elizabeth Parker.

Here Hannah Todhunter Jones had sent her son, James, to become associated with him. Jacob attempted to arrange a marriage for James, but his thoughts went back to his Virginia sweetheart and accordingly, in October, 1798, he went back and married Mary Buster and brought her to Lexington. She was the daughter of John Buster and Jane Woods. The Busters had come from Ireland to Virginia and Jane Woods was daughter of Michael Woods, Jr., son of Michael Woods, Sr., from Ireland, and Mary Campbell of the Scotch Clan of Argyllshire.

James Jones and Mary Buster were married October 10, 1798, at Wytheville, Virginia, and came to Fayette County, Kentucky, where James' uncle, Jacob Todhunter, lived. They remained there until the following autumn. After the birth of their first child (a daughter named Susan, who grew up and married Alvin Cullom) they went to Wayne. They were the first of the Joshua Jones family to go there but all of the family came in a short time. Joshua's wife, Hannah, had stopped with her brother, Jacob Todhunter, near Lexington, until a home was ready for her.

In the summer of 1825 James Jones and Mary Buster Jones visited the old home in Virginia that they had left so long before for the Kentucky frontier. They lived northeast of Monticello where they are both buried. They had been separated only once, while James was absent in the campaign of 1812-13.

Joshua and Hannah Jones's children were: Sarah, James, John, Joshua, Margaret, Martha, Jane, Hiram, Alben, Evan, Mary, and William.

Sarah married, first, Charles Buster; her son, Joshua Buster, was a prominent citizen of Wayne, and her daughter, Mary, married George W. Berry. Her other children were William, Elizabeth, James, and John Buster. Charles Buster died in 1802, and his widow in 1804 married John Sanders. To this union were born Minerva, Julia, and Hiram B. Sanders.

James Jones's and Mary Buster's children were: (1) Susan, married Alvin Cullom and went to Tennessee, where he was later elected to Congress. (2) Hannah married Dr. Jonathan Frisbie. Their children were Susan, who married Joseph Russell; Eliza, who married Sanders; Marietta, who married first L. P. Baker, second Cosby Oatts; Irene, who married Cosby Oatts; J. Smith Frisbie, who married Artema Bartleson.

(3) Jane married first, Hannibal Clemens, uncle of Mark Twain (Dr. John M. Clemens was their son), second, John L. Sallee, and their children were Caroline who married William Francis; Mary who married P. W. Hardin; Joseph who married Lina Owens; Dr. Walter Sallee.

(4) Frances married Milton Mills. Their daughter, Mary, married Dr. John Hall.

(5) Mary married Benoni Mills.

(6) Margaret married William Richardson. Their son, James Jones Richardson, was father of Vernon Richardson of Danville.

(7) Sarah married John McBeath. Their son, Andrew, who married Susan Gholson, had a daughter, Susan, who married John Warden.

(8) Eliza married Micajah Phillips. Their children were James, Juan (Elliott), Mary (Duncan), Henry, Hiram, Hannah, Ephraim, Lula.

(9) Juan, youngest child of James Jones, married Hiram Hall. Their children were Zachary T., William, Marshall, Dr. John, Hiram, Susan (Stone), Mary (Stone).

Of the sons of James Jones, Ledford died young, J. Shrewsbury married Jane Pierce, and Logan left the county.

John, third child of Joshua and Hannah, married Margaret Best. Their son, Jefferson Jones, married Emily Coffey.

Joshua Jones, Jr., married Elizabeth Dean and went to Pulaski County. A mortgage bond from him to Cyrenius Wait, on a slave, is recorded in the courthouse at Somerset.

Margaret Jones, daughter of Joshua Jones, Sr., married James Stone. They are buried in the old cemetery at Monticello.

Martha Jones married Thomas Jackson. They went to Indiana. Dr. Evan Jones Jackson, her son, was grandfather of Mr. Guy H. Humphreys, an attorney of Bloomfield, Indiana.

Jane Jones married William Hudson. They are buried in the old cemetery, also. Their daughter, Amanda, first married a Stone; second, Coleman Coffey.

Hiram Jones married Ann Shrewsbury. They had a daughter, Jane, who married a Hudson.

Alben Jones. No further record of him has been found.

Evan Jones married and moved to Barbourville where his daughter, Amanda, married Dr. J. H. S. Morrison. Their daughter married a Richmond. These last were the parents of Dr. James H. Richmond, former Superintendent of Public Education and State Commissioner of Education.

Mary Jones married Roger Oatts and one of their sons, Joshua Oatts, married Polly Coffey. Their children: Cleveland, James, Cosby, William, John, Lewis, Russell, Thomas J., Emily, and Sophronia.

William Jones, son of Joshua, married Sarah Shipp, in Virginia. Their son, James Jones, born January 28, 1800, died June 30, 1877, married Frances West, born 1802, died 1896. They were married by Raccoon John Smith, Sept. 14, 1826. Frances West was daughter of Isaac West and Margaret Russell. The children of James Jones and Frances West as recorded in an old Bible, were:

Russell Jones, born July 10, 1827, died April 29, 1906.

G. Milton Jones, born Sept. 13, 1828, died March 7, 1908.

Isaac Jones, born Dec. 14, 1829.

Ann Jones, born March 9, 1831, died April 18, 1904.

Mary Belle Jones, born August 28, 1832, died June 19, 1925.
John Jones, born Nov. 23, 1834, died Dec. 18, 1858.
Nancy Emily Jones, born May 6, 1836, died June 20, 1908.
Eliza Jones, born Sept. 8, 1838, died June 29, 1921.
James Jones, born March 8, 1840, died Nov. 14, 1840.
Sarah Frances Jones, born Nov. 1, 1842, died 1926.
William P. Jones, born Feb. 6, 1844, died April 2, 1891.
Elijah Marshall Jones, born Jan. 21, 1846, died June 26, 1901.

Russell Jones married Martha Burkhart. Their children were: John, James, Mary, Will, Elizabeth, Charlie.

Milton Jones married Matilda Kennedy. They had one son, William Kendrick Jones.

Isaac Jones married Margaret Cowan. Their sons were: Robert, John, Joshua, and Edgar.

Ann Jones married Tunstall Hatchett. Their children were: Molly, Oscar, Maggie, and Sallie.

Mary Belle Jones married J. H. Bartleson first. Their children were John and Anna. Second, she married Robert McBeath. Their children were Robert and Jessie.

Nancy E. Jones married E. E. Wright. Their children were: Joseph, Maude, Mabel, James, and Ethel.

Eliza Jones married Joseph Wright. Their children were: Fanny, Kate, Effie, Mamie, Robert, and Alma.

Sarah Frances Jones married Captain L. J. Stephenson.

William P. Jones married Sue Bohon. They had one son, James Jones.

Elijah Marshall Jones married Mary Elizabeth Sallee. They had two children, Charles Edwin and Cora Amanda.

Extract from Sketch of Joshua Jones, from E. Polk Johnson's *History of Kentucky* (Vol. III):

"Joshua Jones came as a very early pioneer to Kentucky, being a member of that plucky little band which first subdued the virgin acres of the new state, and paved the way for present day advancement. He laid out the town of Monticello, in 1801, and made the first surveys of Wayne County. He was a prominent man in his day and generation, an influence for good in the many sided life of his time. At one time, not long ago, count was made of the living descendants of this good pioneer, and it was found there were two thousand scattered over the United States—evidence he did his share to make the name of Jones a familiar one. His wife was Hannah Todhunter whose family had the distinction of importing the first race horse, Tranby, to America. Joshua Jones brought his surveyor's instruments across the mountains from Virginia and they are now in the possession of one of his descendants, Mrs. Mary Cecil Cantrill of Georgetown, Kentucky. The bones of this pioneer lie in Wayne County."

Joshua Jones left an honored name, one his numerous descendants are proud to claim. He was of unmixed Welsh stock, his family being easily traced to about 1100.

His remarkable physical endurance, his sturdy honesty and tenacity of purpose, and a canny thrift enabled him to wrest from the wilderness a sizable fortune for his day. His descendants will be found in every state in the Union today.

Herewith follows copy of the last Will and Testament of Joshua Jones, taken from the records of the Wayne County Court, recorded on page 3 of Will Book A.

## WILL OF JOSHUA JONES

I, Joshua Jones, calling to mind the certainty of death and the uncertainty of life, have a mind to dispose of my property in the following manner:

I bequeath to my beloved son Alben Jones the land I now live on and I do request him to take care of my beloved wife during her life, and

I do bequeath to my beloved daughter Jane Hudson five hundred dollars out of a judgment that I hold on McDermod, and

I do bequeath to my beloved daughter Martha five hundred dollars of the said judgment on McDermod, and

I do bequeath to my beloved son Evan Jones five hundred dollars of the judgment I hold on McDermod, and

I do bequeath to my beloved wife Hannah Jones the benefit of the money that Lawyer Sheffey has in his hands to collect for me during her life, and at her death, I bequeath it to my beloved son Evan Jones; and if the money is not got from McDermod my daughter Martha is to have one-half of the money that Lawyer Sheffey has to collect for me in Virginia.

I do bequeath unto my beloved daughter Martha Jones one bed and furniture and one cow and calf, and I bequeath to my beloved wife Hannah Jones the household furniture to dispose of as she thinks proper and also two cows and calves, and the balance of the judgment that I hold on McDermod is to be equally divided among all my children. And I bequeath unto my beloved son Joshua Jones my surveying instruments; and I do appoint my son James Jones and my son Alben Jones Executors to administer on my estate and to settle with Crockett about the Furnace land and to give the legatees an equal part of the balance of the Furnace land.

This is my last Will and Testament made in my right mind but frail in body. Whereunto I set my hand this 18th day of October 1816.

Attest
John Beatty
Joshua Buster                                          JOSHUA JONES.


MORTGAGE BOND

Recorded in the Clerk's Office of Pulaski County:

This Indenture of Bargain and Sale made and Entered into this first day of January 1831 between Joshua Jones of the one part & Cyrenius Wait of the other part and both of County of Pulaski and the State of Kentucky. Witnesseth that I, Joshua Jones hath this day sold unto Cyrenius Wait and do by these Presents sell and deliver a certain Negro Girl, named Suzan, about nineteen years of age, for the sum of Two Hundred & Sixty Two Dollars and Eighty two Cents the Receipt whereof I hereby acknowledge upon the Terms & Conditions following to wit that whereas I, Joshua Jones, am justly indebted in the Sum aforesaid in two Notes to wit: one note for One Hundred & Thirty dollars & Eighteen cents dated the 25th of December 1830 and another Note for One Hundred & Thirty Two Dollars & Sixty four Cents dated this day & date above written—And being willing to secure the payment thereof with Lawful Interest unto the said Cyrenius Wait. The Conditions of the above Obligation is such that if the aforesaid Joshua Jones shall well & duly pay unto the said Cyrenius Wait the sums aforesaid with Lawful Interest thereon within Twelve Months from the Day & Date above written. Then and in that case this agreement to be void & of no effect. But if the said Joshua Jones Shall Fail, Refuse or Neglect to pay the sums aforesaid with Lawful Interest at the time aforesaid then this agreement to be in full Force and Virtue in the Law.

Given under My Hand & Seal This Day and Date above written in Presents of

Witness
Gideon P. Hail
Edward Stanton (Signed) JOSHUA JONES.

This Joshua was a son of Joshua Jones and Hannah Todhunter.

## THE TODHUNTER FAMILY AS TOLD BY RYLAND TODHUNTER

Lexington, Missouri,
May 9, 1910.

My dear Wm. H. Todhunter, Esq.:

As near as I can learn there is but one family of the name Todhunter in America, all descendants of that "John Todhunter of England who was excommunicated (?) from the Church of England in 1687 for becoming a Quaker and refusing to pay tithes, taxes, etc." The similarity of given names in the list you sent confirms my impression that you are of the line of one of the brothers of my grandfather, Jacob Todhunter, who settled near Nicholasville, Ky. in 1789. He married Elizabeth Parker (d. of Mary Todd and James Parker). They had one son, my father, Parker Evans Todhunter, who was born, reared, and died in the old brick mansion erected upon part of the large estate which he owned in Jessamine Co., Ky., just ten miles from Lexington, Ky.

I am the youngest of five sons and the only one living. My eldest brother, Jacob T., died one year ago aged 89 years.

My father was three times a cousin of Mrs. Abraham Lincoln by the numerous Todd-Parker marriage connection of the line.

My father during the war was arrested and sent to Camp Chase, Ohio, a prisoner, but was pardoned and granted every privilege by a written communication from the President himself, which was so generous in its terms that we did not allow my father to understand the full extent of his liberty, lest he fall into trouble thereby.

I am hoping to elicit your interest in order that together, we may be able to clear up the line of descent, and complete a record of the family in a genealogical order, that may prove a source of pride and satisfaction to future generations of the name.

At least I am determined to do all I can to afford my children intelligent history and family record. I should like to obtain the Todhunter coat of arms also. You know the name means Foxhunter. The crest is a fox.

The great mathematician or writer of textbooks on the subject, I am satisfied, is one of the family, as all the old wills lay stress upon education. I have a photograph of a will of John Todhunter, the progenitor, dated 1714, before the birth of his son John, which mentions his daughter, Sarah.

Later, the will of his widow sets aside a sum for the education of their son John, born after the date of his father's will.

Sarah died young, but John grew up and after being "brought up in a manner becoming a gentleman," and the sum set aside for his education was expended thereon, he was left "a gold watch, a fine two-year-old mare and a plantation and a Bible." His half-brother, Stephen Beakes, was executor of his mother's estate and proved most worthy of the trust. One item I'll add of childish recollections of mine and then give in outline some of the family records so far received.

When a child I remember that some relatives whom my parents called "cousin John Todhunter" visited our home in Kentucky and I was impressed that they were people of prominence. I think there was some connection with the Andes Insurance Company of Ohio. That was before the Civil War.

Some years ago I met at the St. Louis Fair, a Mrs. Bennett who was a descendant of a Todhunter, who was a Revolutionary soldier of Penn., a relative of my grandfather, but I forgot the name. Her maiden name was Annie Todhunter. Her husband was Wm. Bennett, at that time Insurance Commissioner of the States of Missouri and Kentucky and was living in St. Louis. Later he removed to Indianapolis, Ind., and I have not been able to locate them. She was a woman of large frame, and had the full large gray eye of the Todhunters. They are all large men of health and great strength, with a Scotch featuring.

The name is to be found still in Cumberland County, England. Tradition has it that the family was originally Todd. That those Scotch-Irish Todds were once visiting one of the ancestral homes of their relatives, descendants of Lord John Todd, or Tod, and the visiting Todds, or Tods, became so fascinated with the sport of foxhunting that the new name was given them and has stood. Certain it is that both names have the fox for a crest. The Todhunters are Quakers. From the Quaker records of Westchester, Penn., I find that John Todhunter married in Bucks Co., Penn., after 1703, Margaret Hoopes, widow of Stephen Beakes. The Hoopes were from Wales.

The parents of Margaret were Joshua and Isabella. John and Margaret T. had Sarah and John. Sarah died young. John married in the same community Margaret Evans (d. of Evan Evans). They had children, Sarah, Abraham, John, Margaret, Hannah, Jacob, Isaac, Joseph, Mary, Evan, and Martha. All members of the Quaker Church of Westchester, Penn. Sarah married Judge Beale and remained in Penn. Abraham married in Pennsylvania, and was in the militia, 1777-82, from Cumberland County.

In 1767 John Todhunter and wife, Margaret, and nine children obtained certificates to Fairfax Monthly Meeting in Fairfax Co., Va. Hannah married Joshua Jones and removed to Wythe Co., Va., and then to Wayne Co., Ky. Margaret married a Mr. Burgoyne. Martha married George Gregg, 1780. John was disowned. Jacob refused to heed advice of friends and removed himself from among them. Jacob later returned to Pennsylvania, and I have his record of service in the Continental army from 1777-82. He then removed to Logan's Ft., and became associated with Col. Robert Todd, Gen. Levi Todd and others noted in the vicinity in pioneer days. Joseph, one of the brothers of this family, I think, remained in Fairfax Co. and later his descendants are to be found in Baltimore.

Evans was disowned by Fairfax Meeting. This ends the Friend's records obtained at some expense, much time and effort spent, and a patient perseverance. But I count nothing lost if I succeed even no further.

I lately obtained a post card view of the old Fairfax Meeting House which is now in Loudoun Co., Va. The county has divided since 1775. The graves of John and Margaret are in the cemetery which is in the churchyard.

Respectfully,
RYLAND TODHUNTER.

RYLAND TODHUNTER'S ACCOUNT OF FIRST RACE HORSE IN KENTUCKY, WRITTEN FEBRUARY, 1916.

Imp. Tranby was brought to America prior to or about 1840. Purchased in England by Hon. John M. Botts of near Richmond, Va., and P. E. Todhunter of Lexington, Ky. Tranby remained a short time in Virginia and was brought to Parker E. Todhunter farm, "Oakland," near Lexington, Ky., where he remained several years doing a prosperous business at highest price for services of any stallion in America up to that time. Tranby spent one year near Columbia, Mo., and was returned to Mr. Todhunter's farm in Kentucky, where he died a few years later. P. E. Todhunter owned many fine thoroughbred race horses, but Tranby being probably the best. His skull was tacked up on his stable and remained until near the beginning of the War of States in 1861 to '65.

Tranby was purchased in England at $12,000. Afterward P. E. Todhunter sent to England and purchased, as he thought, the next best horse in England, Imp. Zingaree, who lived but a few years in Kentucky, leaving some splendid colts, but in playing in the paddock at "Oakland" he broke his front leg and got so vicious when put in a sling that Mr. Todhunter got his friend,

Dr. A. K. Marshall (brother to the great orator, Thomas Marshall), to destroy Zingaree.

John Todhunter (and his wife Polly) lived and died in Jessamine Co., Kentucky, near Nicholasville. John Todhunter was a first cousin to Parker E. Todhunter. Parker E. Todhunter was a son of Jacob Todhunter and his only child. Jacob Todhunter son of John G., brother of Hannah (wife of Joshua Jones) was born in Pennsylvania, 1760, served in the Revolution, married and died on his fine estate, "Oakland," near Lexington, Ky. Jacob Todhunter owned many slaves and conducted a tannery at "Oakland."

My father, Parker E. Todhunter, lived and died at the same estate where I also was born and reared. These are the only Todhunters who lived in Kentucky, but my father, P. E. Todhunter, knew and visited his Jones kin in Southern Kentucky.

---

Taken from the Records of Fairfax Monthly Meeting of Friends in Loudoun County, Virginia, established 1745.

Book A. Page 261: "At our Monthly Meeting of Fairfax, held 25th. of 4th. Month 1767.

"John Todhunter produced a Certificate from Uwchland Monthly Meeting, dated 9th. of 4th. Month 1767, Recomending himself, Margaret his wife, and their children, Viz. Hannah, Mary, Margaret, Isaac, Jacob, Joseph, & Evan, as members of our society, which was read and accepted."

Page 262: "At our Monthly Meeting of Fairfax, held 25th. of 4th. Month 1767.

"Our women friends request our assistance in drawing a Testimony against Hannah Todhunter, for out going in marriage; Mahlon Janney is, accordingly, appointed for the service."

Page 262: "At our Monthly Meeting of Fairfax, held 4th. of 6th. Mo. 1767.

"Mahlon Janney is appointed to assist our women friends in shewing a Testimony to Hannah Jones, formerly Todhunter, if she declines an appeal, to read it at the close of some public meeting, at Fairfax, and return the paper to be recorded."

Page 268: "At our Monthly Meeting of Fairfax, held 25th. of 7th. Month 1767.

"The friends appointed to assist our women friends in reading a Testimony against Hannah Jones have performed the service, and returned the paper, which is as follows." (Note: this paper was not recorded, a space is left for the recording).

"At our Monthly Meeting of Fairfax held 26th. of 11th. Month 1772.

"Margaret Todhunter requests a Certificate for herself and youngest child, a minor, to Uwchland Monthly Meeting. The son's name was Evan. Francis Hogue and Joseph Hough are appointed to assist the women friends to make enquiry concerning her conduct and conversation."

Page 404: "At our Monthly Meeting of Fairfax held 27th. of 2nd. Month 1773.

"One of the friends appointed respecting Margaret Todhunter, Certificate, reports her business is not settled."

Page 434: "At our Monthly Meeting of Fairfax held 28th. of 5th. Month 1774.

"Margaret Todhunter, a widow, lying under some difficulty in settleing the business relating to her deceased husband's estate, made application to friends for further assistance therein, Therefore this meeting appoints Mahlon Janney, Israel Thompson, Joseph Janney, John Hough, and Abel Janney, for that service.

Page 448: "At our Monthly Meeting of Fairfax, held 31st. of 12th. Month 1774.

"The friends in the case of Margaret Todhunter, report she and her son have chosen men, entered into bonds to abide their award, therefore we think the present care of this meeting may be discontinued."

## Colonial Service of Joshua Hoopes

Colonial Records—*Minutes of Provincial Council of Pennsylvania*, Vol. 1, page 601:

"Att a council in the Assembly Held att Philadelphia die Veneris 10th May 1700 The Sheriff of Bucks Countie his return of Representatives for Assembly was produced, whereby it appeared yt ther wer elected Jno. Swift, Phineas Pemberton, Joshua Hoopes, Wm. Paxton, Jeremiah Langhorne, Sam'll Darck."

This Joshua Hoopes was great-grandfather of Hannah Todhunter. Joshua Hoopes and Isabella his wife came from Wales in 1683.

Their daughter Margaret married John Todhunter I. Their son, John Todhunter II, married Margaret Evans, and Hannah Todhunter, their daughter, married Joshua Jones.

## THE BUSTER-WOODS FAMILY

Macon, Mo., July 11, 1906.

Mrs. Ryland Todhunter,
Lexington, Mo.

Dear Madam:

In reply to your letter of April 25th, but recently received, will say I was very much pleased to hear from you. I, like you, am very much interested in my family history. I have never yet found a person by the name of "Buster" who was not related to me. I have never been able to trace our family further back than Virginia and about the year 1790. As I have it, four Busters came from Virginia to Wayne County, Kentucky, many years ago and settled just northeast of Monticello. I have been on the ground and made inquiry concerning the family. There were four boys; Mike, who came to this State and died; John, a Hardshell Baptist preacher and my grandfather, who came to this county and died leaving quite a family; "Jockey" Bill, who went to Texas and succeeded, he and his son, in making quite a fortune. One of his boys, John W., now lives in Texas. A few years ago I helped buy him a train load of thoroughbred cattle to stock his ranch. The other son lived and died in Wayne County, Kentucky, and I now have an aunt living in Clinton County, Kentucky.

I was in Kentucky in 1893 and went out to the old neighborhood in which my family lived. I found my family had been quite prominent in the early history of Wayne County, having held quite a few of the offices in that county. My grandfather married into the family of Tuttles and later into the Baker family, both Kentucky families. My great-grandfather's name was Charles Buster. You will see how we have kept the name down to the present, and they came from Virginia to Kentucky. My grandfather certainly had Irish blood in him as his language indicated it. He used to tell me when I was a very small boy that his grandfather, if I am not mistaken, anyway some one of his relatives was a soldier in the Revolutionary War. My grandfather was a soldier in the War of 1812. I have heard your name spoken of by my grandfather, but I was such a small boy when he died that I don't remember much about it.

C. G. BUSTER.

Macon, Mo., July 18, 1911.

Mrs. Jas. E. Cantrill,
Georgetown, Kentucky.

My Dear Madam:

In reply to your very welcome letter will say it gives me pleasure to give you all the information in my power concerning our family tree, and while my knowledge is very limited, I know that we are related; and as you are going to Monticello will say I was there in 1893, and, in conversation with the older inhabitants, I found that my grandfather, John Buster, came from Virginia when a small boy with his family and that he afterwards moved to Missouri, and preached the Gospel as a "hardshell," for his entire life, dying at the age of eighty-five years; that he was a pensioner of the War of 1812 and I have his picture with a like company of soldiers taken in 1874. My grandfather had a cousin that came to Missouri about the time that he did by the name of Mike Buster, and also a cousin moved to Texas by the name of J. W. Buster, who grew wealthy in the cattle business. I do not know my grandfather's family except that I was informed that he was one of a large family and was one of the youngest children, in fact, was born as a diminutive child of three pounds; that he has four brothers that I have heard him speak of and one in particular by the name of Charley. In fact, my father's name is Charley and my name is Charley and we have two or three other Charleys—hence, you see, the name is a favorite name.

Again referring to my trip to Monticello, will say I examined the old records and found that several of our relatives were office holders in the county of Wayne; that the family lived just northeast of town on what is now known as "Sinking Creek." Of course, I will be glad to hear from you as to what you find out and I will ask you to write me.

Now, coming to the more modern family history, will say, I have never met a Buster that did not trace his ancestry back to my relations. My grandfather was a man of large influence in the pioneer days of Missouri and I yet hear of the old people recalling some of his characteristics. He boasted of his Scotch blood and was known as a wise and witty preacher. He preached during the Civil War and notwithstanding our border warfare he was never disturbed—a very remarkable thing.

C. G. BUSTER.

Wm. H. Miller, in his *Histories and Genealogies,* published in Richmond, Kentucky, 1907, in chapter on Soldiers in Indian Colonial and Frontier Wars, on page 12, says:

"John Buster, Virginia Frontier, died 1820, Kentucky. P. 208 (Buster) Chapter 13, Art. I."

"Michael Woods, Jr., son of Michael Woods, Sr., of Blair Park, emigrant from Ireland (and Mary Campbell of the Scotch Clan Campbell, of Argyleshire, Scotland, his wife), was born in Ireland, 1708, and came to America with his parents and went with them from Pennsylvania to Virginia and settled in Albemarle County and lived southwest of Ivey's Depot 'til 1773—moved to Botetourt County and lived on a plantation on the south side of James River a few miles below Buchanan where he died 1777. He had married Ann Garth. Their children were Jane Woods, married John Buster, and they removed to Kentucky. Their daughter, Mary Buster, married James Jones."

McAlister's data gives copy of Pension granted Claudius Buster, son of John Buster, grant obtained in Kentucky for service in Virginia.

Archibald Woods, Jr., son of Archibald Woods, Sr., was born in Albemarle County, Virginia, in 1771. He was grandson of Michael Woods, Jr. At an early date, Archibald Woods, Jr., came to Wayne County where he settled on Meadow Creek. He married Mary McBeath. His son, Thomas J. LeGrande Woods, married Charity Elizabeth Henninger. They were the parents of Robert E. Woods, former postmaster of Louisville. Charity Henninger's father, Henry, was son of Conrad Henninger, Revolutionary soldier, who received a pension in Wayne County.

## THE PHILLIPS FAMILY

At Maidenhead, New Jersey, Philip Phillips, son of Theophilus, died in 1740, leaving children Philip, Abner, Samuel, John, and Ruth. To Abner, he left a legacy of land. Abner married his cousin, Elizabeth Phillips. (*New Jersey Archives, First Series*, Vol. XXX—Abstracts of Wills, Vol. II, page 378.)

Abner moved to Virginia, near Alexandria, and from there to Surry County, North Carolina, in 1780. He bought 103 acres on the Yadkin River. He had children: Philip, Richard, Micajah, Cornelius, George, Ephraim. Cornelius married Rhoda Shores, in 1791, and removed to Wayne in 1799 and settled on the land where some of the Kendricks later lived. He and Rhoda Shores Phillips and his son James and wife Jane and their son Charles, and Cornelius's grandson, Jack, and others are buried there.

Richard, son of Abner, emigrated to Tennessee. Micajah went first to Ohio, then to New York and became wealthy. Cornelius's son, Micajah, married Eliza Jones, granddaughter of

Joshua Jones. Cornelius had other children: John, Ephraim, George, Alfred, Pleasant, Hiram, Abner, James, Nancy, Lucinda, Mary. Lucinda married Henry Gatewood. Mary married Micajah Van Winkle. Alfred married Susannah Cullom and moved to Illinois and became wealthy. John married Elizabeth Berry. Hiram married Susan Berry and went to Cedartown, Georgia, where he owned a large plantation, which he sold when he moved to Texas. George Phillips remained in Wayne where he married a Weaver of the Meadow Creek Section.

From *Phillips and Thruston Families*, by Gates Phillips Thruston:

"Theophilus Phillips, who died in New Jersey in 1758, was son of Samuel, a minister of Newton, Massachusetts. He was son of Samuel, of Rowley, Massachusetts, who was son of George, a Puritan preacher who came to Watertown, Massachusetts, in 1630, with Governor Winthrop. He was a Cambridge graduate. He was son of Christopher Phillips, of Boxted, Rainham, England. The family was of Welsh origin."

Birmingham, Ky., April 27, 1882.

Dear Isaac [Newton Phillips]:

Can I make an apology for my great negligence in not replying to your very kind and interesting letter of last November the 28th, which was received early in December? About the time I received it the rain began to fall in torrents, continued, until the water courses overspread the country so much it was with difficulty to get in or out of our town which is situated on the bank of the Tennessee River. The river was so high by the first day of January, steamboat navigation was suspended; many of the railroad bridges were washed away and the mails stopped for over a month.

After I received your letter which gave me so much pleasure, I calculated to answer it in a week or two, but the excitement of the rainfall, and continued increase of the waters, caused me to put off writing until the mails stopped. True I would now and then get your letter, read it, think I would answer in a few days; a promised duty or a pleasure, once procrastinated, is the foreboding of a failure. I hope you will accept this as an apology. I will notice the request in your letter.

In relation to the paternal side of our ancestors: at an early date a large family of our name emigrated from Wales to America, and settled on the Potomac River, in Virginia, near Georgetown or Alexandria. The most of the family drifted into Pennsylvania, settled in and about Philadelphia, engaged in commerce and trade, amassed large fortunes. My great-grandfather remained on the Potomac. My grandfather moved to North Carolina where he raised his family. His sons' names were Cornelius (my father and your grandfather), Richard, and Micajah. Richard moved to Tennessee where he raised a large family, who were honest and industrious, but without much culture of mind. Micajah came to this state several years after my father and remained some time, thence to Springfield, Ohio, where he married and raised a son and daughter—his son, James Abner, visited us in Wayne County some thirty years ago. He was a fine looking man and well accomplished. He returned to Ohio, thence to New York City, where he engaged in the commercial business. We received letters from him for two or three years when the correspondence ceased. I never learned whether the old stock took any part in the Revolutionary War, but presume from their location they were supporters of the independence of the colonies.

On the maternal side, the maiden name of my mother was Rhoda Shores. Her parents were raised in New Jersey. Her father was of Irish descent and her mother was an English lady. Some of her brothers moved to Tennessee and were extensive farmers.

Father's family have drifted over the western and southern states. Brother Alfred was the oldest and I the youngest sons. Out of eight sons, all are dead but Brother Micajah and myself; he is nearly eighty-six years old and I am in my seventy-second year. My wife is about six years younger; her maiden name was Elizabeth F. Berry. It may be that your Aunt Pamela has seen her when a child. Our children are all in Missouri but one, who is in Wayne County. We have only ourselves in family. Today we will start to Malden, Missouri, to see our children. Will be gone five or six weeks. We have three sons, one of them married. My oldest son, Harrison B., at the age of about sixteen years, joined the Third Kentucky Regiment of Infantry under Colonel Bramlette. He had been in the war for nearly three years, and in making a charge on the Rebels at Kennesaw Mountain was wounded with a minnie ball in the left side of his breast on the 27th day of June, 1864, and died on the first of September. I brought him home, but the wound overcame him in about two months. My sons' names are James H., Samuel L., and Charles P., all in Missouri. All my family are doing very well.

I am truly sorry to hear of the great affliction of your Aunt Pamela Brown. I sympathize very much in her sufferings. Give her my high regard and my prayers that she may be restored to good health with ability to walk; and visit her friends and enjoy life for years. When a little boy I went to see your father; he was living on the Cumberland River. He was planting corn. She was a few years the oldest; she flattered me very much; I thought she was the best and prettiest person in the world.

I highly appreciate your photo. It very much resembles my son Samuel's. I have placed it in the next leaf to his in my family album where they can both be seen at one view. It would give me much pleasure to see you and all of Brother Alfred's family. The oldest in a few years will be placed on the old list. How short is life. One generation passes away, the other follows at its heels. I am now old; out of a hundred, one does not live to my age. Take off the first twenty-five years of my age, then my life appears but a span. Perhaps God in his wisdom has allotted to man only time in this life to qualify him to enjoy an eternal life with so much pleasure; he may, if he could reflect back on the time spent on the earth, feel the loss of the joys he had missed during his stay in this life. My time to start is nearly here. Write to me when I come home and I will be more prompt. My wife joins in with our love to you and all the relations.

Your uncle,
JOHN H. PHILLIPS.

## WILL OF ABNER PHILLIPS

In the name of God Amen. This tenth day of November in the year of our Lord 1812. I, Abner Phillips, of Surry County, and State of North Carolina, being sick and weak in body but in perfect mind and memory, thanks be given to God for the same, calling unto mind the mortality of my order this my last Will and Testament (that is to say) first of all, I give and recommend my soul unto the hand of the Almighty God, that at the discretion of my Executors nothing doubting but the general resurrection I shall receive the same again by the mighty power of God, and as touching such worldly estate wherewith it hath pleased God to help me in this life. I give and dispose of the same in the following manner and form.

I give and bequeath to my beloved wife, Elizabeth, all my real and personal estate for her natural life and at her death I give and bequeath all my land and property that my wife at death holds, to my son, Philip, and he shall give to each and every one of my children thirty dollars in trade, except my son, Cornelius; he shall give him one dollar, all to be paid in one year after my wife's death.

And I do appoint my beloved wife executrix and Philip, my son, executor to pay and collect all my just debts.

In Witness Whereof, I have set my hand and seal the day above wrote in presents of.

Test.
Wm. Hurt,
John Baily.                                   ABNER PHILLIPS (Seal)


North Carolina,
Surry County.

I, John G. Llewellyn, Deputy Clerk Superior Court of Surry County, North Carolina, do hereby certify that the foregoing is a true and perfect copy of Will of Abner Phillips, same bearing date of November 10, 1812, as same is taken from and compared with the original record of this office.—John G. Llewellyn, Deputy Clerk, November 11, 1928.

## THE KENNEDY FAMILY

No family has given more distinguished service to Wayne County, in later years, than the Kennedy family, having furnished two sons who have served the people loyally and honorably for many years. The name is found in the records of the old church at Powersburg and in the county records, showing that each generation of the family was active in the life of his day.

The Kennedy's are of Scotch ancestry. They came from Scotland to Bucks County, Pennsylvania. They moved to Virginia and in 1820 Samuel Kennedy came from Lee County, Virginia, to Duncan's Valley, in Wayne. He later removed to Otter Creek. At the time of his removal to Kentucky, his son, Levi, was six years of age, having been born in Lee County, Virginia, in 1814. His son, William Kennedy, had seven daughters and two sons, H. C. Kennedy, of Somerset, and John Kennedy, of Monticello. H. C. Kennedy was elected County Clerk, of Wayne County, in 1894; County Judge in 1905. In 1921 he was elected Circuit Judge of the 28th Judicial District.

John Kennedy was postmaster at Monticello for eight years, County Attorney of Wayne County for ten years, and at present has been Commonwealth's Attorney of the 28th Judicial District for five years.

An entry in Micajah Phillips' Minute Book of organization of the county into common school districts gives the limits of District 29 thus:

Beginning at Samuel Canady's (Kennedy) on the road leading from Monticello to Jamestown, Tennessee, thence up Otter Creek to the mouth of Carpenter's Fork, thence up said Fork including all persons living on both sides of Carpenter's Fork and its waters to the county line and bounded by said line on the south side and west by the line of Districts Nos. 13 and 14 and east by the line of Districts Nos. 27 and 28.

## THE CHRISMAN-McDOWELL FAMILY

The first Chrisman came from Swabia. He was a German, and he married in 1730 Magdalena Hite. On their bridal tour they went into Virginia and settled on a large tract at a great spring, that is known as Chrisman Springs, and is now one of the landmarks of the country. A large body of land was surveyed for this homestead and boundaries fixed, report made to the Governor and Council at Williamsburg, and a grant ordered to be issued. Reference in old deeds describe this land as the "grass land prairie." Chrisman purchased it from George Bowman.

Children of Jacob Chrisman and Magdalena Hite:
Abraham—born October 15, 1733.
Sara—born September 23, 1734.
Anna Marie—born November 9, 1735.
Isaac—born November 9, 1736.
Johannes—born March 9, 1739.
Jacob, George, Henry, and Rebecca.

Consulting war records of old Vincennes expeditions, the name of Henry Chrisman appears as a private in Captain Joseph Bowman's Company. The family record shows that a Chrisman married a daughter of Joseph McDowell, of Quaker Meadows, Frederick County, Virginia. She had a brother, General Charles McDowell, who married Lizzie Greenlee, widow of Captain John Bowman. It is believed this was the Henry mentioned above (other records say George). Two sons of this marriage, Hugh and Joseph, lived and died in Kentucky. The two sons seemed to be attached to the McDowell family, for it is shown that Hugh's daughter, Betsy Chrisman, married Samuel McDowell, son of Major John McDowell, and Joseph Chrisman married a daughter of Caleb W. McDowell, of North Carolina. One daughter of Joseph married a son of Joseph McDowell Lewis. Another daughter married Hon. Marcus Cruikshank, of Talladega, Alabama.

Major John McDowell's second wife, Lucy LeGrand, was descended from a French Huguenot, who after leaving Bohair, of which he was a native, was naturalized in England, whence he emigrated to New York. From there his descendants went to Virginia, where one of them, the Rev. Nash LeGrand, became a Presbyterian minister.

Betsy, daughter of Major John and Lucy LeGrand, married Henderson Bell. Their daughter, Lucy Nelson Bell, married James S. Chrisman. Lucy, the youngest daughter of Major John and Lucy LeGrand, married David Meade Woodson.

The McDowells came to this country and settled in Virginia about the same time that the Chrismans did. They were in the same county. Hannah, who married George Chrisman, was the daughter of Joseph McDowell and Margaret O'Neil. The Chrismans and McDowells intermarried in every generation, cousins married each other several times.

About 1708 Johannes Joost Heydt married in Holland, Anna Maria Dubois. They came to America and settled in Virginia. Magdalena Hite (Heydt), their daughter, married Jacob Chrisman. Their son, George Chrisman, married Hannah McDowell. Their son, John Chrisman, married Sallie Stone, in Wayne County, Kentucky, and their son, James S. Chrisman, married Lucy Nelson Bell. Their daughter, Alice, married Henry L. Phillips, son of Micajah Phillips.

## THE GHOLSON FAMILY

Anthony Gholson, born ——, was perhaps the first of the name who settled in Virginia. In June, 1763, he was living in St. Thomas Parish, in the County of Orange, but as he was then the owner of considerable estate, consisting of lands in that county, and Negroes, it is probable that he had been a resident there for some time. Orange was formed from Spottsylvania in 1734, and it is possible that the records of the latter county would give much earlier information regarding him. Nothing is known as to the date and locality of his marriage. His son, John Gholson, was married prior to 1741, as is evidenced by the deed to him and his wife, Esther, from the latter's father, Thomas Cook. Granting that John was the eldest son, which is by no means certain, this would put the date of the first Anthony's birth at least prior to 1700, and it was, doubtless, much earlier, as in 1763 we find him dividing his entire estate amongst his children and grandchildren, and it is reasonable to conclude from this that he felt himself unable, either by reason of age or infirmity, to retain the management of his affairs. He died some time prior to December 3, 1764; his widow, Jane, in a deed of that date referring to his recent death. How long she survived him does not appear, this deed being the last reference to her upon the Orange County records. The children of Anthony and Jane (———) Gholson as mentioned in the several deeds of gift referred to above were:

William Gholson, Elizabeth Gholson, Lucy Gholson, John Gholson, Anthony Gholson, Jr. (from whom probably descended the Gholsons of Kentucky).

Monticello, Ky., September 30, 1898.

Dear Cousin Mary (Cecil Cantrill):

It gave us pleasure to get your letter and to know that Mr. Norman enjoyed his trip to this hill country of Gholson memories. You said, in your letter sent by him, you wanted us to investigate the dates and records bearing on the Gholson history. Did you mean for us to get them from the county records? Mr. Norman didn't give me time to make many investigations, he was here such a short time and we were just delighted with him. He is indeed a gentleman, and Ma says reminded her so much of her grandfather, John Gholson. He was a very dignified, handsome gentleman and had that same culture that Norman had.

Anthony Gholson came to this country from Virginia, settled at Steubenville, and gave the Baptists a church there and a burying ground. His bones rest there and Norman and I called up his spirit to tell us all these things you wanted to know, but he slept on and the grass waved gently over his grave, "which is not marked." Isn't that too shabby of his descendants? We met a gentleman who had helped to tear down the old Gholson Church. He said it was built with pegs—no nails in it.

Anthony Gholson had a great many Negroes and seemed to be rich, though Norman says that he was disinherited. His children were Kitty, Dolly, Mollie, and Sallie (who died in Virginia), and James, John, Benjamin, and Sam. John was Ma's grandfather, his daughter, Anna Gholson, being Ma's mother. She married Mr. Hussey, from Dublin, Ireland, and moved to Indiana, and Ma was raised there. Kitty Gholson married Bartholomew Hayden and his daughter, Julia Hayden Buster, was your grandmother. Mother of Sarah Buster Cecil and first cousin to Ma's mother, Anna Gholson, making you and Ma third cousins. Susan Gholson McBeath was sister to Ma's mother and cousin, of course, to your grandmother. Her children are Linna Berry, living in Sacramento, California; Sue Masden, in Louisville, down in Portland—don't know her address; Lizzie Stoddard, of Nappa, California; and Loretta Huffaker, who married a cousin of my father's, and lives in Wheatland, California. The sons are Lem, who is in Texas, but is coming back here soon, and Anthony, of Bell County, Texas. Sam Gholson was very wild and did a great many naughty things and Ma says every time she asks the early settlers here about them, they tell her about Sam. They seem to remember him better than the rest. Ma says if she could see you she could trace out a little of all of Anthony's children, but can't write it this time. She says you are very much like Peggie Gholson, her Aunt, who married Moose, and lived in Indiana. Micah Taul married Ma's Aunt, Dorothy Gholson, and was the first clerk this county ever had. He wrote a very fine hand.

John Gholson, Ma's grandfather, was out hunting in the woods of Virginia, met a party of girls that had gotten lost in the woods. He took them home and one of them was his wife, a case of love at first sight. She says they were very elegant people and wouldn't work, but loved to hunt. I am disgusted with them for not marking Anthony's grave. Julia Hayden Buster's mother died and left two children and Anthony Gholson (her father) took them to his house and kept them till they were grown. That was Julia Hayden and Anthony Hayden. Jim Buster's son from South Carolina called here yesterday. He was summoned here to see his mother, who is very ill. Ma says he looks quite a good deal like his father.

I am very much interested in the Gholson family. The more I know of them, the more I want to know. I want you or Mr. Edwin Gholson one to write me all you know about them. I am fond of tracing families. One of my cousins and I sent to Dublin and had my grandfather Hussey's family traced out. We are coming to Paris, Kentucky, in the spring to look after my sister Emerine's grave. Will call on you then. Ma loved your mother so much. She is very anxious to see more of you. We will go south this winter and move to our city home in the spring. I suppose you know that Anthony Gholson was the first trustee this town ever had. Will see Mollie Perry and find the address of Hannah Buster if she knows it.

ADA H.

## THE HARDIN-WORSHAM FAMILY

The Hardins were of Huguenot origin. Martin, the first, had a son Captain John, who married Lydia Waters. His son, Martin, married Elizabeth Strawbridge. Their son, Benjamin, married Sarah Hardin, and Martin, a son, married Judith Calhoun. They had a son, James, who married Mary, daughter of Timothy Burgess. They lived in Lincoln County, Kentucky.

They had sons, James, William, Samuel, Mark, Martin D., Timothy, and one daughter, Sarah.

Martin D. Hardin was born in 1810 and came to Wayne County as a very young man. He married first, in 1834, Mary McKinney, mother of Mary Hardin, second wife of Joshua Berry, and lived where the Moses Simpson family lived later. She died and he married in 1840, her sister, Martha Ann, who lived only a short time. He married Emily Worsham in 1846.

Their children were: Martha (Phillips), Helen, Emily (Oatts), Sallie (Ramsey), Amelia (Back), Sam C., James, Mark, William, Ben, and Joseph.

The Worshams were one of the earliest families in the settlement of Virginia.

William and George Worsham, brothers, had a grant of 400 acres at Old Town on Appomattox. George was Justice of the Peace in Henrico County in 1648. He had a son, Captain George, who was Justice of the Peace in 1707. He died in 1735. He had married Mary Pigott. They had sons, Joseph, Richard, and Charles. This Charles had a son Charles who enlisted in the militia of Virginia, in Henrico County, and, after the Revolution, came to Wayne County. His son Cannon, who married Margaret, daughter of William and Margaret Mullins, was father of Emily Worsham, who married Martin Hardin.

The immigrant ancestor was known as William Pride.

## THE LANIER FAMILY

The Lanier family was of French origin. Sidney Lanier, the poet, who belonged to the same family as the Wayne Laniers, found that a single family of that name lived in France. They first went to England where they were musicians and artists. Jerome Lanier, son of Nicholas, was a celebrated musician. They were friends of Van Dyck, Pepys, Ben Jonson, and others of that day. Sir John Lanier was knighted. The branch that came to America were members of the Huguenot settlement in Virginia, Manakan Town. They became prosperous planters. One branch joined the pioneers who went up through Tennessee into Kentucky and on to Indiana. J. F. D. Lanier, who built the beautiful Lanier House at Madison, Indiana, was of the same branch. Sidney's family went to Rockingham, North Carolina. His grandfather, Sterling Lanier, was descended from Thomas, who settled in Virginia early in 1700.

The Wayne County branch came up the Cumberland River from Tennessee and settled at Mill Springs in the first half of the 19th century. From them have come some of the finest citizens of Wayne, Boyle, and other localities.

From Robert Lanier's account of his family, the following is taken:

"Lloyd Addison Lanier, the first of the name in Wayne County, was born near Nashville, Tennessee, on what is still known as 'Granny White's Pike.' At the age of fourteen he got a job on a river packet. He got a pilot's license when he was older and ran on a palatial Mississippi River packet. He became an expert and finally received a Master's license, thus realizing his boyish ambition.

"He loved the upper Cumberland, and saving his wages he rented a small store room at Roberts Port, a landing about three miles down river from Mill Springs, Kentucky, and put in a stock of merchandise and was successful in building up a nice country trade and at the same time met, loved, and married Amanda Brown of Wayne County, who with five other young ladies ferried the river at Roberts Port each Monday morning, and Friday evening, going to and returning from the home of Uncle Johny Rousseau who for years taught a class of young ladies each winter.

"Thompson Brown, the brother of L. A. Lanier's wife, owned a farm of twelve hundred acres at Mill Springs, and Mr. Lanier told his brother-in-law, Mr. Brown, if ever he wanted to sell the place, write to him, as he and wife were moving to Nashville, Tennessee. In 1869, Mr. Lanier bought this farm, and he with his family of four sons and three daughters and wife moved up the Cumberland from Nashville and took possession of this wonderful farm. The farm residence was a large and beautiful two-story frame building having nine rooms and kitchen, with long double porches, fronting south and west. These porches had red cedar floors, and while not matched, were hand planed and accurately jointed, and only a few years ago, his son, T. S. Lanier, who then owned his part of this farm, remodeled the old home and in taking up the old cedar porch flooring, found the boards as sound as when lain in the early sixties, and being reworked these same cedar boards were used in the remodeling.

"When the Battle of Mill Springs was fought, Zollicoffer used this old home as his headquarters before the battle was fought and after the fight the Confederates retreated, going south.

"A few days later the Union forces brought down from the battlefield their artillery and stationed a field piece high up on the north side of the Cumberland, almost a couple of miles off and centering their effort toward the headquarter's building, put two shells through that lovely old building; one made a clean passage through the parlor and hall and fell as a spent shell in a meadow. In passing through what was then known as the parlor room, it smashed an ink well resting on an old marble-top table, and ink was smeared and splotched on the ceiling, and L. A. Lanier would never in his lifetime allow it to be calcimined over. After demolishing the ink well the shell went through a hall door that stood half ajar. The door was preserved until 1932, when a son, R. L. Lanier, went into business in Monticello, Kentucky, and placed it in his show window that tourists might see it and read its inscription. A fire in 1932 wiped out a block on Main Street and R. L. Lanier's place of business went up in smoke, as did that much loved relic.

"When L. A. Lanier took over the Mill Springs farm, there was a store, a mill, and several tenant houses thereon, and a post office was in the old store, and the old water mill was operating, however, it did not belong to the farm; also a carding factory and a cotton gin, both belonging to a neighbor, Mr. I. P. Lynch. A short while after Mr. Lanier came into possession of the farm, he bought the old mill and the two factories. The old mill was operated just as it was in 1869 until '77, when it and the two factories were razed and on the factory site Mr. Lanier erected a forty by forty three-story, twenty-foot basement modern building in which went the machinery to equip a first-class flouring mill. The framing timber for this job was cut and hewn several miles above Burnside on the Cumberland and was of white oak and yellow poplar and all hewn to sixteen inches square. It was rafted and floated to Mill Springs and went into this building in 1877. The grinding was done on two sets of burrs dressed for wheat, and one set for corn. The water wheel was twenty-eight feet in diameter with three feet breast. Before the death of L. A. Lanier in February, 1879, he sold it to a son, I. T. Lanier, and a son-in-law, J. M. Sallee. In 1884, a son, R. L. Lanier, and a son-in-law, Dr. J. A. Jones, bought the plant, operating it as it was until '85. Dr. Jones sold an interest to I. D. Ruffner, who had been head miller for several years, and the new firm of J. A. Jones & Company remodeled the plant to the roller system. The property was sold a few years later to Bolan E. Roberts & Sons. They made a lot of improvements, adding a 'sifter' which took the place of the long bolting reels, and made the 'purifier' useless. They took out the old twenty-eight-foot wooden water wheel installing a forty-foot steel wheel which was a great gain in power, and this wheel is said to be the next largest water wheel in America."

### Lanier Family Record

L. H. Lanier, son of B. H. Lanier and Nancy Lanier, his wife, was born May 27, 1812.

Isaac E. Lanier, son of B. H. Lanier and Nancy Lanier, his wife, was born November 17, 1817.

Lloyd Addison Lanier, son of B. H. Lanier and Nancy Lanier, his wife, was born June 17, 1820.

William H. Lanier, son of B. H. Lanier and Nancy Lanier, his wife, was born February 21, 1822.

Mary Ann Lanier, daughter of B. H. Lanier and Nancy Lanier, his wife, was born February 16, 1824.

Martha P. Lanier, daughter of B. H. Lanier and Nancy Lanier, his wife, was born June 9, 1826.

Leamiza Elizabeth Lanier, daughter of B. H. Lanier and Nancy Lanier, his wife, was born October 20, 1827.

B. II. Lanier, son of B. H. Lanier and Nancy Lanier, his wife, was born March 4, 1829.

Mrs. Buchanan Earthman Lanier, daughter of Isaac and Mary Holt Earthman, was mother of L. H., Lloyd Addison, William, Mary, Martha, Elizabeth, and Buchanan, Jr., Lanier. Her name was Nancy Earthman. The great-grandparents, Isaac and Mary Earthman, were married in Pennsylvania. After their marriage, they moved to North Carolina, then to Tennessee just after the state was admitted to the Union. The Holts now living in Williamson County are distant relatives. The Lanier branch of the family settled on the Dickerson Road and the Earthmans on the White Creek Pike in Davidson County, Tennessee, near Nashville. Some of the property is still in the Earthman family.

This is a true statement.—*Martha Lanier Wilson.*

Buchanan H. Lanier, son of William and Penny Lanier, his wife, departed this life April 20, 1830, about nine o'clock in the morning. "His spirit has reached the undiscovered land from whose border no traveller returns, till Christ shall come to arouse the slumbering dead. Farewell, pale lifeless clay, a long farewell. Sweet be thy sleep beneath the green trees' shade, where I have laid thee in thy lonely cell."

Nancy McLane, formerly the wife of B. H. Lanier, daughter of Isaac and Mary Earthman, died January 31, 1856.

Lloyd Addison Lanier married Amanda Brown.
Elizabeth married Sam Cowan.
Buchanan married Mary West.
Isaac married Amanda Sallee.
Mollie married Joe Allen Jones.
Thomas S. married Peggy Sallee.
Margaret married Jeff Sallee.
Robert married Mattie West.

John Jones, born October, 1742, died May, 1824, near Hustonville, Kentucky; married Elizabeth Elrod.

Robert Jones, born June, 1775, died June, 1843; married Nancy Talbott.

Green Jones, born August, 1812, died December, 1883; married Nancy Caldwell.

Josiah Allen Jones, born July, 1839, died February, 1925; married Mollie Lanier.

## THE WARDEN-DUNCAN-McBEATH FAMILIES

In 1623 the ship Anne, with Captain Eppes, brought a company of thirty, who had obtained a patent to an extensive tract in Virginia. Among them was Thomas Warden, the first of the name in America. He had a son, Thomas, whose son, John, married Elisabeth Shearwood, in Princess Anne County. Their son, John, became an attorney and is frequently mentioned in the records of that county. He enlisted in the militia of Virginia during the Revolution, and when the war was over, returned to the practice of his profession. His son, John, came to Wayne County, Kentucky, with his family, about 1810.

The Duncans are of Scotch ancestry. The first of the name in Wayne County was George, who came from North Carolina, in 1801, and settled on Beaver Creek. He had two sons, George and William. George married Rhoda, daughter of William and Nancy Miller Bartleson. Their children were Samuel, John, Granville, Charles, William, and Harvey, and two daughters. Samuel married Mary Phillips. John married Martha Stone. Granville married a Miss Menifee, of Lincoln County. Charles married Nettie Warden. Harvey married Mary Tuggle.

The McBeaths came from Scotland also. They first settled in Southwest Virginia, at an early date, coming to Wayne with the family of Archibald Woods, who married Mary McBeath. John McBeath married Mary Jones, daughter of James and Mary Buster Jones. Their son, Andrew, married Susan Gholson, and their daughter, Susan, married John Warden.

There were other members of these families of whom information is not at hand.

## THE WEST FAMILY

In 1622, John West, Captain Francis West, and Nathaniel West, with others, acquired a tract of land in Virginia, which included the plantation of Westover, one of the celebrated colonial homes still standing. This historic shrine was bought by William Byrd in 1678. The West family is of distinguished English origin. Benjamin West, the famous artist, was of the same stock. Isaac West came into Wayne before 1800 and settled in the upper part of the county. It was at his home that Micah Taul met Dorothy Gholson in 1801, at the wedding of Abel Shrewsbury and Tebitha Van Hoogan.

The name is frequently found in the early annals of the county. They intermarried with the Lanier family, many of whose descendants are found in Boyle County and Wayne today, whence they have scattered over the United States.

Isaac West married Margaret Russell. Their son, Russell West, built the first brick house in Wayne County.

## THE SALLEE FAMILY

The Sallees were Huguenots who came very early in the 17th Century to Virginia. They were members of the group at "Manakan Town," near Richmond, who were given a grant there. A branch came down into North Carolina and thence to Kentucky. The first of the name to come to Wayne was Peter Sallee, who married Charity Van Winkle in North Carolina. They were the parents of John L. Sallee who married Jane Jones (Clemens), granddaughter of Joshua Jones. John and Jane (Jones) Sallee's children were: Caroline (Francis) and Mary (Hardin), Joseph, who married Pauline Owens, and Walter. John L. Sallee was born in Wayne County in 1813 and died there in 1886. He filled with credit many places of trust. He was county judge, circuit clerk, county clerk, and representative in the State Legislature.

Martin Phillips Sallee was born March 16, 1828, in Wayne County, Kentucky, where he lived until 1883, when he removed to Boyle County, and located two miles east of Danville. His father, Captain Moses Sallee, of Wayne County, was long a magistrate and member of the Court of Claims, and a representative of the Legislature. He was a Whig, a farmer and slave owner, and died in 1840 at the age of fifty-five years. He was the son of Peter Sallee, whose offspring were John, Joseph, Moses, Charity (Van Winkle), and Susan (Bruton). Moses married Mary Deering of Wayne County (died in 1858, aged about sixty years), and their union was favored by the birth of Harrison M., Lucinda (Redman), Melinda (Redman), Martha (Huff), Anna (Hurt), Martin P., and Cyrina (Parmley).

Martin Phillips Sallee had been twice married; first, on August 21, 1849, to Margaret A., daughter of Jefferson and Rachael (Coffey) Jones, of Wayne County (born in 1830, died January 11, 1862); and from their union sprang Elizabeth (Jones), Jefferson, Amanda (Lanier), and Margaret (Lanier). On May 18, 1864, he was united in marriage with Miss Susan, daughter of Harrison and Elizabeth (Carter) Berry, of Wayne County (born July 18, 1842).

## THE HEDRICK-TATE FAMILIES

Back in the "horse and buggy" days, a young man went to Monticello from the upper part of the county, and set himself up in business in a small way. This young man was George Hedrick. His only capital was an unlimited capacity for hard work, a determination to succeed, and sound business judgment. Coupled with these qualities was an unswerving honesty and sense of fair dealing. Step by step he came up, gradually expanding his plant until, by the beginning of the present century, he was operating an extensive hardware business. From the horse-drawn vehicle, he went into the sale of automobiles and amassed a fortune. Liberal in his business policies, and always ready to lend a helping hand to struggling young men, it may well be said that no man in the county has contributed more to the civic and commercial development of this section than he.

Mr. Hedrick married Miss Ellen Tate, daughter of Judge Stephen H. Tate, who was an active force in the business and political life of his day.

Of the Tate family, it is noted that each member has taken a prominent part in the life of the community in which he lived.

## THE BERRY-EWING-CARTER FAMILIES

George Berry, of Culpepper Court House, Virginia, married Mary Buster, daughter of Charles Buster, of Monticello. They had the following children:

William Harrison Berry married Elizabeth Carter.

Charles Berry married a Louisville woman and went to Paris, Texas.

James Berry married Jennie Jones.

George Berry married a widow in Arkansas.

Joshua Berry married (1) Emerine Huffaker, (2) Mary Hardin, Monticello.

Vienna Berry married Hiram Phillips.

Elizabeth Berry married John Phillips.

Margaret Berry married Samuel Long, Albany, Kentucky; moved to Texas.

Mary Berry died.

---

William Harrison Berry, born in Monticello, April 18, 1813, died in Monticello, September, 1864; married Elizabeth Ewing Carter, born in Monticello, December 13, 1817, died in Danville, 1911, age 94; children:

Mary Carter Berry married Chesley Toler.
George Ewing Berry died during Civil War.
Susan Elizabeth Berry married Martin Phillips Sallee.
Vienna Phillips Berry married Robert Baylor Metcalf.
Unity Catherine Berry died unmarried.
Emily Jane Berry married N. Dienecis Ingram.
Laura Ewing Berry died unmarried.
John Carter Berry died unmarried.
James Berry married Emma Crawford.
Braxton Carter Berry unmarried, living in Danville.
Vienna Berry Toler married John Gheens Cramer.
Minnie Laura Toler unmarried.
Chesley Toler went away and not heard from for years.

Vienna Berry Toler had two children, Minnie Toler Cramer and Vie Toler Cramer married Maury Crutcher.

William Carter, of Wythe County, Virginia, married Unity Bates. They moved to Kentucky and settled on the Cumberland River on a big farm. They had the following children:

Elizabeth Carter married twice (1) Crockett, (2) R. Montgomery.

Susan Carter married John Moore of Monticello.

Mildred Carter married Anthony Dibrell, of Sparta, Tennessee.

Jackson Carter moved to Tennessee, married a Carter cousin.

Braxton Carter married three times: Mary Ewing, Mrs. Burnetta Taylor, Mrs. Ellen Worsham Chaplin.

Children of Braxton Carter and Mary Ewing:

Elizabeth Ewing Carter married William Harrison Berry.

William Wallace Carter married Mary Metcalf, Mill Springs, Kentucky.

George Ewing Carter married Theresa Van Winkle, Wayne County, Kentucky.

Unity Bates Carter married James Meadows, Wayne County, Kentucky.

Susan Moore Carter, unmarried.

Mary Catherine Carter married William Meadows, Wayne County, Kentucky.

John Anthony Carter married Margaret Bobbitt, Wayne County, Kentucky.

---

George Ewing, of Virginia, married Elizabeth Wallace and they came to Kentucky and settled on the Cumberland near William Carter, when their children were about grown. They had two children:

Mary Ewing married Braxton Carter.
Katherine Ewing married Leo Hayden, of Stanford, Kentucky.
Elizabeth Wallace's father was Andrew Wallace.

---

The Ewings came from Scotland to North Ireland and then to America. Two brothers came over. Their names were Finis and Baker Ewing. Baker Ewing was my great-great-great-great-great-grandfather.—*Minnie Toler.*

## THE SHEARER FAMILY

When Cromwell disbanded his famous Ironsides, he settled them on the confiscated estates in Northern Ireland. Among them were Shearers, whom we are unable to trace by name throughout the first two generations. They were English Puritans and Presbyterians. They preserve their identity and traditions to this day, with but little admixture of Scotch-Irish blood on the one hand or Celtic blood on the other. All were at first

Presbyterians and Old Line Whigs in this country, and all seemed to need or to care for a stimulant.

Some time before the Revolutionary War, about 1740, four brothers of this Puritan stock came to America with their families from the County of Armagh and Province of Ulster, Ireland. Their names were George, John, William I, and James. One settled in New York, two in Pennsylvania, and one in South Carolina. The South Carolina branch of the family are traceable throughout North Carolina, Kentucky, Texas, Oklahoma, Missouri, Iowa, and Nebraska, and the other branches and their families are found in almost every state in the Union. Wherever found they preserve their traditions—personal, social, and religious, and their physical characteristics and conformation, gait and features are easily recognized. These Shearers are not to be confounded with the German Lutherans of about the same name —Scherer, Schearer, and Sherer, of whom there are a great number in this country.

One of these brothers was the father of William Shearer II who married in South Carolina, and was the father of William Shearer III. This was the William Christian Shearer, our ancestor, born about 1760, North Carolina, died about 1830, in Wayne County, Kentucky, buried at Bethesda Churchyard.

William Christian Shearer was married twice in North Carolina. First wife, Hannah Hoover, buried in Ashe County, North Carolina. Her children were Daniel, Jacob, Henry, Sallie, Mary, David. The second wife (from whom J. B. Shearer, of Emerson, Nebraska, descended) was a German Hessian, named Sallie Walters. Her children were Susan, Jane, Hannah, Solomon, Walter, Margaret, Catherine, William, Hester, Elizabeth, and Nancy.

This William Christian Shearer was one of the early settlers of Wayne County; came about 1812. John Shearer's family in Monticello are descended from Jacob of the first family. The others from Daniel, whose wife was Margaret Vickery, their children being: Violet Roten, Polly Huffaker, Adam N., Margaret Huffaker, Rebecca Hicks, Caroline Rankin, Sallie Hicks-Marshall, Louisa Simpson, J. Jenkins, Frank, Broyles.

J. Jenkins Shearer married Zerelda Ingram, daughter of Samuel Ingram and Elizabeth Parmley. Their children were: Lousetta married Shelby Ragan, Emma C. married Thomas J. Rankin, Samuel married Mollie Huffaker, Menifee married Mary Wray, James.

Samuel was son of James Ingram.

## THE OATTS FAMILY

Roger Oatts, the first of the name in Wayne County, was there before 1800. Thereafter he was prominently identified with the life of the county.

He had the first tavern in Monticello. He served several years as Justice. He came from Southwest Virginia.

Rogers Oatts is noted as a juror in Fincastle County, Virginia, in 1793. He was son of William Oatts, a Revolutionary soldier. He married Mary Jones, daughter of Joshua Jones, in 1790. His oldest son, Joshua, married Polly Coffey. Their children were: Cleveland; James, married Harriet Worsham; Cosby, married (1) Irene Frisbie, (2) Marietta Frisbie; William; John R.; Lewis; Russell, married Emily Hardin; Emily, married Eben Jones; T. J., married Nancy Ingram; Sophronia.

Roger Oatts' descendants have been noted for their high qualities of citizenship and business acumen.

### From the Oatts Bible

Roger Oatts, born 1760, died 1837.
Mary Jones, born 1772, died 1840.
They were married in 1790.

Joshua Oatts, born 1791, died 1856.
Polly Coffey, born 1800, died 1855.
They were married in 1821.

T. J. Oatts, born 1837, died 1913.
Nancy Ingram, born 1860.
They were married in 1888.

## THE INGRAM FAMILY

The Ingram family is of Scotch ancestry by way of England. The name was originally Ingraham and some of them still retain this spelling in England and Scotland. The armorial bearings are similar. The family is of aristocratic ancestry wherever found.

James Ingram, founder of the family in Wayne, was born in England, June 26, 1761, and died in Wayne, August 1, 1854. He came to America with his parents when he was four years old. He married in Virginia, Rhoda Menifee. Their children were: Samuel, Nimrod, James, William, and Rhoda.

The Ingram records, following, are from Bibles of different Ingram families, descendants of the first James.

### From the Old Ingram Bible

Jas. Ingram, born 1796, April 18; died 1880, September 25.

Jemima M. Ingram, born January 10, 1797; died August 7, 1876.

Geo. W. Ingram, born November 22, 1823; died April 24, 1889.

Jas. R. Ingram, born July 21, 1824; died April 18, 1891.

Marietta Ingram, born April 23, 1827; died December 29, 1839.

Nimrod Ingram and Nancy Cecil were married February 8, 1825.

Charles Buster and Mary E. Ingram were married November 9, 1841.

James M. Ingram, born October 6, 1820.
Louisa Ingram, born July 12, 1822.
Emerine Ingram, born December 12, 1823.
Granville C. Ingram, born June 5, 1826.
John Borlen Ingram, born February 17, 1829.
Nimrod D. Ingram, born January 16, 1832.
William Perry Ingram, born January 16, 1834.

Louisa Ingram, died December 1, 1823.

Nimrod Ingram departed this life on 4th day of October, about 2:00 o'clock, in the year 1828.

James M. Ingram departed this life on 19th of April, in the year 1843, age 23 years, 5 months, and 12 days.

Nancy Ingram, consort of Nimrod Ingram, departed this life the 13th of June, about five o'clock, 1864.

Granville C. Ingram died February 7, 1880.

W. P. Ingram died February 8, 1885.

J. B. Ingram died March 14, 1887.

Mary Emerine Ingram Buster died May 25, 1891.

Nimrod Dyancus Ingram.

## From the Bates Bible

Thomas Shelby Bates and Evaline Matilda Simpson were married the 29th day of September, 1842, and the said T. S. Bates was born 7th day of October, 1818.

Reuben Thomas Bates, son of T. S. Bates and E. M. Bates, his wife, was born 1845.

Mary Jane Bates was born 22nd day of May, 1848.

James J. Bates was born 16th June, 1850.

Moses Simpson Bates born 1853.

William Bates born 1854.

Elisha Lankford Bates born 1856.

## From William Simpson's Bible

William Simpson, son of Reuben Simpson, Jr., born 15th July, 1806.

Isaac Simpson born 1807.
Rebecca Simpson born 1809.
Sally Simpson born 1811.
Thomas Simpson born 1813.
Mary Simpson born 1814.
Elisha Simpson born 1816.
Samuel Simpson born 1818.
Moses Simpson born 1825.
Ruth Simpson born 1822.
Reuben Simpson born 1820.
Evaline Simpson born 1827.

Wm. Simpson, son of Reuben and Martha, born July 15, 1806; died 1869.
Sarah Chrisman, 1st consort of Wm. Simpson.
John C. Simpson, November 22, 1834.
Sallie Fleming, 2nd consort of Wm. Simpson.
Joab Rigney.

### From the Buster Bible

Bartholomew Hayden married Julia Gholson. Their children were: Augustus Hayden, married Miss Dibrell; Kitty Hayden, married General Joshua Buster. Their children were: Charles Buster, married Mary Emerine Ingram; William Buster; James Buster, married Eliza West; Milton Buster, married Louisa Parker; Kitty Buster, married William Kendrick; Sarah Buster, married Granville Cecil.

Zachariah Cecil married Julia Howe, in Montgomery County, Virginia. Their children were: Nancy Cecil, married Nimrod Ingram; Russell Cecil, married Lucy, daughter of Micajah Phillips; Granville Cecil, married Sarah Buster, daughter of Joshua Buster; Minerva Cecil, married James Ingram.

Nimrod and Nancy C. Ingram's children were: Mary Emerine, married Charles Buster; Granville; John B.; William, married Betty Allen; Dyancus, married Emma Berry.

James and Minerva C. Ingram's children were: George Ingram, Rufus Ingram, Virginia Ingram, Perry Ingram.

William and Betty Allen Cecil's children were: Nancy, Ethel, John L., Bessie.

Dyancus Ingram and Emma Berry's children were: Dyancus, Minnie, John.

George Ingram's children were: Marietta, Emerine, and James.

### From an Old Bible Presented in 1870 to Mrs. Mary Cecil Cantrill, by William Buster, son of Joshua Buster and Julia Gholson Hayden; Edinburgh, 1775.

*(Evidently written with quill pen, ink much faded, almost indecipherable)*

Charles Buster and Sarah Jones married March 13 1788.
Mary Buster was born June ye 12th 1789.

William Buster was born June ye 5th 1791.
Joshua Buster was born April ye 8th 1793.
Elizabeth Buster was born Dec. ye 25th 1795.
James Buster was born June ye 26th 1798.
John Buster was born June ye 24 1800.

Charles Buster departed this life Nov. ye 12th 1802.

John Sanders and Sarah Buster were married June 10th 1804.

Minerva Sanders was born April 30th 1805.
Julia Sanders was born Feb. 7th 1808.
Hiram Bewley Sanders, born Sept. 22nd 1810.

Sarah Sanders departed this life Jan. 24th 1832.

## THE BARTLESON-MILLER FAMILIES

"Pearson Miller and Nancy Huff married in Virginia and started on journey to Kentucky with one horse, feather bed, and rifle. Pearson Miller walked before the horse carrying rifle, and his wife rode upon the horse on top of the feather bed. They settled in Duvall Valley, in Clinton County, Kentucky, and after their first son, Absalom, was born they moved to Tennessee, three miles above Three Forks of Wolf Creek near Jamestown and resided there the balance of their lives. Unto them were born eleven children. Pearson Miller was a fleshy man. His wife was tall and was not fleshy."—*Miss Fayette Miller.*

"My grandfather, William Bartleson, came to Virginia from Ireland, then to Illinois, and later to Tennessee. He married a Miss Grier and raised eight children.

"My father married Nancy Miller at her father's home, Three Forks of Wolf Creek.

"My mother was as fine looking a woman as anybody knew. She was 5 feet 10 inches tall; very fair, smooth skin; wore 2½ size shoes, weighed in prime of life 170 pounds; had auburn hair that lay on floor when she sat down; had a common school education; was born in England. There was always love in our home."—*Lola B. Ralston.*

## From the Bartleson Bible

William Bartleson (first) married Miss Grier. Children:
William Bartleson married Nancy Miller.
Harvey Bartleson married Belle Jones.
Nellie Bartleson married Van Winkle—went to Illinois.
Peggy Bartleson married Ingram—went to Missouri.
Rhoda Bartleson married George Duncan.
Betsy Bartleson married William Duncan.
Hannah Bartleson married Absalom Miller.

William Bartleson, born October 2, 1808; died January 13, 1873. Nancy Miller, born September 20, 1818; died October 27, 1875. Married September 14, 1837. Children:

Emerine Bartleson, born December 4, 1838; married Perry Taylor.

James Bartleson, born September 10, 1840.

Artema Bartleson, born May 29, 1842; married Jonathan S. Frisbie.

Amanda Bartleson, born May 5, 1844; married Joseph Denham.

John Bartleson, born August 25, 1846; married May Sloan.

Hannah Bartleson, born October 6, 1848; married Wesley Duncan.

Pearson M. Bartleson, born January 19, 1851; married Hannah C. Oatts.

Telitha Bartleson, born May 27, 1853.

Wm. H. Bartleson, born October 12, 1855; married Alice Chrisman.

Rufus Ingram Bartleson, born July 9, 1858; married Fannie Tuttle.

Nancy Bartleson, born June 10, 1861.

Jonathan Smith Frisbie married Artema Bartleson, August 20, 1868.

Pearson Miller Bartleson married Hannah Clementine Oatts, November 15, 1882.

Dr. Jonathan Smith Frisbie married Hannah Jones. Children:

Jonathan Smith Frisbie, Jr., married Artema Bartleson.
Susan Frisbie married Joseph Russell.
Eliza Frisbie married (1) Sanders, (2) Oldacre.
Etta Frisbie married (1) Baker, (2) Oatts.
Julia Frisbie married William Burton.
Dr. J. B. S. Frisbie married Harriet Phillips.
Irene Frisbie married Cosby Oatts.

## From the Cooper Bible

Frederick Cooper and Dorothy Brown were married 1783.

Katy Cooper, born 1784.
Anne Cooper, born February, 1786.
Henry Cooper, born 1790.
John Cooper, born June 9, 1793.
William Cooper, born November 25, 1795.
Abraham Cooper, born November 9, 1798.
Isaac Cooper, born December 20, 1805.
Jacob Cooper, born April, 1808.

## Bible Record of William Tarleton Taylor

William Tarleton Taylor and Elizabeth Hampton, daughter of Jeremiah Hampton, Loudoun County, Virginia.

William T. Taylor, born August 24, 1759.
Elizabeth H. Taylor, born March 25, 1762.
William and Elizabeth Taylor were married August 4, 1778.

John Taylor and Amy Weeks were married January 8, 1807.
Burgess French and Sally Taylor were married April 13, 1807.
Reuben Smart and Nancy Taylor were married November 16, 1809.

Levi T. Taylor, born Loudoun County, Virginia, April 26, 1779.

Levi T. Taylor and Nancy Downing were married January 6, 1799.

Nancy Taylor, born October 6, 1792.
Ignatius Taylor, born August 25, 1795.

Eliza Taylor, born February 28, 1798.
Alfred Taylor, born October 11, 1799.
Elizabeth Taylor, born March 25, 1800.
Jenefer Taylor, born March 23, 1801.
Ellender Taylor, born December 13, 1802.
William T. Taylor, born August 26, 1804.
Joseph Taylor, born March 15, 1805.
Levi T. Taylor, Jr., born July 20, 1806.
Abednego Taylor, born October 7, 1808.

### John H. Taylor's Children

Levi T. Taylor, born April 26, 1779.
John Taylor, born January 27, 1782.
Tarlton Taylor, born December 11, 1784.
Sally Taylor, born June 9, 1787.
Hampton Taylor, born December 4, 1789.
William T. Taylor, born July 26, 1808.
Elizabeth Taylor, born March 15, 1810.
Joseph Hampton Taylor, born May 3, 1810.
Sarah Ann Taylor, born January 15, 1812.
John T. Taylor, born January 21, 1812.

### Burgess French's Children

Louisa French, born October 16, 1808.
Marian French, born July 28, 1810.
Anna French, born October 5, 1813.
Mahala French, born July 9, 1819.
John W. French, born June 2, 1822.
Sarah Ellender French, born September 25, 1823.

### Eads Bible

Charles Eads and Sarah Piborn were married in 1785. Children:

Gabriel Eads, born February 10, 1787.
Nancy Eads, born February 9, 1789.

Polly Eads, born February 4, 1790.
Rachael Eads, born August 31, 1792.
Jacob Eads, born October 30, 1796.
Ruth Eads, born March 11, 1799.

### John Francis' Bible

John Francis and Nancy, his wife, married May 15, 1784.
Leah Francis, born October 5, 1785.
Mary Francis, born July 10, 1787.
Henry Francis, born May 16, 1789.
Tabetha Francis, born March 22, 1791.
Nancy Francis, born November 6, 1795.
John Francis, born September 24, 1797.
Elisha Francis, born July 5, 1799.
Peggy Francis, born November 11, 1802.
George Francis, born May 21, 1805.
Elisha Francis and Sally Blevins.
Henry Francis and Peggy Conwell were married September 20, 1805.
Mahala Francis and Robert Travis were married October 2, 1828.

## KENDRICK-SAUNDERS FAMILY

George Saunders and Lockie Arthur were married January 12, 1805, Bedford County, Virginia.

Creed Saunders, born 1810, died 1843.

George Woodward Saunders, born 1814, married Jane Kinkead Long, November 7, 1839.

John Kendrick, born 1750 (Washington County, Virginia), died 1812. Served in American Revolutionary War, was in Battle of King's Mountain, lived on the Holston River. He married in 1805, Elizabeth Summers, born ——, died 1857.

William Kendrick, born 1804, died 1889. Married October 13, 1824, Catherine Buster (daughter of Joshua Buster), born July 25, 1818, died February 6, 1849.

Joshua Buster Kendrick, born March 5, 1846, married Mary E. Saunders, September 20, 1842.

### WILLIAM J. KENDRICK, SEN.

June 13, 1889.

Born in Washington County, Virginia, October 13, 1804, died in Wayne County, Kentucky, June 10, 1889. Such is the record upon the tablets of "Old Mortality," of the beginning and end of the earthly career of one of the most remarkable men who ever figured in the annals of our county.

About the year 1822, when about eighteen years of age, with but a limited education, no capital but his native talents and strong right arm, and no guaranty of success but his indomitable will, energy, and habits of industry, he came to this, then, newly settled part of Kentucky to seek his fortune.

The first business in which he was engaged was as a clerk in the store of Ambrose Bramlette in Clinton County, where he remained about two years, when he was recalled to Virginia by the death of his stepfather. He remained in Virginia for three years, taking care of his mother and other members of the family, and managing the farm. He came to Wayne County about the year 1828, and resided near Monticello from that time until his death, a period of more than threescore years. The first business in which he engaged, after returning to Kentucky, was making rails on the present John R. Oatts and Brothers farm at 25 cents per hundred, and working on the farm eight months for $40, after which he carried on a blacksmith shop, in which he for some time labored at the bellows and wielded the sledge. He was afterwards engaged as clerk in the store of his uncles William and Samuel Summers, in Monticello, Kentucky.

He was twice married, first about 1836 to Miss Catherine Buster, daughter of General Joshua Buster, and second, about 1851, to Mrs. Abbie Rachael Coffey, widow of Cullom Coffey. He had six children by his first wife and five by his last.

Somewhere in the thirties, in partnership with Granville Cecil, he embarked in merchandising. The firm of Cecil & Kendrick did a large and prosperous business in merchandise and extended its operations to trading largely in cattle and other farm stock, which they marketed in Virginia and the cotton states at a large profit, up to the dissolution of the firm in 1847, when Cecil removed to Boyle County.

In the meantime Mr. Kendrick had bought the Albert Epperson and Charles Mills farms which he united into one and farmed and raised stock on a large scale on his own account.

After the dissolution of the firm of Cecil & Kendrick he continued merchandising on his own account until the outbreak of the war. On the organization of the branch of the Commercial Bank of Kentucky at Monticello, he took stock in it to a considerable amount and was its president during its continuance in business. During the fifties and after the war in the sixties, and for some time in the seventies, he turned his attention to the investment of his means into land. He also made considerable investments in Government and County and City bonds. On the organization of the National Bank of Monticello in 1872, he took a large amount of stock in it and was its president from its organization to 1877 when it went into liquidation. During part of 1877 and 1878 he carried on a private bank, under the style of Kendrick, Sallee & Company. He was the founder of the Kendrick Institution and its largest stockholder, and president from its institution in 1866 to the time it was unfortunately burned in 1872. He was the largest stockholder and for many years the president of the Monticello and Burnside Turnpike Company, and subsequently its treasurer to the time of his death. Besides an active participation in all these things, though far advanced in years, he personally superintended extensive farming operations on several large farms, even down to the smallest details.

Possessed of a powerful frame and vigorous constitution, unimpaired almost to the last, he seemed to go everywhere and to attend to everything on his extensive possessions that required attention. His capacity for business during at least fifty years of his life among us was truly wonderful. During that time he transacted more business, it is safe to say, than any other ten men that ever lived in the county during the same time. His sound judgment and sagacity in business was proverbial, and while connected with a vast amount of business affairs of his own, he was consulted by nearly all the citizens of the county on embarking in, or conducting enterprises of their own.

He was a man of the strictest integrity in all his dealings with his fellow men, and his long and honorable career found its just reward, not only in the accumulation of a considerable fortune, but in securing for him the most implicit and abiding confidence and esteem of all who knew him.

No man who ever lived in the county dispensed charity more liberally or with less ostentation. Besides that he was ever the helper of poor young men struggling for a start in life. In addition to lending a helping hand to hundreds who needed help in business; he furnished money to more than a score of young men to aid them in qualifying themselves for professions, never asking security and trusting to their honor and his judgment of their merits and prospects of successful repayment. He has often remarked with gratification that he was never deceived in any of them, or never lost anything in helping them, except perhaps a very trivial balance that one or two of them failed to pay, owing to misfortune, and for which he attached no blame.

Some years ago he attached himself to the Christian Church, since which he has lived and died an exemplary and consistent member of that fold. His many good traits and deeds would fill a volume, but circumstances prevent a more extended notice at this time. "Taken all in all, we shall never see his like again."—*Monticello Signal*.

This is an exact copy of a letter found by Samuel Duncan of Nicholasville, now owned by Miss Amelia Saunders, Somerset, Kentucky:

Knoxville, Tennessee, September 9, 1821.

Tunstall Quarles,
   Somerset,

Dear Sir:

I want you to see Mr. Dollarhide and tell him he can have that sorrel horse which I promised to him by paying 50 dollars. I could get more money for such a horse if I had him here in Knoxville, but as Mr. Dollarhide is an old friend he may have the horse for the sum mentioned above. Tell George Saunders I was in Bedford County, Virginia, two weeks ago and attended the burial of Julius, his father. He was buried in honors of war as he was in the capture of that old Skoundrell Cornwallis at Little Fork, sixty-one years ago. Julius was a good soldier. I was in the funeral escort. More than a thousand people were at his burial. Rev. James Shelburne, a Baptist preacher, delivered a sermon at the grave. He was four years younger than myself. I was born in 1754; he was born in New Kent, 1758. I will be in Somerset in October or 1st of November.

SAMUEL NEWELL.

## THE RAMSEY FAMILY

The Ramsey family is of Scotch ancestry. They came to Wayne after 1816. The first of whom we have a record was John Ramsey whose son, Richard, was father of R. S. Ramsey. Another son, I. C. Ramsey, was prominent in the life of the county. He taught in the county as a young man and became superintendent of schools. For a time he was in the mercantile business.

G. T. Ramsey, his brother, was sheriff of Wayne County, a fearless and popular official. Logan, another brother, became wealthy, owning extensive fertile lands in the rich Cumberland River bottoms. Preston moved to Missouri when he was very young.

R. S. Ramsey served with the Union Army in the Civil War. Alert and active at the age of ninety-four, he attended the reunion at Gettysburg. His prowess on horseback excited the admiration of his friends. A recent picture shows him taking a jump few younger men would attempt.

Many of the family served in the Revolution. It is thought that Thomas Ramsey, of Southwest Virginia, was the progenitor of the Wayne family.

Thomas Ramsey, Revolutionary soldier, emigrated to Lincoln County after the war. He received a pension in Garrard which had been created from Lincoln.

He was born in Botetourt County, Virginia in 1732, son of Thomas Ramsey. He was surveyor of that county in 1770, juror in 1773.

John Ramsey, his son, was deputy sheriff in Fincastle County in 1788.

## HISTORIC HOUSES

"THE OLD FRENCH FEWSTON. J. T. Alexander Tavern is one of the older buildings of the town, the oldest building in town being a part of the John Marcum property on Short Street, which was the original post office of the town, built in about 1800. The courthouse was then located on the lot where T. M. Ragan's oil house stands, afterwards known as the old Stone stable."—*Wayne County Outlook*, August, 1938.

In this house on Short Street, William Hardin lived with his family. His brother, Martin D. Hardin, born in Lincoln County in 1810, came as a very young man to Wayne and lived there with him. He remembered living there "when the stars fell in '33." His sister, Sarah, was visiting here at the time.

### THE METCALFE HOME

"One of the most historic and interesting places in Wayne is the Metcalfe homestead on State Route 90, the old Monticello and Burnside toll pike, just south of Mill Springs post office. This house, built originally of brick, now has added a frame addition, which was built in the year 1800 when it was then in Pulaski County. The farm is the same as that patented by a governor of Kentucky to a lineal ancestor of the present owners and occupants and has been continuously owned and occupied by descendants of this pioneer whose name was West, of the fifth generation from him.

"The present owners, the Metcalfe family, have many antique pieces of furniture and bric-a-brac that have come down to them, that are of much interest especially to admirers of antiques, two especially prized pieces being a pair of old walnut tables. It was one of these tables that was used as a writing table by General Felix K. Zollicoffer who made his headquarters several months at this home, just prior to his tragic death in the Civil War Battle of Mill Springs, about six or seven miles north near the present national cemetery in 1863. A huge shaft of native limestone marks the spot where he is said to have been killed by opposing Union forces. The battle, by the way, is known as the

Battle of Fishing Creek, by Southern sympathizers in that conflict between the states.

"The Metcalfe home with its old historic association lies in a beautiful valley surrounded by high knobs, is a splendid example of a remnant of the beginning of civilization in Kentucky. It is on a splendid highway and easily accessible—but antique buyers had better save time for there is nothing for sale."—*Somerset Commonwealth*, May, 1934.

### BIRTHPLACE OF SHELBY CULLOM

"One hundred years ago, when the surging, restless sea of humanity in the tier of states along the Atlantic burst its banks and came sweeping westward, inundating the Western plains, a diverging stream, diverted by a narrow channel, turned south and sought its level in what is now Wayne County, Kentucky. Strong rugged, fearless Anglo-Saxons were the men who sought homes on the frontier, ready to do battle with the red man for supremacy, to establish themselves there by untiring labor, and maintain their families by the sweat of the brow.

"Four miles from Monticello, on the Elk Spring Valley road, stands the oldest house in that section. Placed hospitably near the roadside, as was the custom in building in those days, when men were more considerate of each other's convenience, it remains a monument to the industry of a past generation, and a type of architecture now fast disappearing. Built of logs, then weatherboarded, making it a little more pretentious than the ordinary log house of the settler, with a queer low-ceiled porch running the full length of the house, it has successfully defied the ravages of time for a century. For a long time it has been unoccupied save by bats, until recently, a Negress, with a half dozen pickaninnies, has made one wing habitable. This house was built in 1798 by Lewis Coffey, a native Virginian, who came to Kentucky the same year with his wife.

"This old house was the birthplace of Shelby M. Cullom, the war Governor of Illinois and afterward United States Senator.

"Not half a mile away from the old house referred to a circular drive leads to the new home of T. J. Oatts. Built of brick and complete in every detail of modern convenience and artistic beauty, it is one of the most attractive country places in South Central Kentucky.

"And these two houses stand—the one a monument to the indomitable will and courage of a past generation, the other an indication of the thrift and industry of the present—the first house built in the county and the last."—Augusta LeGrande Phillips, *Courier-Journal,* October 23, 1897.

### EARLY HOME OF JOHN CATRON

"In a sequestered corner of Wayne County, Kentucky, stands an old house of particular interest to Tennesseans, as it was the home of one of her most eminent jurists, John Catron. Tottering as it is under the withering touch of time, whose impartial, irresistible march devastates alike the home of the well known and the obscure, this house is a type of the homes of the earliest settlers and one of the landmarks, fast disappearing, of the frontier days of Kentucky and Tennessee.

"At that time each log cabin contained the seeds of an embryo empire, that, under the touch of tyranny, merged in the common cause of liberty, have developed into a mighty republic. Yet, cosmopolitan as the society necessarily was, the lines of national demarcation were clearly drawn. And among the few local survivors of a time fraught with such history-building material. John Catron is still referred to as a 'Dutchman.' He was of German parentage on both sides. Realizing his inability to succeed in his chosen profession, the law, in Monticello, then a village of not more than 100 inhabitants, he removed in 1825 to Nashville, where he became a member of the bar. He served the people of Tennessee in different official capacities for a number of years. It was while he was judge of the court of appeals of the district in which he lived that he was enabled to befriend John Smith, the noted opposer of Calvinism in Kentucky. It was in 1832. The court was in session at Sparta, with some brilliant legal lights in evidence.

"As was customary, Smith had sent word to have the announcement made that he would preach in Sparta at a certain time. But the people, in the violent opposition to what was termed Smith's heresy, refused to make the announcement and the church doors were closed against him.

"Catron learned of this and remembering Smith as a friend of his boyhood in Kentucky, made the announcement, opened the courthouse to him, and with his colleagues turned out to hear him preach. Catron early evinced an inclination to the study of law, in which he was encouraged by both parents, who having had no opportunities themselves for education, realized the necessity of such equipment for the battle of life, and directed their son's study to the classics, deeming a wide range of information a requisite for legal success—thus proving themselves prudent judges. In Andrew Jackson's last administration Catron received the appointment of associate justice of the supreme court of the United States—the highest tribunal in the land—in which judicial capacity he served till his death.

"The ruling passion of the Kentuckian was strong in John Catron's make-up, for the first thing he did upon attaining his majority was to purchase a Kentucky thoroughbred, naming him Agricola, in honor of that grand old Roman who fought the ancient Britons so bravely.

"There lives at Monticello today the tailor—a man of fourscore and eight years—who made the suit of broadcloth in which the old man Catron went to Washington to see John in all the dignity and majesty of his new position. What a privilege allowed to man, thus to span the centuries and note the mighty changes as the decades pass in rapid succession! But the path of glory—as all other paths—leads but to the grave, and John Catron lives but in the memory of the few of his surviving contemporaries."—Augusta LeGrande Phillips, *Chattanooga Times*.

(The above article was published in 1897.)

John Catron was born in Grayson County, Virginia, son of Peter Catron who was son of Christopher Catron of Holland.

Peter Catron received pension for his services in the American Revolution.

## EARLY MARRIAGES

The earliest marriage recorded in Wayne County was that of Thomas Stewart and Hannah Allen, May 27, 1801. The ceremony was performed by the Rev. Elliot Jones. Other early marriages were:

| | |
|---|---|
| Charles Hart and Fannie Hugens | May 28, 1801 |
| John Mercer and Ann Caldwell | May 28, 1801 |
| Abel Shrewsbery and Letta Vanhoozer | May 28, 1801 |
| Samuel Gholson and Polly Staton | June 24, 1801 |
| Jonathon Chandler and Elizabeth Elrod | June 24, 1801 |
| Thomas Bowes and Callender Allen | September 30, 1801 |
| George McGaham and Peggy Caldwell | October 9, 1801 |
| John Coffey and Patty Harbord | December 28, 1801 |
| Stephen Nicholas and Betsy Spurlock | January 13, 1802 |
| William Harbord and Jane Coffey | January 20, 1802 |
| William Johnson and Retta Hammond | March 1, 1802 |
| Micah Taul and Dorothy Gholson | May 22, 1802 |
| Benjamin Gholson and Polly Hardin | November 3, 1803 |
| Samuel Johnson and Rachel Smith | June 5, 1805 |
| Joshua Jones and Elizabeth Dean | October 3, 1805 |
| John Dick and Elizabeth Chrisman | February 22, 1806 |
| Samuel Cecil and Jane Chrisman | May 8, 1806 |
| George Berry and Mary Buster | June 1, 1807 |
| William Wray and Sarah Phillips | June 8, 1807 |
| William Hudson and Jane Jones | November 26, 1810 |

The Rev. Elliot Jones solemnized most of these marriages, The Rev. Mr. Hill marrying two couples. Micah Taul and Dorothy Gholson were married by North East, J. P.

Marriages recorded as solemnized by Elder John Smith:

| | |
|---|---|
| James Bertram and Tilly Heaton | 1815 |
| John Chrisman and Sallie Stone | 1816 |
| Jacob Eads and Ada Norman | 1817 |
| Silas Young and Elizabeth Donaldson | 1817 |
| John Williams and Lavinia Bertram | 1817 |
| Joseph Hurt and Polly Eades | 1817 |
| Joshua Buster and Julia Haden | 1817 |
| Silas Shepherd and Polly Stone | 1817 |

Some later marriages:

| | |
|---|---|
| Alex Bobbitt and Sopronia Coffey | 1831 |
| Andrew McBeath and Susan Gholson | 1832 |
| Berry Gatewood and Nancy Phillips | 1833 |
| Isaac Sheppard and Susan Moore | 1834 |
| M. D. Hardin and Mary E. McKinney | 1834 |
| Benoni Mills and Polly Jones | 1834 |
| H. W. Tuttle and Courtney Metcalfe | 1834 |
| John H. Phillips and Elizabeth Berry | 1835 |
| Edmund Cook and Mary Simpson | 1837 |
| Moses Simpson and Nancy Higginbottom | 1838 |
| Leo Hayden and Catherine Ewing | 1838 |
| Henry Gatewood and Lucinda Phillips | 1838 |
| Henry Huffaker and Zilpha Mills | 1838 |
| Martin D. Hardin and Martha A. McKinney | 1840 |
| Micajah Phillips and Eliza Jones | 1841 |
| Henry Huffaker and Elizabeth Brown | 1841 |
| H. T. Hall and Juan Jones | 1842 |
| Harvey Roberts and Miely Maxie | 1842 |
| John L. Sallee and Jane H. Clemmons | 1842 |
| William Oldacre and Susan Buster | 1843 |
| James S. Chrisman and Lucy Bell | 1845 |
| William Burton and Mary E. Frisbie | 1847 |
| Russell Cecil and Lucy Ann Phillips | 1848 |

# FIRST MARRIAGE BOOK OF WAYNE COUNTY, KENTUCKY, 1801–1813

| Groom | Bride | Date |
|---|---|---|
| Charles Hart | Fannie Hugens | December 12, 1801 |
| Abel Shrewsbury | Letta Vanhoozer | October 22, 1801 |
| Samuel Gholson | Polly Staton | June 24, 1801 |
| Jonathan Chandler | Elizabeth Elrod | September 30, 1801 |
| Thomas Bowes | Ellender Allen | December 20, 1801 |
| John W. Coffey | Polly Harbord | December 27, 1801 |
| George Pointer | Joannah Tackett | ......................., 1801 |
| George McGaughan | Peggy Caldwell | October 9, 1801 |
| Thomas Stewart | Hannah Alexander | December 11, 1801 |
| John Mercer | Anne Caldwell | May 28, 1801 |
| William Harbord | Jane Coffey | January 26, 1802 |
| Stephen Nicholas | Betsy Spurlock | January 13, 1802 |
| Hugh Carrigan | Patsy Langston | January 16, 1802 |
| Henry Guffey | Elizabeth Adams | December 21, 1802 |
| William Johnson | Retta Hammond | March 1, 1802 |
| John Scott | Betsey Livingston | March 6, 1802 |
| William Adams | Elizabeth Johnson | March 2, 1802 |
| John Harris | Leah Sharp | March 25, 1802 |
| Anthony Cooke | Jane Caldwell | March 30, 1802 |
| Absalom Mounce | Sally Beaver | May 6, 1802 |
| Solomon Brents | Eliz. McWhorter | May 19, 1802 |
| Micah Taul | Dorothy Gholson | May 22, 1802 |
| John Austin | Rachel Denney | June 21, 1802 |
| Daniel Andrews | Anne Mary Cooper | July 21, 1802 |
| Solomon West | Martha Norton | July 27, 1802 |
| Phillip Tackett | ................ Pointer | August 23, 1802 |
| William Robins | Polley Reed | October 5, 1802 |
| John Morris | Sally Franklin | October 26, 1802 |
| Peter Troxall | Sally Saratte | December 7, 1802 |
| James Martin | Ellender Yocum | November 15, 1802 |
| Jacob Lilly | Susannah Jackson | ...................., 1802 |
| Joel Melton | Winney Newell | January 17, 1803 |
| John Anderson | Mary Roberts | February 3, 1803 |
| Richard Guffey | Phoebe Adams | April 11, 1803 |
| Francis Martin | Nancy Shores | April 16, 1803 |
| Henry Harryford | Jenny Wade | April 30, 1803 |
| John Robards | Betsy Scallon | May 7, 1803 |

| Groom | Bride | Date |
|---|---|---|
| Jesse Robards | Rebekah Blevins | June 4, 1803 |
| William Chaney | Sarah Scott | July 7, 1803 |
| Ephraim Guffey | Salley Denney | July 9, 1803 |
| William Small | Mary Morrow | July 9, 1803 |
| Zach Martin | Lydia Hinds | August 3, 1803 |
| William Chasteen | Elizabeth Reed | August 23, 1803 |
| Jonathon Blevins | Katy Troxall | April 7, 1803 |
| James Coffey | Frances Lane | October 1, 1803 |
| Alexander Conner | Elizabeth Jackman | October 17, 1803 |
| Henry Miller | Mary Smith | November 1, 1803 |
| William Simpson | Peggy Mattox | November 2, 1803 |
| Tarlton Blevins | Polly Troxall | November 2, 1803 |
| John Caldwell | Nancy Mercer | November 7, 1803 |
| Benjamin Gholson | Polley Haden | November 17, 1803 |
| Jacob Lefever | Sarah Davis | November 19, 1803 |
| William Brown | Anne Martin | November 29, 1803 |
| Peter Troxall | Jenny Stevenson | December 7, 1803 |
| John Dean | Susannah Bartleson | December 18, 1803 |
| Charles Harrison | Polly Cowan | December 18, 1803 |
| Jacob Gross | Nancy Summers | May 30, 1803 |
| William Norton | Easter James | ------------------, 1803 |
| John Wright | Peggy Wolfscale | ------------------, 1803 |
| Joseph James | ------------ Skaggs | January 2, 1804 |
| Sampson Vanhoozer | Elizabeth Cowan | January 4, 1804 |
| David Moore | Anne Craig | February 4, 1804 |
| James Brooks | Nancy Isbel | March 5, 1804 |
| Martin Musick | Sarah Ballew | March 8, 1804 |
| David Maxwell | Elizabeth Stevenson | April 2, 1804 |
| James McKamie | Annabel Vanoozer | May 12, 1804 |
| John Saunders | Sally Bustard | June 9, 1804 |
| William Denney | Margaret Scott | June 19, 1804 |
| Moses Simpson | Sarah Penn | June 26, 1804 |
| Thomas Isbel | Leah Frances | June 30, 1804 |
| David Bruton | Nancy Pemberton | July 16, 1804 |
| William Tackett | Hannah Cardwell | July 17, 1804 |
| Peter Fry | Nancy Johnson | September 1, 1804 |
| John Rutherford | Sarah Sloan | September 17, 1804 |
| James Burke | Anne Robins | October 1, 1804 |
| Reuben Ralread | Mary Warmsley | October 22, 1804 |
| William Davis | Polly McWhorter | November 7, 1804 |
| James Thompson | Peggy Norton | December 5, 1804 |
| Samuel Scisscell | Catherine Pevyhouse | December 16, 1804 |
| William Rush | Rachel Wolfscale | December 27, 1804 |
| Phillip Copple | Patsy Wright | ------------------, 1804 |
| James Welch | Sarah Hughes | January 16, 1805 |

| Groom | Bride | Date |
|---|---|---|
| William Hambleton | Betsy Cotton | February 18, 1805 |
| Samuel Allen | Polley Hambleton | January 18, 1805 |
| Reuben Johnson | Martha Hall | February 18, 1805 |
| Isconias Langston | Nancy Dodson | March 16, 1805 |
| Preston Beck | Eliza Simpson | March 18, 1805 |
| James Johnson | Mary Ingram | March 18, 1805 |
| Jacob Whitson | Sarah Adams | April 12, 1805 |
| James Kerr | Lydia Dodson | April 20, 1805 |
| Edward Ryan | Eliza Bartleson | May 6, 1805 |
| Hugh Roberts | Sabine Hatfield | May 27, 1805 |
| William Savage | Elizabeth Anne Wade | May 22, 1805 |
| John Mills, Jr. | Rebekah Stephens | May 24, 1805 |
| Henley Moore | Mary Jones | June 22, 1805 |
| Jonathon Barrow | Betsey Fox | August 6, 1805 |
| James Neville | Polly McCorkle | August 20, 1805 |
| Matthew Henry | Hannah Whitacre | August 23, 1805 |
| John Goodrich | Polly McHenry | September 9, 1805 |
| John Turner | Catharine Butler | September 9, 1805 |
| Henry Hicks | Rhoda Renfro | September 16, 1805 |
| Stephen Renfro | Betsy Hicks | September 16, 1805 |
| Henry Francis | Peggy Conwell | September 19, 1805 |
| George Waggoner | Betsey Ritter | September 21, 1805 |
| Reuben Simpson | Patsey Merrill | September 23, 1805 |
| George Berry | Polly Bustard | September 24, 1805 |
| Samuel Johnson | Rachel Smith | October 1, 1805 |
| John Davis | Patsey McCollum | November 6, 1805 |
| Thomas Woods | Polly Bruton | November 11, 1805 |
| Joel Bond | Jane Hinds | November 11, 1805 |
| Valentine Fry | Peggy Fulton | November 12, 1805 |
| William McClendon | Lucy McGowan | November 14, 1805 |
| James Royal | Polley Frances | October 24, 1805 |
| Edward Mattix | Elizabeth Bond | March 31, 1805 |
| James S. Cowan | Anne Buchannan | ----------------, 1805 |
| George Stringer | Mary Ballend | ----------------, 1805 |
| John Allen | Mary Livingston | December 9, 1805 |
| Thomas Hansford | Alcey Martin | December 14, 1805 |
| Benjamin Sloan | Betsey Dick | January 6, 1806 |
| Joshua Jones | Elizabeth Dean | February 9, 1806 |
| William Hereford | Ann Ingram | February 10, 1806 |
| William Denney | Patsy Burnett | February 10, 1806 |
| John Davis | Mary Meadows | February 13, 1806 |
| John Dick | Elizabeth Chrisman | February 20, 1806 |
| Stephen English | Mercy Maddox | March 4, 1806 |
| Jeremiah Summers | Elizabeth Baker | March 4, 1806 |

| Groom | Bride | Date |
|---|---|---|
| Aaron Roberts | Betsey Hansford | March 20, 1806 |
| George Neville | Betsey Ward | March 28, 1806 |
| Martin Cowan | Nelly Allen | March 29, 1806 |
| Thomas Smiley | Nancy Stevens | April 7, 1806 |
| Stephen Blevins | Sally Mounts | April 9, 1806 |
| Thomas Collins | Mary Bach | May 7, 1806 |
| William Bruton | Magdalen Sallee | June 16, 1806 |
| James Evans | Elizabeth Williams | July 17, 1806 |
| John Fox | Elizabeth Rush | July 16, 1806 |
| John Hancock | Tabitha Ballew | July 5, 1806 |
| William Shores, Jr. | Rhoda Pipes | July 5, 1806 |
| Isaac Bond | Anne Mercer | August 11, 1806 |
| Samuel Cecil | Jane Chrisman | August 16, 1806 |
| John Crockett | Elizabeth Elkins | August 19, 1806 |
| James Dockery | Anne Blanchet | August 27, 1806 |
| James Belcher | Susannah Ingram | October 8, 1806 |
| Joshua Cook | Elizabeth Hall | October 9, 1806 |
| Elias Kelley | Nancy Caldwell | October 12, 1806 |
| David Duncan | Sally Duncan | October 20, 1806 |
| George Yocum | Jane Ballew | October 20, 1806 |
| John Coger | Hester Jones | October 23, 1806 |
| James Mullens | Rebekah Smith | November 3, 1806 |
| Jesse Alcorn | Polly Duncan | November 31, 1806 |
| John Smith | Anne Townsend | December 6, 1806 |
| George Hereford | Lucy Burton | December 7, 1806 |
| Adam Bowyer | Catherine Worley | December 21, 1806 |
| William Shores | Abigail Pipes | December 31, 1806 |
| Samuel Mason | Nancy Moore | ----------, 1806 |
| John Balch | Nancy Bashma | ----------, 1806 |
| Samuel Owens | Jane Mercer | ----------, 1806 |
| Amos Wright | Peggy Davis | January 15, 1807 |
| James Murray | Rebekah Scott | January 24, 1807 |
| Solomon West | Kitty Norton | November 21, 1806 |
| Gideon Foster | Polly Pemberton | February 3, 1807 |
| Samuel Rector | Ruth Simpson | February 14, 1807 |
| Henry Robson | Elizabeth Shores | February 16, 1807 |
| William Ward | Polly Casse | February 26, 1807 |
| Francis Cullom | Polly McConkey | February 28, 1807 |
| Jesse Yocum | Jenny Mullins | March 2, 1807 |
| Solomon McGowan | Phoebe Pipes | March 4, 1807 |
| Squire Crabtree | Chloe Crabtree | March 4, 1807 |
| John Haden | Rhoda Stephens | March 18, 1807 |
| Henry Guffey | Candys Lessley | March 24, 1807 |
| James Morgan | Amy Raines | March 25, 1807 |
| John Walker | Peggy Weddle | April 3, 1807 |

| Groom | Bride | Date |
|---|---|---|
| Hugh McKee | Betsy Davis | April 3, 1807 |
| Samuel Simpson | Betsy Fulton | April 6, 1807 |
| Benjamin Price | Gincey Simpson | April 14, 1807 |
| John Wright | Nancy Perlee | April 29, 1807 |
| William Meek | Judith Popplewell | May 18, 1807 |
| Michael Elrod | Elizabeth Davis | June 20, 1807 |
| Aaron Cotton | Nancy Hatfield | June 30, 1807 |
| William Westberry | Margaret Elliot | July 6, 1807 |
| Jesse Dobbs | Phoebe Maxwell | July 13, 1807 |
| Andrew Alexander | Elizabeth Summers | July 13, 1807 |
| William Richardson | Elizabeth Hiatte | July 23, 1807 |
| Davids Potts | Jane Kennedy | August 4, 1807 |
| Hiram Gregory | Mary Logsdon | August 4, 1807 |
| William Ray | Sarah Philips | August 17, 1807 |
| William Lovelace | Nancy Dougherty | August 18, 1807 |
| James Barber | Patsy Haden | August 24, 1807 |
| Samuel Kelly | Nancy Kennedy | September 1, 1807 |
| Nathan Melton | Betsey Hammond | September 5, 1807 |
| Daniel Ward | Susan Nevill | September 9, 1807 |
| John Wilson | Sarah Belcher | September 19, 1807 |
| Richard Basham | Phoebe Pennicuff | September 28, 1807 |
| Solomon Aughtwell | Anne McDermed | November 3, 1807 |
| William Bowman | Jane Hall | November 7, 1807 |
| George Hall | Nancy Bowman | November 7, 1807 |
| Jonathon Fox | Fanny Ambers | November 11, 1807 |
| Benjamin Harris | Ruth Pendleton | November 16, 1807 |
| Stephen Loveall | Becky Roberts | December 7, 1807 |
| Alexander Thomas | Polly Blevins | December 9, 1807 |
| Elijah Franklin | Elizabeth Coke | December 19, 1807 |
| George Templeton | Peggy Turpin | December 20, 1807 |
| William Rayn | Keziah Blevins | ....................., 1807 |
| John Day | Sarah Ballenger | February 9, 1808 |
| Moses Summers | Celia McDermid | January 15, 1808 |
| John Watts | Polly Ross | January 15, 1808 |
| Lewis Green | Margaret Smith | January 18, 1808 |
| Benjamin Davis | Susanna Fields | January 23, 1808 |
| Henry Nevill | Sally Canady | February 8, 1808 |
| John Kennedy | Nancy Ferrill | February 24, 1808 |
| Cornelius Pointer | Rebekah Snow | February 24, 1808 |
| Thomas Asher | Sally Sumpter | March 2, 1808 |
| Dennis Gaterell | Agnes Payne | March 9, 1808 |
| John Jackman | Mary Williams | March 19, 1808 |
| Jeremiah Gray | Polly Yocum | January 1, 1808 |
| Christian Steel | Elizabeth Blevins | March 28, 1808 |
| James Hix | Milly Adams | March 23, 1808 |

| Groom | Bride | Date |
|---|---|---|
| Robert Wray | Elizabeth Scott | April 12, 1808 |
| Ephraim Acre | Valerie Warren | April 14, 1808 |
| Thomas Russell | Mary Dorphin | April 18, 1808 |
| John Hatfield | Polly Craig | May 5, 1808 |
| Robert Pendleton | Sally Casperson | May 16, 1808 |
| William Bond | Charity Hinds | May 25, 1808 |
| John Martin | Jane McGee | May 31, 1808 |
| Ebenezer Lester | Anne Scallon | June 24, 1808 |
| Benjamin Denney | Agnes Ballew | July 19, 1808 |
| Jesse Musick | Sally Crabtree | July 20, 1808 |
| William Smith | Polly Black | August 27, 1808 |
| Edward Jenkins | Mary Beard | September 19, 1808 |
| Am. Thompson | Polly Harris | October 4, 1808 |
| Hiram Kilgore | Nancy Grant | October 6, 1808 |
| William Maxwell | Celia Hix | October 8, 1808 |
| David Hall | Hannah Wilson | December 16, 1808 |
| William Rice | Jean Baker | December 5, 1808 |
| Jonathon Loveall | Elizabeth Kennedy | December 5, 1808 |
| Marvel Marcum | Polly Watts | December 5, 1808 |
| Samuel Martin | Dorothy Chrisman | November 22, 1808 |
| John Williams | Sally Hunter | November 15, 1808 |
| Archibald Gipson | Priscilla Cecil | November 15, 1808 |
| James Townsend | Sally Warren | November 4, 1808 |
| Alexander Warm | Anne Collins | October 27, 1808 |
| Gabriel Eads | Leah Garner | October 27, 1808 |
| Cornelius Cooper | Nancy Dell | December 27, 1808 |
| Jeremiah Brannon | Jane Smith | January 10, 1809 |
| James Crabtree | Polly Wallace | January 14, 1809 |
| John Huff | Sally Kelsoe | January 17, 1809 |
| Nicholas Mercer | Sarah Hinds | January 20, 1809 |
| Uriah Raines | Elizabeth Chasteen | January 21, 1809 |
| Joseph Menzes | Peggy Summers | January 20, 1809 |
| Nimrod Ingram | Rebeckah Summers | February 28, 1809 |
| Elias Thomas | Easter West | February 24, 1809 |
| Joseph Decker | Sally Brown | February 20, 1809 |
| William Raines | Sarah Hancock | February 20, 1809 |
| Enos Ray | Agatha Dodson | February 15, 1809 |
| James Lasley | Rebekah Dobbs | January 8, 1809 |
| David Cox | Mary McGee | February 7, 1809 |
| William Robards | Jennie McCollum | March 1, 1809 |
| William Logsdon | Jenny Potts | March 10, 1809 |
| Robert Belshe | Elizabeth Gill | March 28, 1809 |
| George Brown | Betsy Mason | March 30, 1809 |
| Abraham Mays | Mary Guffey | April 12, 1809 |
| Benjamin Brown | Nancy Finn | April 4, 1809 |

| Groom | Bride | Date |
|---|---|---|
| Davidson Brown | Jane McCorkle | June 3, 1809 |
| Richard Davis | Elizabeth Flinn | June 19, 1809 |
| Russell Garret | Polly Rutherford | June 21, 1809 |
| Jeremiah Aulger | Peggy Nowling | June 24, 1809 |
| James Bell | Peggy Troxall | July 5, 1809 |
| John Duffey | Margaret Johnston | July 5, 1809 |
| Anthony Cox | Mary Gilbert | July 6, 1809 |
| Joshua Hunter | Judy Gentry | July 7, 1809 |
| John Hill | Jemima Polly | July 15, 1809 |
| Isaac Shipley | Elizabeth Polly | July 15, 1809 |
| William Scott | Celia Cowan | July 18, 1809 |
| Thomas Norman | Nancy Williams | July 27, 1809 |
| John Worley | Sally Sharp | August 8, 1809 |
| James Spradlin | Betsy Mounce | September 11, 1809 |
| John Hambleton | Ellender Collett | October 2, 1809 |
| James Dollarhide | Barbara Samples | October 4, 1809 |
| Samuel Turpin | Elizabeth Ralston | October 9, 1809 |
| David Roberts | Linea West | October 18, 1809 |
| Isaac Prather | Catherine Nicholas | August 26, 1809 |
| Martin Turpin | Patsy Ralston | October 31, 1809 |
| Andrew Kinnetzar | Mary Anne Blevins | November 15, 1809 |
| Robert Parmley | Barbara Adair | November 20, 1809 |
| David Sparks | Doshea Roberts | November 20, 1809 |
| John Price | Isabella Simpson | November 28, 1809 |
| Michael Fry | Susanna Johnson | December 18, 1809 |
| William Calhoun | Elizabeth Ross | December 19, 1809 |
| Allen Fuller | Catharine Southard | December 25, 1809 |
| Mesheck Gregory | Anne Beeson | December 27, 1809 |
| Ignatius Owens | Betsy Shepherd | December 30, 1809 |
| William Burton | Elizabeth Roberts | December 31, 1809 |
| Abel Summers | Elizabeth Clark | January 2, 1810 |
| John Guffey | Polly Nicholas | February 5, 1810 |
| James Craig | Jenny Brown | February 10, 1810 |
| Thomas Holt | Cinthy Waters | February 10, 1810 |
| Reuben Sullens | Jean Turpin | February 19, 1810 |
| Jesse Hancock | Milly Morrow | February 19, 1810 |
| Richard Pilson | Hannah Peele | February 19, 1810 |
| Lewis Foust | Rebekah Parmley | February 19, 1810 |
| Thomas Watts | Eady Markham | February 21, 1810 |
| Casper W. Lewis | Stella Stoner | February 27, 1810 |
| John Mills | Polly Asberry | February 27, 1810 |
| Samuel Ford | Eliz. Shrewsberry | February 28, 1810 |
| William Hall | Rachel Markham | March 19, 1810 |
| Lewis Green | Nancy Lloyd | March 27, 1810 |
| Robert Craig | Susannah Raines | March 31, 1810 |

| Groom | Bride | Date |
|---|---|---|
| James Blanchet | Elizabeth Kinnetzar | April 4, 1810 |
| Joseph Baker | Martha Wolfscale | April 7, 1810 |
| George W. Gibbs | Susannah Dibrell | April 12, 1810 |
| Lewis Whitesides | Sally Dunn | April 23, 1810 |
| James Barnett | Polly Scott | May 28, 1810 |
| John Kennedy | Sally New | June 5, 1810 |
| Jesse Gray | Nancy Rainbolt | June 29, 1810 |
| Rowland Branscomb | Nancy Barrow | June 30, 1810 |
| William Sturman | Sally Dabney | July 9, 1810 |
| Joshua Whitaker | Hannah Hambleton | July 26, 1810 |
| John Lee | Tabitha Francis | July 31, 1810 |
| Mason French | Peggy Conn | August 6, 1810 |
| William Coger | Polly Bookout | June 6, 1810 |
| Samuel Hannah | Jean McCasland | August 16, 1810 |
| John Hopkins | Patsy Brush | August 14, 1810 |
| John Gilbert | Elizabeth Gilbert | August 22, 1810 |
| Baker Mills | Joannah Stephens | August 15, 1810 |
| Jesse Mullanix | Betsy Wright | August 25, 1810 |
| Temple Poston | Judith Dibrell | September 3, 1810 |
| Allen Cox | Polly English | September 4, 1810 |
| John Dent | Catherine Fryer | September 12, 1810 |
| James Neville | Marcum Dodson | September 17, 1810 |
| James Ryan | Elizabeth Wolfscale | September 17, 1810 |
| Jacob Shearer | Violet Vickory | September 17, 1810 |
| Elisha Lloyd | Phoebe Evans | September 25, 1810 |
| Joseph Wray | Polly Carnes | September 26, 1810 |
| Abner Jones | Rebekah Hambleton | October 1, 1810 |
| Daniel Cooper | Nancy Back | October 1, 1810 |
| Edward Harper | Nelly S—— | October 1, 1810 |
| Johnson Walker | Fanny Burnett | October 1, 1810 |
| Nicholas Harris | Sally Elrod | October 16, 1810 |
| Peter Stephens | Elizabeth Arbuckle | October 17, 1810 |
| James Ward | Jane Hutchinson | November 7, 1810 |
| James Hunter | Winnaford Elam | November 19, 1810 |
| John Hudson | Sally Barnes | November 20, 1810 |
| John Summers | Sally Summers | November 22, 1810 |
| Henry Garner | Elizabeth Decker | November 24, 1810 |
| William Hudson | Jane Jones | November 26, 1810 |
| Jeremiah Denney | Rachel Holt | December 3, 1810 |
| James Barnes | Mary Acre | December 10, 1810 |
| Reuben Warren | Margaret Hancock | January 3, 1811 |
| James Whitesides | Elizabeth Dick | January 5, 1811 |
| Henry Cooper | Patience Back | January 11, 1811 |
| Charles Harris | Dicey Davis | January 22, 1811 |
| Joseph Mays | Nancy Davis | January 22, 1811 |

| Groom | Bride | Date |
|---|---|---|
| Rice Phipps | Elizabeth Gann | January 26, 1811 |
| Wardman Summers | Nancy Summers | February 8, 1811 |
| James Melton | Rachel Rutherford | February 21, 1811 |
| Samuel Evans | Patience Shepherd | February 26, 1811 |
| George Barret | Patsy Neville | March 18, 1811 |
| Joseph West | Ruth Murry | April 8, 1811 |
| James Ashbrooke | Christiana Fry | April 23, 1811 |
| Anthony Dibrell | Milly Carter | April 24, 1811 |
| John Southwood | Sally Gaines | May 10, 1811 |
| David Bruton | Rosanna Thadford | May 24, 1811 |
| Solomon Summers | Mazey Mullinix | June 8, 1811 |
| Henry Shearer | Polly Summers | July 15, 1811 |
| Gabriel Graham | ........................... | June 12, 1811 |
| Hugh Weir | Elizabeth Wallace | July 25, 1811 |
| Silas Bell | Lucretia Walker | August 30, 1811 |
| George Dougherty | Sally Wilkerson | August 31, 1811 |
| Francis Holt | Sally Denney | September 10, 1811 |
| John Eames | Elizabeth Wood | September 17, 1811 |
| George Bridgehammer | Nancy Atkinson | October 12, 1811 |
| Joseph Bookout | Polly Overstreet | October 25, 1811 |
| Cornelius Bertram | Catherine Kidwell | October 25, 1811 |
| Simeon Popplewell | ............................... | October 25, 1811 |
| James White | Ruth Walker | October 28, 1811 |
| Henry Moss | Sally Pennicuff | October 29, 1811 |
| Mordecai Layne | Seila Atkinson | November 2, 1811 |
| Edward Dolan | Anne Burk | November 2, 1811 |
| Benjamin Jones | Viney Wallace | November 3, 1811 |
| John Vaughn | Polly Lewis | November 13, 1811 |
| Richard Radford | Polly Ward | November 21, 1811 |
| John Ally | Sarah Starling | November 21, 1811 |
| James Baker | Rebekah Small | November 25, 1811 |
| George Hinds | Mary Hinkle | November 28, 1811 |
| Nicholas Smith | Sarah Henry | December 10, 1811 |
| Solomon Evans | Jane Bartleson | December 10, 1811 |
| Nathaniel Scott | Elizabeth Wade | December 10, 1811 |
| Jubal Bramblette | Betsey Shrewsberry | December 17, 1811 |
| Jesse Yearles | ......................... | December 25, 1811 |
| Alexander West | Sally Murray | January 4, 1812 |
| Lewis Stinson | Sally Sullens | January 8, 1812 |
| Hezekiah Carman | Nancy Craig | January 11, 1812 |
| John Hall | Lydia Patton | January 12, 1812 |
| James Dupre | Polly Bohon | January 14, 1812 |
| John Roberts | Jemima Blevins | January 20, 1812 |
| David Beckman | Rachel Eads | January 22, 1812 |

| Groom | Bride | Date |
|---|---|---|
| Jesse Evans | Easter Newell | January 25, 1812 |
| William Hall | Sophia Dabney | February 3, 1812 |
| William Turpin | Rolsten ................. | February 12, 1812 |
| James Trumble | Nancy Turpin | February 12, 1812 |
| Elisha Mullinix | Charity McCollum | February 24, 1812 |
| John Dirkson | Catherine Calhoun | March 2, 1812 |
| David Bell | Polly .................... | March 2, 1812 |
| Samuel Moore | Nancy Layne | March 3, 1812 |
| Carter Robertson | Polly Shrewsberry | March 4, 1812 |
| Stephen Raines | Margaret Shasteen | March 14, 1812 |
| Robert Upton | Rhoda Winter | April 1, 1812 |
| Isaac Steel | Elizabeth Smith | April 7, 1812 |
| David Vestie | Sally Wade | April 6, 1812 |
| Samuel McLaughlin | Sally Baker | April 8, 1812 |
| William Warren | Lydia Stockton | May 5, 1812 |
| John McCollum | Polly Beeson | May 14, 1812 |
| Joseph Dodson | Judith Bradshaw | May 17, 1812 |
| Fielding Prather | Betsey Merideth | May 16, 1812 |
| Alexander Worley | Sally Denney | May 23, 1812 |
| James Evans | Polly Stockton | May 30, 1812 |
| Jacob Vestie | Selah Summers | July 5, 1812 |
| Adam Vickory | Polly Baker | July 11, 1812 |
| John Renfro | Sally Buster | July 18, 1812 |
| Andrew E. Hays | Hannah Evans | August 15, 1812 |
| Daniel East | Elizabeth Deekam | August 15, 1812 |
| Martin Turpin | Charity Hinkle | September 2, 1812 |
| James Vaughn | Elizabeth Troxall | September 17, 1812 |
| John Crabtree | Winnaford Gilstrap | September 22, 1813 |

# BIBLIOGRAPHY USED IN COMPILING THIS BOOK

Appleton's Encyclopedia of American Biography.
Collins, Richard H.: *History of Kentucky.*
Dorris, Jonathan T.: *Old Cane Springs.*
Funkhouser, Wm. and Webb, Wm.: *Ancient Life in Kentucky.*
Jillson, Willard Rouse: *Kentucky Land Grants.*
Johnson, E. Polk: *History of Kentucky.*
Kennamer, L. G.: Wayne County (Radio Address).
Littell, William: Acts of Kentucky.
Miller, W. H.: Histories and Genealogies.
Smith, Z. T.: *History of Kentucky.*
Summers, Lewis Preston: *History of Southwest Virginia.*
Williams, John Augustus: *Life of John Smith.*
Young, H. F.: *History of Education in Wayne County.*
Records of Bethel Church at Parmleysville.
Records of Pleasant Hill Church at Powersburg.
Records of Fairfax Monthly Meeting of Friends.
Deed Books, Marriage Book, Will Books, Minute Books of Wayne County.
*Courier-Journal* and *Times*—Louisville, Kentucky.
*Mt. Sterling Gazette and Courier.*
*Somerset Commonwealth.*
*Wayne County Outlook* and *Monticello Signal.*
Bible Records and Tombstone Inscriptions.
Old Letters.
Captain Tuttle's Diary.
Rodes Garth's Journal.
Coleman, J. Winston, Jr.: *Stage-Coach Days in the Bluegrass.*

# INDEX

# INDEX

## A

Abston, James, 84
Acre, Peter, 60
Acre, William, 6, 10
Adair, John, 6, 7, 21, 76
Adair, William, 87
Adams, William, 20
Adkins, Berry, 21
Akin, Josiah, 47
Albertson, N., 84
Alcorn, James, 20
Alcorn, John, 20
Alexander, Andrew, 60
Alexander, Joseph, 20
Alexander, R. C., 79
Alexander, Wm., 80
Allen, George, 47
Allen, Hannah, 75
Allen, James, 12
Allen, James L., 81
Allen, John, 33
Allen, William, 3, 4
Anderson, Moses, 21
Anderson, Rufus K., 34
Andrews, Daniel, 20
Ard, James, 60
Ayres, Samuel, 20

## B

Bailey, Benjamin, 13
Baker, Edward, 21
Baker, James, 60
Baker, L. P., 159
Baker, Squire, 29, 46
Ballard, Professor, 114
Ballew, Alfred, 46
Ballew, Ned, 11
Ballou, Joseph, 81, 110
Barbee, Col., 47, 50, 51, 52
Barbee, Captain, 48, 52
Barnes, Enos, 60
Barnes, Moses, 60
Barnes, William, 46, 60
Barnett, Samuel, 121
Barney, L., 191
Barrier, Richard, 76, 83
Barry, W. T., 32
Bartleson, Ensign, 59
Bartleson, John, 46, 56, 183
Bartleson Family, 241
Bates, James, 20
Bates, Nannie, 115
Bates, Thomas, 99, 239
Bates Family, 239
Baugh, A. H., 81, 110
Baugh, Marcellus, 110
Baxter, Joshua, 46
Baylor, Frances N., 132
Baylor, John, 132
Baylor, Walker, 132
Bays, Abednego, 47
Beakley, Robert, 6
Beard, Joseph, 20, 21, 22, 28
Beard, Littleton, 98, 101, 109
Beard, William, 21, 22, 28
Beason, Henry, 21
Beaty, Martin, 66, 67, 71, 100, 101, 108, 184
Beauregard, 146
Beckett, Josiah, 46
Beecher, Henry Ward, 132
Bell, David, 21
Bell, Dr. J. W., 135
Bell, James, 21
Bell, John, 60
Bell, Lucy, 176
Bell, William, 21
Belshe, Joseph C., 101
Belshe, Robert, 120
Berry, B. C., 112, 173
Berry, George, 101, 184
Berry, Joshua, 100, 133, 139, 191
Berry Family, 233

Bertram, Abial, 83
Bertram, Alvin, 83
Bertram, Camealy, 83
Bertram, Cornelius, 60
Bertram, Elijah, 21, 83
Bertram, Elizabeth, 83
Bertram, Ephraim, 83
Bertram, Feroby, 83
Bertram, Jacob, 21
Bertram, James, 83, 86
Bertram, Joel, 83
Bertram, Jonathan, 83
Bertram, Joseph, 9, 97, 100, 114
Bertram, Laruhanna, 83
Bertram, Lavina, 83, 86
Bertram, Nancy, 83
Bertram, Rowena, 83
Bertram, W. C. C., 84
Bertram, William, Jr., 83
Bertram, William, Sr., 6, 83
Bibb, William, 67
Blackburn, J. W., 82
Blackwell, Samuel, 121
Blackwood, Richard, 47
Blair, Dr., 152
Blair, William, 46
Blankenship, Abel, 46
Bledsoe, Abraham, 3, 4
Bledsoe, Jane, 132
Blevins, Henry, 83, 84
Blount, Major, 13
Bobbitt, Alex, 255
Boone, Daniel, 4
Boone, Kirk, 184
Bosley, E. M., 82
Bowles, Colonel, 139
Bradley, R. M., 90
Bradshaw, William, 119
Bramlette, Thomas E., 88, 136
Bramlette, Wm., 132
Branscomb, John, 21
Breckinridge, John C., 141
Breckinridge, Robert J., 110
Brennan, Major, 156
Brents, J. A., 136
Brents, Samuel, 21, 86, 87

Brents, Solomon, 23
Bridges, Robert, 139
Bright, William, 46
Bristow, James M., 132, 139
Bristow, Richard, 132
Brock, Georgia, 113
Brook, Wm., 47
Brooks, Cassius, 3, 7
Bromley, George, 46
Brown, Alexander, 60
Brown, Barnabas, 60
Brown, J. A., 99, 115
Brown, J. N., 140
Brown, Dorothy, 10
Brown, James, 47
Brown, Joseph, 6
Brown, Lewis, 60
Brown, Thomas, 60
Brown, William, 20
Brumett, James, 20
Bruton, Major George, 9
Bryan, Edmund, 102
Buchanan, Roxie, 113
Buchanan, Welsher, 46, 56, 59
Buchanan, William, 5
Buckner, Richard, 87
Buckner, ——, 174
Bullock, David, 30
Bunyard, Ephraim, 83
Burbridge, General, 131
Burcham, Isaiah, 46
Burke, William, 80
Burnett, Captain, 57
Burnett, Isaac, 21
Burnett, Reuben, 21
Burnett, Richard, 139
Burton, Charles, 172
Burton, Mack, 172
Burton, Professor, 174
Burton, William, 108
Buster, C. W., 135
Buster, Charles, 8
Buster, Claudius, 215
Buster, Dr. James, 103
Buster, John, 20, 29, 46
Buster, Joshua, 61, 81, 86, 98, 107

Buster, Michael, 132
Buster, Milton, 87, 100
Buster Family, 212ff
Butler, Edward, 90

C

Cabell, Captain, 10
Caldwell, John, 20, 121
Calfey, William, 110, 112
Calhoun, James, 46
Calhoun, Thomas, 20
Calloway, Richard, 5
Campbell, Alexander, 80
Campbell, John, 5
Campbell, William, 7
Canada, Samuel, 220
Cantrill, Mary Cecil, 98
Carpenter, John, 46
Carpenter, William, 6
Carrigan, Arthur, 47
Carrigan, James, 121
Carter, Braxton, 108
Carter, Charles, 132
Carter, Harrison, 132
Carter, John, 46
Carter, William, 20, 47
Carter Family, 233
Cary, Nathan, 47
Cary, Robert, 8
Casson, John, 60
Castillo, Dr. J. W., 103
Castillo, John, 163
Castillo, Mike, 70, 77
Catron, Jeremiah, 110
Catron, John, 163f, 252
Catron, Peter, 6, 20, 251
Cecil, Granville, 98, 171, 240
Cecil, Russell, 240, 255
Chafin, W. T., 113
Chamberland, William, 47
Cheatham, Josiah, 47
Chilton, Thomas, 34, 80
Chrisman, Elijah, 47
Chrisman, Isaac, 22, 28, 33
Chrisman, James S., 90, 91f, 101, 119f

Chrisman, John, 31, 33, 86
Chrisman, Joseph S., 7, 29, 33
Chrisman, Micah T., 87, 101, 108
Chrisman, Thomas, 12
Chrisman Family, 221
Clark, Benjamin, 46
Clark, Beverly, 37
Clark, George Rogers, 7, 18, 31
Clark, Raleigh, 22, 28
Clelland, Thos., 80
Cleveland, Benjamin, 8
Cochran, James, 121
Cocke, William, 5
Coffey, Andrew, 120
Coffey, Coleman, 8
Coffey, Emma, 128
Coffey, Fannie, 133
Coffey, Frank, 8, 81
Coffey, Gen. B. F., 135
Coffey, Henderson, 8
Coffey, James, 8, 20, 21, 120
Coffey, John, 120
Coffey, Lee, Miss, 184
Coffey, Lewis, 8, 11, 20, 29, 35, 45, 46, 59, 61, 100, 120, 173, 191
Coffey, Reuben, 6, 8
Coffey, Sallie, 134
Coffey, Shelby, 8, 101
Coffey, Shelby, Jr., 101
Coffey Family, 8
Coger, John, 21
Cole, William, 47
Coleman, J. Winston, 172
Colyer, Martin, 120
Conaldson, Elizabeth, 86
Conley, Charles, 120
Conley, James, 120
Conn, James, 20
Conn, Stephen T., 65, 66
Cook, Dr. A. S., 103
Cook, Edmund, 255
Cook, Enos, 61
Cook, Dr. John, 103
Cook, Dr. Littleton, 103
Cook, Dr. Will, 103

Cooke, Thomas, 100
Cooksey, John, 46
Cooksey, William, 46
Cooper, Caleb, 7, 61
Cooper, Fount, 113
Cooper, Fred, 6
Cooper, Fredrick, 9, 20
Cooper, William, 81, 82, 83
Cooper Family, 243
Copenhaven, John, 120
Cotton, James, 46
Coughron, Wm., 61
Covington, Robert, 6
Cowan, Andrew, 46
Cowan, Edward, 3, 23
Cowan, F., 120
Cowan, James, 46
Cowan, Samuel, 46, 120
Cowan, Thomas, 46
Cox, Dr. C. A., 180
Cox, Charles, 38
Cox, David, 61
Cox, Rebecca, 39
Coyle, Patrick, 6
Crabtree, Isaac, 7, 22, 100
Craig, John, 60
Cress, W. R., 100
Crews, Michael, 47
Crockett, Robert, 3
Cross, William, 46
Crutchfield, Seaborn, 120
Cullom, Edward, 22, 23, 25, 28, 46, 100
Cullom, Shelby, 176, 251
Cullom, Tillman, 46
Cuzzart, Isah, 47

## D

Dabney, Chas., 61
Dabney, George, 6
Daffron, Rody, 7
Dalton, Roscoe, 100
Davidson, W. R., 84
Davis, Alexander, 46, 58, 82
Davis, Jefferson, 161
Davis, John, 6, 21

Davis, William, 61
Dawes, John, 120
Decker, George, 6
Decker, Thomas, 46
Degraffenreed, William, 47
Denney, Sherman, 115
Denny, Esther, 83
Denny, J. C., 100
Denny, J. S., 140
Denny, John, 10
Denny, Mollie, 99, 113
Denny, Samuel, 20
Denny, Wesley, 83
Denton, Isaac, 76, 86
Desha, I. B., 32
Dibrell, Anthony, 31
Dibrell, Charles, 20, 22, 28
Dick, John, 26, 35, 46, 57
Dick, R. R., 84
Dodson, George, 60
Dodson, John, 46
Dodson, Leonard, 20, 29
Dodson, T. A., 99
Dodson, Thomas, 20
Dop, Ezekiel, 47
Dorris, Jonathan T., 128
Douglas, H. S., 184
Drake, Joseph, 3
Dudley, Guilford, 13
Duffey, John, 61
Dunagan, James, 49
Dunagan, Solomon, 29, 46
Duncan, David, 21
Duncan, George, 230
Duncan, Granville, 173
Duncan, Josie, 115
Duncan, Samuel M., 99
Duncan Family, 230
Dunlap, Colonel, 156
Durham, Constantine, 120
Durham, Judge, 88
Durham, Martin, 6

## E

Eads, Jacob, 86
Eads, Polly, 86

Eads, Thomas, 29, 101
Eads Family, 244
East, Daniel, 46
East, North, 46, 59, 100
Easter, John, 46
Edge, Larkin Decatur, 171
Edrington, J. L., 80
Edward, Major, 59
Ellington, Polly, 12
Elliott, Asa, 47
Elliott, Milton, 112, 128, 179
Elrod, Harmon, 60
Emerson, Francis, 21, 23, 86
Emerson, Walter, 20, 46, 59, 79, 101
England, Samuel, 46
Enoch, Captain, 9
Evans, Andrew, 36
Evans, James, 21, 22, 28
Ewing, David, 20
Ewing Family, 233

F

Fairchild, A., 114
Fairchild, Abijah, 84
Fairchild, Ebenezer, 82
Fairchild, Lewis, 83
Ferguson, Champ, 131, 136
Ferguson, Henry, 120
Ferrill, Robert, 86, 107
Flinn, Jesse C., 46, 120
Flournoy, L. M., 191
Flowers, Thomas M., 46
Floyd, General, 145
Floyd, Matthew, 84
Floyd, William, 82
Ford, Samuel, 46
Ford, William, 46
Foster, John, 46, 61
Fox, Fontaine, T., 89
Fox, W. McKee, 90, 191
Francis, James, 132
Francis, John, 10, 23, 65, 66, 245
Franklin, Elisha, 20
Franklin, Thomas, 46
Frazer, James K. Polk, 95

French Family, 244
Frisbie, Eliza, 133
Frisbie, Dr. John S., Jr., 81, 102, 133, 174
Frisbie, Dr. John S., Sr., 81, 102, 107, 109
Frisbie, Julia, 174
Frisbie, Tine, 174
Fritz, William, 120
Fulton, John H., 67
Funkhouser, Dr. W. D., 3
Fuston, Elizabeth, 20
Fuston (Fewston) Tavern, 250

G

Gabbert, David, 46
Gabbert, Henry, 46
Gabbert, James, 120
Gaither, Nat, 90, 120
Garland, Anderson, 46
Garner, Henry, 20, 22, 28, 29
Garner, John, 60
Garovir, John, 46
Garth, Jack, 135
Garth, Rodes, 45, 46, 47, 50, 59, 60, 87, 100, 107
Gates, General, 9
Gatewood, Henry, 255
Geary, Captain, 189
Gholson, Anthony, 22, 29, 33, 59, 76
Gholson, Ben, 28
Gholson, Dorothy, 32, 33
Gholson, James, 36
Gholson, Nancy, 34
Gholson, Samuel, 61
Gholson Family, 222
Gibbs, John, 20
Gibson, Edward, 20
Gibson, Stephen, 61
Gilmore, Colonel, 140
Givens, James, 46
Goddard, John W., 99
Goddard, Francis, 108
Gooding, Abraham, 61

Gooding, William, 82
Graves, Miss, 113
Gray, Jesse, 61
Graham, James, 120
Green, Gardner, 47
Green, General, 11
Green, Richmond, 47
Green, William, 20
Gregory, Fleming, 21
Gregory, Hiram, 60
Gregory, Mordecai, 46
Gresham, Green, 120
Gresham, William, 120
Griffin, Joseph, 132
Grizzard, William, 121
Gross, John, 46
Grubbs, Hayden, 114
Guffey, J. W., 115
Guffey, Henry, 20

## H

Hayden, G. C., 133
Hayden, Julia, 86
Hayden, Leo, 26, 101
Haines, John, 61
Hall, Dr., 174
Hall, C. T., 139
Hall, Henry, 61
Hall, Joseph, 159f, 176ff
Hall, John W., 171f
Hall, Dr. John, 102
Hall, Mrs. Juan, 81, 128
Hall, Lapsley, 60
Hall, Walter, 101
Hall, William, 46
Hall, Z. T., 139
Hammond, John, 22
Hansford, Thomas, 101
Hardin, Ben, 87
Hardin, Emily W., 174f
Hardin, James G., 99
Hardin, James L., 180
Hardin, M. D., 175, 250, 255
Hardin, Mary E., 133
Hardin, P. W., 94
Hardin, Parker, 90

Hardin, Sam C., 95f
Hardin, William, 26, 100, 250
Hardin Family, 225
Hardwick, James, 121
Harper, Asa, 46
Harper, James, 46
Harris, Isaac, 47
Harris, Richard, 20
Harrison, General, 45, 48, 61
Harrison, J. P., 96f
Harrison, Thos. G., 76
Harvey, John, 47
Haskins, W. A., 133
Hatchett, Arch, 121
Hatchett, Sallie, 114
Havens, John, 59
Hawley, Zebedee, 46
Hayden, Bartholomew, 20, 29, 33
Hayden, Gordon, 174
Haynes, E. A., 100
Hays, Andrew, 120
Hays, H. R., 99
Hays, Joseph E., 90
Heaton, Gilly, 86
Hedrick George, 233
Heaven, Thomas, 184
Henderson, Mr., 174
Henderson, Lilburn, L., 66
Henninger, Conrad, 7
Hibbitts, Charles, 47
Hicks, John, 46
Higginbottom, Andrew, 21
Hill, Reverend, 75
Hill, Thomas Peyton, 93
Hill, Wm., 61
Hinds, Berry, 56
Hinds, Samuel, 22
Hines, Stephen, 46
Hines, Woods, 121
Hogan, Humphrey, 3
Holland, John, 47
Hooker, General, 156
Hope, A. H., 81
Hopkins, Elias, 83
Hovey, A. H., 189
Howard, Portman, 46, 49

Hubbard, Colonel, 10
Hubbard, Mr., 179
Hudson, Marshall N., 101, 102
Hudson, William, 132
Huff, Preston, 158
Huffaker, Barton W. S., 100, 101
Huffaker, Christopher, 20
Huffaker, J. C., 99
Huffaker, Henry, 158
Huffaker, Marion, 113
Huffaker, Michael, 107
Huffaker, Mollie, 115
Huffaker, Tobias, 113
Huffaker, W. G., 99
Hughes, ——, 3
Hughes, James, 121
Huling, Marcus, 67, 68
Hull, Samuel, 132
Hunt, Curtis, 121
Hunter, William, 121
Hurt, Abraham, 7
Hurt, Jacob, 110
Hurt, Joseph, 86
Hurt, Nancy, 86
Hurt, Virginia, 110
Hurt, William, 60
Hutchins, Benjamin, 87
Hutchins, William, 121

## I

Ingram, J. P., 173
Ingram, J. R., 140
Ingram, James, 20
Ingram, Jonathan, 20
Ingram, M. E., 191
Ingram, Nannie, Miss, 114
Ingram, Nimrod, 101
Ingram, Samuel, 46, 59, 62
Ingram Family, 238

## J

James, A. J., 88
James, Henry, 38
Jarvis, John C., 132
Jefferson, Thomas, 35
Jeffries, Calvin, 132

Jennings, Colonel, 49, 51, 52, 54
Jillson, Willard Rouse, 21, 71
Job, T. C., 113
Johnson, Adam, 122
Johnson, Augustus, 46
Johnson, John, 58
Johnson, R. M., 54
Johnson, Wesley, 121
Johnson, William, 7
Johnston, Thomas, 17, 18
Jones, H. C., 113
Jones, Abner, 82
Jones, Alben S., 121
Jones, Benjamin, 46
Jones, David, 11
Jones, Rev. Elliott, 75, 254
Jones, Lucy, 114
Jones, James, 7, 20, 21, 22, 26, 28,
    35, 45, 46, 48, 62, 100
Jones, James, Jr., 7
Jones, Jimmie ("Tanner"), 35
Jones, John, 201
Jones, Joseph, 101
Jones, Joshua, 5, 6, 8, 18, 19, 22,
    24, 25, 26, 28, 34, 191
Jones, Reuben, 83
Jones, William, 20, 23, 34, 46, 61
Jones Family, 199ff

## K

Kearns, Charles, 132
Keeton, Allen, 21
Keeton, Julius, 21
Keith, William, 7
Kelley, Elias, Sr., 20
Kelley, Nettie, 115
Kelley, Emma, 113, 115
Kendrick, Eula, 113, 115
Kendrick, J. B., 113
Kendrick, Rucker, 173
Kendrick, Sallie, 113, 115
Kendrick, William, 81, 98, 112,
    113, 171, 184, 246f
Kendrick Family, 245
Kennamer, Dr. L. G., 191
Kennedy, H. C., 99, 100

Kennedy, James, 46
Kennedy, Thomas, 20
Kennedy Family, 220
Kinne, W. A., 69
King, John, 87, 140
Kinkead, John, 5
Knox, James, 3
Knox, Richard, 3
Kogar, Wm., 61
Koger, Nicholas, 20

## L

Lacy, Henry, 47
Lair, James, 80
Lambert, Henry, 61
Langston, James, 46
Lanier Family, 226ff
Lankford, John, 107, 109
Lanphier, William, 191
Larton, Joseph, 47
Lawrence, Robert, 58
Lawson, General, 8, 11
Lawton, Robert, 47
Layton, E., 159
Ledford, William, 46
Lee, John, 61
LeGrand, James, 46
Lester, Abraham, 46
Lester, John, 61
Lincoln, Abraham, 159
Linn, Samuel, 46
Littrell, James, 110, 114
Livingston, Robert, 61
Lloyd, Giles W., 110
Lloyd, Nicholas, 20, 100
Lockett, Matilda, 78
Lockett, William, 76, 78
Logan, Cyrus, 46
Logan, Thomas, 46
Long, Andrew, 47
Long, John, 20
Long, Samuel, 234
Long, Vi, 174
Loveall, John, 20
Low, William, 20
Lucke, W. A., 47

Lynch, David, 3
Lyon, Matthew, 24, 25

## M

McBeath, Anthony, 166f
McBeath, Mark, 176
McBeath, Robert, 112, 176
McBeath, Thomas, 112, 176
McBeath, William, 166f
McBeath Family, 230
McClung, James, 34
McConnaghy, Charles, 100
McCreary, James B., 121f
McCullom, John, 20
McDermott, Hugh, 21, 22, 28, 29
McDowell, Ephraim, 176
McDowell, Joshua, 23
McDowell, Major, 57
McDowell, Samuel, 33
McDowell Family, 221
McFarland, Alexander, 17, 18
McGee, Amanda, 110
McGee, James, 7, 12
McGowan, Samuel, 61
McGready, James, 80
McHenry, James, 7, 20
McKee, Colonel, 29, 141
McKee, Samuel, 29
McMahan, Dr., 152
McMillan, Joseph, 56
McNair, David, 47
McNutt, ——, 20, 28
McTeer, ——, 189
Mackey, William, 46, 47
Madison, Thomas, 5
Malone, Locky, 162
Mansco, Kasper, 3
Marat, Captain, 145
Marcum, G. K., 99, 100
Marshall, Peter, 81
Marshall, Thos., 37
Martin, George, 47
Martin, James, 46
Martin, John, 20
Martin, Nathan, 47
Mary, John, 47

Mathews, Lott R., 46
Maxwell, Nimrod, 47
Mays, Captain, 10, 11
Mays, Daniel, 31
Mays, David, 61
Meadows, J. H., 145
Meeks, Samuel, 121
Mercer, Frisbie, 121
Merritt, Thomas, 7, 12, 20, 21
Metcalfe, Courtney, 132
Metcalfe Home, 250
Metcalfe, John, 132
Michel, Elijah, 47
Middleton, John A., 134
Miles, Robert J., 191
Miller Brothers, 173
Miller, Fred, 6, 21
Miller, George, 61
Miller, Isaac, 46
Miller, Pearson, 101
Miller, Thomas, 36, 45, 59
Miller, William, 46
Miller Family, 241
Milton, Mollie, 132
Mills, Arch E., 100
Mills, Benoni, 201
Mills, Charles E., 108
Mills, Mary, 174
Mills, Milton, 87, 101
Mills, Thomas, 46
Montgomery, James, 22, 28
Montgomery, John, 3, 46
Montgomery, Judge, 36, 38
Montgomery, William, 46
Moore, John S., 26, 27
Moore, Jonathan, 46
Moore, Mary E., 27
Moore, Samuel, 12
Moore, Sarah Adelaide, 27
Moore, William, 90
Moore, William Perry, 26, 27
Moore, Virgil, 90
Moreland, Dudley, 7
Morgan, General, 9, 10
Morgan, William, 47
Morrow, T. Z., 89, 92

Mosby, Littleberry, 10, 11
Mullins, Professor, 107
Murray, Alfred, 189
Murray, David, 46

N

Nazie, George, 13
Neal, George, 49
Neal, Jesse, 61
Neal, John, 70
Newell, John M., 46
Newell, N., 59
Newell, Samuel, 6, 22, 28, 36
Noland, George, 133
Norman, Ada, 86

O

Oakley, Miss, 113
Oatts Brothers, 173
Oatts, James, 100
Oatts, Joshua, 8, 26
Oatts, Roger, 11, 20, 22, 25, 26, 28
Oatts, Thomas, 120
Oatts Family, 237
Obanion, John, 47
Offerd, ——, 57
Oldacre, William, 255
Oldham, Othniel, 129
Oldham, Thomas, 129
Onton, John, 47
Owens, John, 46
Owens, William, 87
Owsley, Judge, 31
Owsley, M. H., 89

P

Page, J. R., 162
Paris, George, 9
Parker, Lewis, 76, 82
Parker, Nathan, 20
Parmley, Robert, 110
Parmley, Elizabeth, 61
Parmley, John, 20, 21

Pearce, Silas, 121
Pemberton, Thomas C., 46, 57
Pennington, Anthony, 47
Perkins, M. B., 135
Petty, John H., 132
Peveyhouse, Daniel, 46, 56, 59
Peveyhouse, John, 20
Phillips, Cornelius, 20, 25, 95
Phillips, Dr. H. A., 102, 173
Phillips, Harriet, 174
Phillips, Henry L., 113
Phillips, Hiram, 90, 233
Phillips, James A., 24, 28, 46, 99, 100, 184f
Phillips, John H., 218, 233
Phillips, Juan, 128f, 133
Phillips, Micajah, 24, 32, 81, 107
Phillips Family, 215ff
Philpott, R. H., 120
Pierce, James, 7
Poage, Colonel, 49
Porter, Roy L., 81
Powell, Isaac, 70, 82
Powell, John, 57
Powers, D. S., 9, 114
Powers, David, 134
Powers, Jesse, 7, 9
Powers, W. M., 9, 82, 83
Pratt, James, 121
Pratt, Stephen, 7
Preston, William, 4
Price, J. S., 101
Price, James, 47
Price, John, 30, 82
Pults, George, 132

## Q

Quarles, Tunstall, 36

## R

Ragan, Shelby, 173
Rains, John, 3
Ramsey, G. T., 249
Ramsey, I. C., 249
Ramsey, Logan, 249
Ramsey, R. S., 249
Ramsey, Richard, 249
Ramsey Family, 249
Randolph, Colonel, 10
Rapier, Joseph, 101
Ray, John, 46, 61
Rayfield, Isaac, 47
Rector, Samuel, 20
Reed, John, 20
Reneau, Isaac T., 80, 86
Rhoann, Dr., 152
Rice, David, 80
Rice, James, 20
Rice, William, 82
Richardson, Dr. E., 102, 135
Richardson, Martin, 132
Richardson, Vernon, 201
Ridgeway, James, 46
Right, Lewis, 46
Ringer, George, 184
Roberts, B. E., 120, 124f
Roberts, G. E., 100
Roberts, H., 100
Roberts, John, 20, 46
Robertson, George H., 26, 28
Rogers, George, 7, 75
Rogers, John I., 81
Rogers, W. C., 99
Rollin, Gilbert, 47
Rousseau, John, 107
Rowan, John, 37
Rowe, Joab, 46
Rudd, George, 46
Russell, ——, 3
Ryan, G., 189
Ryan, Thomas, 60, 70, 71

## S

Sallee, John L., 81, 92, 100, 101
Sallee, J. W., 99, 115
Sallee, Mollie, Miss, 136
Sallee, Moses, 101
Sallee, William, 61
Sallee Family, 232
Sanders, E. T., 96
Sanders, John, 8, 20, 133

## Index

Sanders, Zachariah, 7
Sanders Family, 241
Sandusky, James, 17
Sandusky, John, 24, 100
Sandusky, William, 113
Saufley, Henry R., 108
Saufley, Jack, 95
Saufley, J. M., 134
Saufley, M. C., 31, 92f, 120
Saunders Family, 245
Savage, Richard, 46
Savage, William, 46
Scott, Richard, 46
Senior, William, 191
Sewell, Caleb, 81
Shannon, John, 46
Sharp, Abraham, 20
Shaw, John, 61
Shearer, Ala, 84, 115
Shearer, A. N., 84
Shearer, Christian, 173
Shearer, Daniel, 84, 110
Shearer, Jacob, 173
Shearer, J. D., 114
Shearer, Jenkins, 84, 191
Shearer, John H., 82, 99
Shearer Family, 235
Shelby, Isaac, 8, 36, 45, 62
Shelby, James, 4, 5
Shelton, James, 61
Sheppard, F. F., 191
Sheppard, Isaac N., 26, 92, 97, 99, 101, 133
Sheppard, Silas, 86
Sheppard, Thomas, 120
Sheppard, W. S., 191
Sherley, Captain, 57
Shrewsbury, Abel, 23, 26, 33, 184
Shrewsbury, John, 46, 51
Shutts, Jacob, 47
Shutts, John, 47
Silvers, John, 121
Silvers, T. J., 121
Simeral, Colonel, 56, 57
Simpson, James, 20, 184
Simpson, John, 20

Simpson, Reuben, 20
Simpson, Thomas, 110
Simpson, William, 11, 32, 75, 81, 108, 110
Simpson Family, 239
Sims, Martin, 22, 28
Singleton, George, 22
Skaggs, Henry, 3
Skaggs, Richard, 3
Slaughter, Capt., 60
Slavey, Richard, 65, 66
Smalley, Andrew, 46
Smith, Alexander, 46
Smith, Allen, 132
Smith, B. B., 109
Smith, George, 61
Smith, Henry, 3, 61
Smith, John ("Raccoon"), 9, 76, 80, 82, 85f, 107
Smith, John, Sr., 47
Smith, Mathew, 20
Smith, Phillips, 82
Smith, William, 20, 47, 61, 121
Souther, Jacob, 46
Southerland, J. C., 139
Southwood, John, 61
Speck, Jacob, 46
Speed, Thomas, 150
Spicer, David, 47
Spradling, John, 68
Stephens, G. C., 36
Stephens, Isaac, 7
Stephens, Peter, 61
Stephenson, John, 20, 41
Stephenson, L. J., 101, 191
Stewart, Thomas, 75
Stinson, Nimrod, 84
Stockton, Isher, 47
Stockton, Lemuel, 47
Stogdon, Hickabod, 58
Stone, Bryan, 121
Stone, F. P., 80, 90
Stone, Frank, 26
Stone, Lucy, 26
Stone, Marshall, 113, 121, 139
Stone, N. B., 88

Stone, Polly, 86
Stone, Sallie, 86
Stone, Shelby, 90
Stone, Uriah, 3
Stone, William, 81
Stoner, Michael, 4
Stoph, Christopher, 3, 4
Story, Isaac, 82
Stowe, Harriet Beecher, 132
Strain, Robert, 20
Strube, William, 189
Summers, Isaac, 20
Summers, Lewis Preston, 4, 5
Summers, William, 20, 46
Sutton, William, 20

### T

Tate, Sam C., 36
Tate, S. H., 99, 100
Tate Family, 233
Taul, Algernon Sidney, 33, 34
Taul, Arthur Thomas, 30
Taul, Micah, 22, 24, 28, 29, 30, 31, 32, 33, 45, 48, 59, 60, 61, 62, 107
Taul, Thomas Payne, 32, 34
Taylor, Amanda, 113
Taylor, Bettie, 115
Taylor, C. S., 139
Taylor, Henry, 90, 132
Taylor, John H., 244
Taylor, Lucy, 113, 114
Taylor, Sam, 139
Taylor, William Tarleton, 9, 243
Terrell, Obadiah, 3
Terrell, Thomas, 46
Thomas, Elisha, 6, 20
Thomas, Mr., 184
Thompson, James, 5
Thompson, T. L., 113, 184
Thornton, John, 61
Thurman, Absalom, 47
Tiller, John, 61
Todd, Dr., 152
Todhunter Family, 206ff
Toler, Chesley, 234

Townsend, Anna, 86
Trimble, Colonel, 56, 58, 59
Troxell, Granville, 121
Tucker, Moses, 46
Tuggle, James, 191
Tuggle, Henry, 20, 83
Tuller, John, 46
Tupper, General, 56
Turner, James, 7
Turpin, Solomon, 20, 110
Tuttle, Henry, 46
Tuttle, H. W., 101
Tuttle, Jabez, 132
Tuttle, James, 20, 46, 57
Tuttle, Jason, 132
Tuttle, J. W., 65, 81, 92, 99, 132ff, 189, 191
Tuttle, William, 99
Tyree, David, 11

### V

Van Hoozer, Jacob, 18, 31
Van Winkle, Abraham, 100, 110
Van Winkle, E. L., 90, 93, 94, 98, 101, 136, 159, 160f, 191
Van Winkle, Isaac, 46
Van Winkle, John S., 90, 92, 93, 94f, 98, 101, 138
Van Winkle, Micajah, 46, 94, 100
Vestol, David, 46
Vickery, Captain Adam, 46, 60, 61
Vicory, Francis, 20

### W

Wade, Ballenger, 46
Wade, Elisha, 61
Wade, John, 20, 61
Wakefield, John, 20
Walker, Isaac, 100
Walker, William, 20
Wallace, Barnabas, 61
Walter, John, 7
Walthal, William A., 47
Warden, Charles, 7
Warden, John, 230

## Index

Warden, Joseph V., 101
Warden Family, 230
Warren, George, 132
Warren, John, 132
Watson, Pierson, 68
Wayne, Anthony, 17
Weatherford, Hardin M., 184
Weaver, Jo, 47
Weaver, William, 121
Webb, Dr. William, 3
Wells, Jesse, 46
Wells, John G., 191
Welsher, Joshua, 61
West, A. R., 140
West, Isaac, 20, 25, 29, 46, 100
West, James H., 108
West, Joseph, 9, 61
West, Solomon, 20
West Family, 231
Wheat, Zack, 88
Wheeler, Joseph, 22
White, John, 132
Wilborn, Z. W., 114
Wilhite, M. S., 184
Wilhite, Noah, 46
Williams, John Augustus, 107
Williams, Mr., 189
Williams, S., 136
Williams, Sherrod, 26, 90, 101, 176
Williams, Thomas, 9, 26
Wilson, Capt., 36
Winfrey, T. C., 90
Winters, Henry, 47
Wisdom, Francis, 47
Wisdom, James, 47
Wisdom, John, 47
Wisdom, William, 47

Witham, John, 46
Wood, General, 146
Wood, James, 46
Wood, Josephus, 132
Woods, Archibald, 26, 80
Woods, James, 61
Woods Family, 214
Woolcott, Ezekiel, 121
Woolfolk, Joseph H., 46, 59
Woolford, Frank, 138
Worley, Valentine, 46
Worsham, Cannon, 12, 26
Worsham, Charles, 7, 10, 11
Worsham, Polly, 12
Worsham, Snowden, 136, 157
Worsham Family, 225
Worsley, Zephaniah, 46
Wray, Daniel, 61
Wray, John, 46, 121
Wright, Alfred, 132
Wright, Amos, 20
Wright, O. F., 121
Wright, Thomas, 9

### Y

Young, Harry, 110, 112
Young, Jacob, 79
Young, J. F., 102, 115, 191
Young, James, 46
Young, John, Jr., 46
Young, Silas, 86
Young, Washington, 21

### Z

Zachary, James, 81
Zimmerman, Andrew, 68, 69
Zollicoffer, General, 129f, 250

www.ingramcontent.com/pod-product-compliance
Lightning Source LLC
Chambersburg PA
CBHW020641300426
44112CB00007B/202